Urban Theory

Also by John Rennie Short

Alabaster Cities: Urban US since 1950

Making Space

Global Metropolitan

The World Through Maps

Globalization and the Margins (co-edited with Richard Grant)

Global Dimensions: Space, Place and the Contemporary World

Representing the Republic

Alternative Geographies

Environmental Discourses and Practice: A Reader (co-authored and co-edited with L. M. Benton)

Globalization and the City (co-authored with Yeong-Hyun Kim)

Environmental Discourses and Practice (co-authored with L. M. Benton)

New Worlds, New Geographies

The Urban Order

An Introduction to Political Geography

Human Settlement (editor)

Imagined Country: Society, Culture and Environment

The Human City

Housebuilding, Planning and Community Action (co-authored with S. Fleming and S. Witt)

Developing Contemporary Marxism (co-edited with Z. Baranski)

The Urban Arena

An Introduction to Urban Geography

The Human Geography of Contemporary Britain (co-edited with A. Kirby)

Housing in Britain

An Introduction to Political Geography

Housing and Residential Structure (co-authored with K. Bassett)

Urban Data Sources

Urban Theory

A Critical Assessment

JOHN RENNIE SHORT

palgrave
macmillan

First published 2006 by
PALGRAVE MACMILLAN
Houndmills, Basingstoke, Hampshire RG21 6XS and
175 Fifth Avenue, New York, N.Y. 10010
Companies and representatives throughout the world

PALGRAVE MACMILLAN is the global academic imprint of the
Palgrave Macmillan division of St. Martin's Press, LLC and of Palgrave
Macmillan Ltd. Macmillan® is a registered trademark in the United
States, United Kingdom and other countries. Palgrave is a registered
trademark in the European Union and other countries.

ISBN-13: 978–1–4039–0658–8 hardback
ISBN 10: 1–4039–0658–0   hardback
ISBN-13: 978–1–4039–0659–5 paperback
ISBN 10: 1–4039–0659–9   paperback

This book is printed on paper suitable for recycling and made
from fully managed and sustained forest sources.

A catalogue record for this book is available from the British Library.

A catalog record for this book is available from the Library of Congress.

10	9	8	7	6	5	4	3	2	1
15	14	13	12	11	10	09	08	07	06

Printed in China

'The city, which should be the symbol and center of civilization, can also be made to function as a concentration camp.'—**Edward Abbey**, *Desert Solitaire*, 1968, 150

'. . . the biggest and most cosmopolitan cities, for all their evident disadvantages and obvious problems, have throughout history been the places that ignited the sacred flame of the human intelligence and the human imagination.'—**Sir Peter Hall**, *Cities in Civilization*, 1998, 7

Contents

List of Tables

1

Introduction

In the past 200 years there has been an urban revolution. In 1800, cities were only tiny island pinpricks in a rural ocean. Out of every 100 people, only three lived in cities. By 2000, almost half lived in cities.

In absolute terms urban populations exploded. Only about 29 million people lived in cities in 1800, but by 2000 this figure had skyrocketed to 2.8 billion. One of the most significant features of this urban trend is the growth of the large cities. In 1800, only four cities had populations of more than 1 million; by 2000, no fewer than 411 cities broke this figure. Not only do more people live in cities, but more people live in very large cities.

If we plot any urban population data statistic the trend is the same: a relatively flat line before 1800, with the line becoming steeper and steeper after that. But the urban revolution is not only a redistribution of the world's population: it is also a fundamental change in the spatial organization of society and the social organization of space. The growth of cities goes hand in hand with the seismic shift in economic structure, from a reliance on agricultural production to economies that hinge around the manufacturing and service sector. The rise of cities is intimately connected to the social change from the local to the global, from close-knit immediate social relations to more dispersed anonymous transactions, and to the development of new and antagonistic social classes. Cities focus both the development and embodiment of social transformation. They are the embryos of socio-economic change.

This book presents the various perspectives of this urban revolution that has been wrought around the world. The narrative is guided by the following questions. How do we understand the city? What models have been employed in the past? What ones are relevant now?

There is an intriguing connection between the city and social theory in that the city is a crucial setting of social change as well as a key site of social theorizing. This book tries to capture both elements: a very ambitious task necessitating a wide combination of approaches. Two broad sweeps are attempted. First, the book concentrates on the rise of the

1

contemporary city and its relationship with modernity, capitalism and postmodernity, investigating the macro-scale links between broad social changes and deep urban changes. The second objective is to provide a broad-ranging assessment of the main theoretical ideas currently employed to understand the city. Introductory chapters place the previously dominant theoretical models in their historical context. Subsequent chapters explore the connection between contemporary urban socio-spatial processes and current theoretical models in order to prise open knotty relationships between space, place and social theorizing with the ambitious goal of theorizing the city and urbanizing theory.

Let us begin with some definition of the fundamental terms used in the title of this book. 'Urban' is an umbrella term that relates to cities and city living. It was first used in English in the early seventeenth century when urban living was associated more directly with a commodification of society and a capitalization of the economy. As an adjective it literally means 'pertaining to a characteristic a city or town'. This begs the question of what do we mean by 'city'? Statistical definitions lend precision but lack subtlety. The US Census, for example, has a population cut-off figure of 2,500 above which a settlement is classified as urban, so a community of 2,600, as well as the New York metro area of almost 18 million, occupy the same category. In this book, the term 'urban' is plastic and elastic; we will use it to refer to cities in general but especially the large sort of cities that are commonly recognizable as more than simply large villages. The term applies across a band of different city sizes, but the emphasis is on places that are both quantitatively and qualitatively different from large rural villages.

Theory is a contentious term. It derives from the Greek, meaning 'looking at', 'to behold', or 'spectacle', translated into Latin as 'contemplation'. But in Latin 'contemplation' also has the sense of partitioning, cutting off: it shares the same root as 'template' and so we get the sense that theories are a priori structures. I use the term more in the original Greek sense to indicate that urban theories arise from people looking at cities. This loose definition allows us to see urban theory less as a formalized set of ideas and more as a response to the spectacle of the city.

In Part I, I examine the rise of the modern capitalist city and the theorizing of the postmodern city. The chapters in Part II, consider the varied urban experiences of the contemporary city and associated theorizations. Each of these chapters is a window on seeing the city, focusing on a key aspect of contemporary urban studies. The final chapter subsumes the main themes, offering a basis for understanding possible future developments in our thinking about the city.

The city is a complex field of study. While the chapters in Part II give different perspectives, it is also important to remember the interconnections that give a fuller understanding of the city. The framework that unites the chapters together is a conceptualization of the city as a nested structure of *power, difference, polity* and *comity*. This structure frames each of the different chapters, sometimes explicitly, often implicitly. The chapters of the book are like windows on the city: they give only a select view and they look out on different vistas, but they are located in a shared structure.

The encircling frame for any understanding of the city is *power*. The operation of power and the struggle for power are the principal organizing features of the city. The city embodies the tensions of power relations and expresses the struggle for power. From the exercise of brute force to the more subtle internalizations of power relations that we carry around in our own heads, power is the determining element of the urban experience. Issues of power and its contestation, from the arena of formal politics to the more everyday sense of self-actualization, run through all the chapters.

The city is also a place where *difference* is created, maintained and sometimes undermined. Social differences are connected to power relations. Differences in class, gender, age, race, ethnicity and stage in the life cycle, to mention just a few of the sources of difference, are all expressed in urban patterns and urban processes. Take one dimension: gender relations are expressed in and through and by urban social space. Urban space is gendered, and gender is spatialized in cities. While there is a specific chapter on gender and the city, the different urban experiences of men and women runs through many of the other chapters.

Power and difference are so central to the understanding the city that they appear in various guises through all the chapters. Thus while Chapter 11 is concerned with urban design, it is impossible to understand architecture without reference to considerations of power and the creation of difference. City planning and urban design are neither politically neutral nor socially indeterminate in their effects. Urban design is intimately connected to issues of power and difference.

Polity is a broader term than politics and refers to the political organization of a group. It is not scale-specific so it covers community organizations as well as city governments and nation states. It ranges from the secular to the religious. I share the perspective of the ancient Greeks who saw humans fundamentally as political animals. Political practices include more than just formal politics. I use the term 'polity' to alert the reader that the sense of political I employ is wider than just formal politics and includes the personal and private as well as the social and the public. The very demarcation of public and private, or social and personal, is a political process.

Comity is complex word. The dictionary definition conjures up notions of civility and respect. I use it in a wider sense to refer to tolerance, trust and the coming together in civil society to get things done. The city as only a place of power and difference is suggestive of a Hobbesian world that at best is one of brutal indifference. Comity softens the harsh edges of marked social difference and unequal power in routines and practices of tolerance. Sometimes these are enshrined in legal codes, in modes of thought and everyday life. Issues of comity run through many of the chapters in this book. Chapter 4 on globalization, for example, raises the issue of cosmopolitanism and the encouragement of difference. Chapter 7 discusses the competitive city and raises the question as to whether the encouragement of tolerance is a prerequisite for successful repositioning of cities in an increasingly competitive world. The formal discussion of the concept of social capital reaches through a number of chapters. In Chapter 12, which looks at nature and the city, there is also a sense that a sense of community needs to be widened to the ecological world if long-term urban sustainability is possible.

The four interlinked elements structure the chapters. Chapter 9, for example, deals with the erotic city and questions of sexual identity; such identity is structured by the legal construction of sexuality (power), differences in sexual orientation (difference), personal politics (polity) and communities of desire (comity). It is impossible to frame the issue of sexual identity without a consideration of the interconnections between power, difference, polity and comity.

Another way to think of the interconnection is to utilize notions of *the authoritarian city, the city of difference, the cosmic city* and *the collective city*. These are ideas of the city as well as of urban social relations; they are intellectual discourses as well as political forces. Elements of these cities are found in all the chapters in Part II.

The Authoritarian City

Cities are sites of social aggregation that involve compulsion, order and discipline as well as freedom, anarchy and self-realization. While it is important to see the city as a site of individual and collective emancipation, a tradition that incorporates Karl Marx and Friedrich Engels as well as Robert Nozick and Milton Friedman, it is just as important to remember that the city is an imposition and adherence to a series of master narratives. From Rameses II to Frank Gehry, through Baron Haussmann and Le Corbusier, the city has been inherently authoritarian, sometimes totalitarian and occasionally fascistic.

All ideas are relational. However, this notion of the urban as discipline is not contrasted to an Arcadia of pastoral freedom. I am not counterpoising a brutal urban with an idealized rural. The countryside, no less than the city, is a place of compunction.

The debate on urban origins has long fascinated me. The traditional holds that the urban revolution was predicated upon the agricultural revolution. Agricultural surplus created cities. Jane Jacobs (1969) outlines an alternative, proposing a reversal of the process: urban trade created agriculture. Thus we can think of an urban–agricultural revolution in which trade played a key role. However, the work of Marshall Sahlins (1972) convincingly shows that the hunter-gathering societies which preceded this revolution spent less time working than agricultural societies; he calls them the 'original affluent society'. In other words, pre-urban, pre-agricultural societies had more disposable time, more freedom. The urban–agricultural revolution marks a loss of freedom, a greater work discipline and more time devoted to the drudgery of work and the compulsion of social order. Cities are a Nietzschean will to power. Let me illustrate this with an example.

There are the remains of an important urban culture in the desert Southwest of the United States known as the Anasazi. This independent urban civilization was centred on Chaco Canyon, New Mexico. The traditional rendition goes like this: between the tenth and twelfth centuries the Anasazi culture, based on efficient agriculture, flowered into cities with vast cliff dwellings, and major feats of engineering, architecture and art. Brilliant pottery, sophisticated irrigation systems and keen solar and astronomical observations round out a picture of an urban civilization that follows the old precept that cities equal civilization.

Yet there is another interpretation of the Anasazi. The work of anthropologist Christy Turner presents a darker side of Anasazi culture, suggesting that the Anasazi culture developed from the Toltec empire which lasted from the ninth to the twelfth century in central Mexico (Preston, 1998). This was an empire centred on human sacrifice and cannibalism. Thugs from the Toltec empire moved north into what is now New Mexico and found a pliant population of docile farmers whom they terrorized into a theocratic society. Social control was maintained through acts of cannibalistic terror. The Anasazi culture, so long admired, was a Charles Manson type of social order where the bad and powerful controlled the weak. The great feats of art and astronomy, road building and city formation were not so much sparks of human ingenuity as the mark of organized social terrorism. While others would want to remind us of the ingenuity in Catal Huyuk, I want to remind us of the terror of Chaco Canyon.

The authoritarian project is not always successful. The city is a place of resistance and contestation and, while these have emerged as important topics in recent years, we would do well to remember that something is being resisted, something is being contested. There is a structure to all this agency. I am not suggesting that the authoritarian project is always bad; we may agree with the classical liberal theorists (such as Locke and Hobbes) that we need some form of social contract in order to save us from the excesses of the more powerful. The city is an embodiment of the social contract.

Cities have an authority embedded in them. Street layouts, traffic lights, police, the location of things: there is an imposed discipline to our lives, our behaviours, the paths that we trace through time and across space. Whatever the question, Lenin once suggested, the answer is always power. The city both reflects and embodies power. Urban society involves an order in time and space, a discipline of space and time. The urban environment is a system of boundaries and transgressions, centres and peripheries, surveillances and gestures, gazes and performances. At a fundamental level there is something inherently fascistic about architecture and urban planning, and something both inhibiting and liberating about city life.

The notion of the authoritarian city is a useful corrective to the idea of urbanism as a sort of Prometheus unbound breaking through the bonds of tradition and established order, a theme best exemplified in Sir Peter Hall's magisterial urban history (Hall, 1998). This has been the dominant rendering of the city for the past 200 years, with versions embraced by the socialist emancipatory project, the mobile gaze of the *flâneur*, modernist sensibilities and a postmodern irony. In recent years this notion has morphed into a market-driven, 'neo-liberal' narrative that has demanded the loosening of planning controls and deregulation. This implied call for freedom attaches itself to the unfettered operation of the market. I want to stress very strongly that this discourse needs to be challenged. Because the city is inherently authoritarian, the demands for less planning and deregulation should be perceived for what they are, as struggles over who is doing the planning and what are the redistributional consequences of regulation. Deregulation is always reregulation. And the real question is not whether to have urban planning or not, but *who* is doing the planning.

If planning controls over land use disappear, more power is transferred to private interests. A perspective of the city as the operation of power shifts the debate from the phony *control versus freedom* to the more politicized question, *who is in control*?

Power is a ritual, a practice, a process wielded by some people over others. It is unevenly distributed and unequally imposed. There is work on the authoritarian city. The work of Michel Foucault interrogates the practices of power, the operations of discipline, the spaces of exclusion and the sites of control. This vision has influenced the work of many scholars looking at the city as site of power relations. Recent work on the control, surveillance and policing of public space extends this fascination (Fyfe, 1998; Mitchell, 2003): these are the more obvious uses of power. Yet power can also be exercised in a number of other ways, from direct coercion through to adherence to community standards. At one extreme are the personnel and techniques of the coercive state and corporatist apparatus, and at the other the social norms that define what is proper and right. The nature of the authoritarian city varies from the direct operation of centralized power – including imprisonment, punishment and bodily torture – to the individual incorporation of values and standards into a taken-for-granted view of the world. A thumbnail history of the authoritarian city reveals a reliance on both, with but a greater use of the latter in democratic capitalist societies.

The authoritarian city comes in a number of thicknesses. Authority is thickest when everyday practices are overlaid with the practice of power, and thinnest when power is part of popular will. Consider the contrasting utopia/dystopia model imagined by Aldous Huxley and George Orwell in their respective novels *Brave New World* and *1984*. These are arguably the most emblematic political novels of the twentieth century. Huxley describes a place where order is maintained by sexual promiscuity and the easy availability of drugs. Orwell's world is puritanical, harsh and bitter. Orwell depicts a thick authoritarian city; Huxley presents a thin authoritarian city.

While the obvious and direct uses of power are worthy of investigation, especially as new and subtler forms of surveillance emerge, it is also important to realize that the more powerful chains are the self-imposed ones that imprison our imagination. When we internalize power relations we become our own repressive police state. There are connections between *Brave New World* and *1984*.

Excavating previous intellectual debates can be useful, not so much for providing old answers but for posing new questions. After the First World War, when the first flush of the revolutionary impulse fizzled throughout much of Western Europe, a number of radical thinkers sought to understand how the social order maintained itself. The tenacity of the capitalist system to survive shattered the Marxist belief in the inexorable dynamic of revolution. This is the context for Antonio Gramsci's notion of hegemony and the Frankfurt School's critical theory. In particular, Herbert Marcuse's *One-Dimensional Man* (1964) describes the process of introjection whereby the values of a capitalist society become embedded into an individual psyche.

A succession of French theorists, rarely seduced by the notion of participatory democracy, outline similar ideas. Louis Althusser writes of an ideological state apparatus, including schools and universities, that maintained loyalty to the capitalist order. And Pierre Bourdieu, echoing Noam Chomsky, argues that social consent is manufactured, representative democracy is an illusion, and the struggle for domination is less in the market place than in the media place, where bourgeois culture perpetuates itself.

Critical theory tends to displace the very notion of struggle. While local struggles over working and living conditions will always occur, we seem to have lost, at least for the moment, the sense of big struggles over the shape of the social order. The real success of capitalism has been to persuade us of its inevitable legitimacy. We are all capitalists now. Through the creation of an all-embracing market mentality, the seductive power of the commodity and the enclosure of fulfilment and desire within purchase and consumption, capitalism shows itself so infinitely adaptable that even resistance and contestation is commodified and sold. There is now a strong and binding connection between commodity and identity, satisfaction and consumption. A linkage between political economy and psychoanalysis, first outlined by Erich Fromm and Charles Reich, and developed by such writers as Jacques Lacan, would seem to be an important way for us to unravel some of the strands that bind us to this tenacious social order.

We should be wary, however, of accepting a hermetically sealed connection between order and consent. If consent is manufactured, how does radical change come about? How does any change come about? One view is that we are recycling notions. From focus groups come advertising campaigns and media strategies that package our beliefs and fears into commodities, a closed cycle of desire and satisfaction, endlessly repeating itself from dream to commodity back to desire and commodity. But change does occur and it takes place when people interact, when discourse is 'real', and that occurs when people come together to talk, discuss, share or complain, and when individual fears and dreams are shared and shaped by comparison and contrast, empathy and argument. And this takes place most palpably in cities. Taking to the streets is not only an age-old political strategy, it has become a contemporary corrective to the imposed media images. Resistance takes place when lived urban space conflicts with the dictates of the market place and the commodified images of the media place.

The City of Difference

Not all dense and large agglomerations of people are cities. We can make a distinction between a city and a large urban settlement. A measure of heterogeneity is necessary for a place to be a real city. Difference is a vital ingredient of the urban experience. The sources of difference are many and include age, gender, sexual orientation, race and ethnicity. We should be careful of imputing biological origins to sources of social difference. While male and female are the biological categories of masculinity and femininity, what it signifies to be a man or what it implies to be a woman is socially produced and reproduced as well as celebrated and challenged. It is a product of social relations, not historical truths or biological verities. Social differences may be codified, reinforced and policed, but they are more plastic than the existing power relations would suggest.

The primary source of difference is power. The most obvious difference is between those who control and those who are controlled, between those who structure decision-making environments and those whose decision-making is constructed. The sources of difference are many, but at root they are a function of power relations. One criticism of contemporary urban studies is the relative lack of interest in the very wealthy and the very powerful. We have a great deal of work on the poor and many studies of sources of difference amongst those in the middle, but we have too few studies that illuminate the world of the most powerful (Beaverstock, Hubbard and Short, 2004).

Social differences are imposed and adopted, resisted and celebrated; they are sources of constraint and platforms for creativity. They are also subject to change. Even the most rigid divisions of gender or sexual orientation can change. We are in the middle of a period of flux when traditional categories are being redefined as well as being held on to. Issues of gender, race, ethnicity and sexual orientation are all being both undermined and reinforced, depending on time and space. We are in a period of restructuring social differences, and the city is the eye of this storm.

The Cosmic City

As an example of polity I want to consider the city as a religious artefact. For modernists this sentence may seem strange, even incomprehensible. Religion has been long counterposed to the continuing Enlightenment project of rationality. The city has been so long associated with the modern and the contemporary in the western imagination that it is read as the site of the irreligious and the secular. But cities always have reflected and embodied cosmologies. The earliest cities mirrored the world. Indeed, they *were* the world. The size, shape, orientation, location, siting and naming of cities is tied to a deeper vision of the connection between the sacred and the profane. Pericles's Athens, often depicted as the birthplace of western rationality, was named after the goddess Athene. She was glorified and worshipped by the citizens and the success of the city was seen as a mark of her benevolence. The Parthenon was dedicated to her and once a year citizens marched in a long procession up the steep slopes of the Acropolis where they presented a sacred garment to the 40-foot high statue of the goddess made from gold and ivory. Ancient Chinese cities, such as Changan and Beijing, were laid out on precise rectangular lines orientated to the four cardinal points to embody the shape of the world. The Aztec city of Tenochtitlan was also laid out in four equal parts, four being a magical number in Aztec cosmology indicating the completeness of the world. The boundaries of the city's four quarters met at a central point occupied by the Great Temple and imperial palaces. City layout and building design were homologies to the wider cosmos. In the Hindu city of Angkor Wat, each step in the temples marked a stage in the solar cycle, and each terrace represented a tier of the world. The earliest cities were market places and living places, but above all they were ceremonial sites of religious recollection and cosmic narrative. The site and shape echoed religious cosmology. Even the grid, a seemingly secular form of urban design, contains a fantasy of turning chaos into order, transforming topography into geometry. The very act of founding a city and planning a city embodied wider human involvement in, and deeper responsibility for, the world. The city was the cosmos; the cosmos was the city. This macrocosm–microcosm also extended from city to body. The walled, quartered medieval city was a microcosm of a larger world, but also a metaphor for a bounded, divided self.

Urban cosmologies justified the social hierarchy. The cities gave substance to the line of descent from the gods to ruling classes to the masses. The social hierarchy was sanctified and legitimized through the built form of the city and its urban rituals. Spectacular festivals and cere-monies united the people and the rulers and the gods.

In the West, the advent of the merchant city, the humanist city and the capitalist city all undermined the city as *the* site of cosmic narrative. The long history of urbanism reveals a steady secularization of the city, a growing disenchantment. Religious observance does not disappear but increases in outbreaks of religious fervour. Yet the city itself has lost its religious significance. The city has become illegible as a religious docu-ment; it is no longer a religious artefact, a text for understanding the world, and even less is it a site for taking part in rituals of cosmic signifi-cance that tie together people and place, the sacred and the profane. The word 'profane', by the way, means *outside the temple*. Over time, more of the city was outside the temple.

The market city, based on individual adherence to the power of the market – 'I am what I consume' – provides little in the way of cosmic significance. Consumption and wealth display form only one superficial layer of meaning and provide little of the spiritual depth and resistance to the contingencies of human life and suffering. The market gives us social positioning rather than human understanding, social ranking rather than communal meaning. At its existentially bleakest, the city becomes a setting for the meaningless passage of the individual through a blind universe, bereft of meaning. James Kelman's novel, *How Late It Was, How Late* (1994), provides a dramatic example: a man wakes up in jail, blind; he proceeds to stumble his way through a Kafkaesque nightmare. There is something heroic about his will to 'batter on' but it is tragically heroic, an act of blind individualism in the face of an indifferent, cold world. Life is meaningless beyond the will to survive.

Such existential crisis is not a global phenomenon. In many non-western cities religion survives, and even in the West, many are looking at religions less as false consciousness or the opiate of the people, and more in terms of collective identity and resistance to globalization. More accurately, it is an accommodation with globalization as extended communities around the world shape their sense of themselves through religion. The postcolonial city is becoming the more religious city. New faith communities enliven many cities as new sites of religious obser-vance. Even club culture is a type of Dionysian celebration as acolytes orgiastically dance the night away. In the city there are many and varied attempts to fill the God-shaped hole at the centre of our materialistic culture. Thomas Moore (1997), for example, writes of the need for, and practice of, more soulful cities. The postmodern city is the site for a rich variety of religious cosmologies.

The Collective City

Cities are sites of collective provision, collective consumption and the workings of civil society. They are shared spaces, places of parallel and sometimes intertwined lives, joint projects, positive and negative externalities and neighbourhood effects. The organization of this collective project varies over time and across space. I will examine briefly two issues: collective goods and services and the notion of civil society.

The city is a site for the provision and consumption of collective goods and services; these goods and services are organized into private or public provision, and private or public consumption. The resultant four-fold structure provides a basic anatomy of the city. Take the case of transport, provided either by the market or by the state, although in most cases the large, capital investment projects tend to be handled by the state, such as motorway construction or mass transit systems. The market shies away from such big, long-term risky projects. The consumption can vary from the more private – such as the car – to the more public, the subway or bus. Around the world the shift has been from public to private consumption, and it is tied to trends of individualism and the decline of civic engagement.

These divisions are more than just alternative ways of providing or consuming goods and services: they are the epicentres of fundamental debates about the social contract. In recent years, an ongoing assault has sought to undermine public provision of the collective. Collective provision and consumption has been associated with the discredited Left. Socialist cities were meant to take away the power of the market to influence social and spatial outcomes. The defeat of communism, the decline of the Eastern bloc and the apparent failure of the socialist agenda to garner mass support have meant a withering away of the collective idea and its influence upon social and spatial outcomes. To be sure this has not prevented the state from assuming huge influence and spending power. In the US, for example, critics of big government and government spending see no apparent paradox in their demands on the one hand for less government, and on the other their calls for more government spending on 'defence' and for giving more power over capital punishment to the state. Under this model, governments cannot be entrusted with providing basic human services, yet they can be given the power to spend billion of dollars on armaments or to take human life.

Collective goods are described less by fiscal realities and more by social and political power. Subsidies to corporate interests – corporate welfare – are less discussed than income support to low-income households.

Subsidies to home-owners are considered less destructive to the social order than subsidies to the unemployed. One is legitimized while the other is delegitimized. The big debates about political control of the market are most vivid in our discussions on collective goods and services. There is a decline of the Keynesian city and a withering away of the socialist city. At this millennial juncture we are in the process of a fundamental shift in the collective organization of the city.

Civil society emerges from the set of rules and practices established in the shared space of the city. The first cities were gated communities and notions of a public good or civic order were slow to develop, and, always it seems, able to be undermined by family and group loyalties. There is now a great deal of interest in civil society, social capital and all those interstitial areas between the realm of formal politics and the market-place. Civil society operates between the state and the market. The decline of the Keynesian and socialist state undermines reliance on the state, while the operation of the market creates inequalities in social and spatial outcomes. For a number of commentators civil society is now a terrain of social opportunity, providing one of the few possibilities of maintaining a progressive project. A number of commentators have stressed the positive forms of civil society. Robert Putnam's (2000) notion of social capital, for example, refers to the ability of civil society to transcend family and group ties, and John Friedmann writes about the possible liberating connections between civil society and urban planning (Friedmann, 1998).

While civil society is important we should be careful of seeing it as a panacea. Civil society contains the Michigan Militia and Ku Klux Klan as well as chess clubs and benign community groups. Moreover, underlying many of the debates concerning civil society and the state is the Greek notion of the *polis*, a small, almost homogeneous community. The contemporary city, however, always problematic for the workings of democracy due to growing heterogeneity, suburbanization and the fragmentation of city governments, has undermined the urban community. The ancient *polis* was small and unitary. The contemporary city, in contrast, has a metropolitan fragmentation that separates the centre from the edges, cities from suburbs, blacks from whites, rich from poor.

A number of years ago, Kenneth Galbraith (1958) wrote of the growing disparity between private affluence and public squalor. In many cities around the world the disparity grows. As the city balkanizes, architecturally into gated communities and politically into exclusive suburbs (abandoning its inner city), simply calling for civic engagement, a major chord in social commentary on the city, is to miss this wider structural context. To be actively involved in your all-white suburban neighbour-hood may be public involvement, but it is not civic engagement.

The city is full of paradoxes: affluence with squalor, civic obligations with individual needs and public duties with private actions. The cities of classical Greece, almost two-and-a-half millennia ago, combined public affluence with private squalor; civic obligations circumscribed private actions and the market place did not dominate over the temple or the *agora*. Contemporary cities are marked by the power of the market over the *polis* and the temple, private affluence (of a minority) alongside public squalor and the valuing of individual rights above civic obliga-tions. It will be interesting to note the changing balance of this urban equation in the future. The city will remain centre-stage in this evolving, contested social order.

A Note to the Discerning Reader

A final draft of this book went out to two anonymous reviewers, both experts in the field. They each came back with a list of names they felt should have been mentioned but were not. The two reviewers had completely different names. One of the reviewers mentioned that too much emphasis was given to one author while the other reviewer felt this same author's work was largely ignored. The point of this story is to remind the reader that this book is partial; it reflects my own views and experiences. It is weighted towards my own research interests and biased towards my own research focus on urban issues in UK and USA. I have sought to provide as wide a coverage as possible, beyond my own imme-diate interests, but inevitably some bias remains. I have also tried to avoid the trap of writing a book that provides essentially a checklist of refer-ences in favour of providing a critical assessment with its own authorial voice.

Finally, urban studies, in common with other sites in the academic production of knowledge, is heavily skewed towards the West. There is an uneven development in our understanding of the world. I am acutely aware of this bias and have written on the problems caused by the domi-nance of English as the academic medium (Short *et al.*, 2001) as well as the marginalization of whole areas of the world even in such ostensibly global discourses as globalization (Grant and Short, 2002). And while I have striven to widen the angle of vision in this book, I fear that the view is still skewed towards the richer cities of the West.

PART I

Theorizing the City

2
Theorizing the Modern City

The year 1927 saw the release of two great classics of the cinema, *Metropolis* and *Berlin: Symphony of a City*. While the first is better known than the second, they share a similar preoccupation with understanding the modern city.

In the 1920s Berlin grew to be an industrial city of almost 4 million people with approximately 790,000 manufacturing jobs, 250,000 of which were in the high-technology electrical sector. Combined with a social dislocation caused by the defeats in the First World War and a failed social revolution, such rapid growth resulted in the general sense of social malaise that was an important source of creative cultural expression across all the arts in Weimar Berlin, which was on the socially disorientating (yet nonetheless stimulating) cusp of an aesthetic, intellectual and cultural response to modernity throughout the 1920s.

Metropolis, directed by Fritz Lang, presents us with a deeply divided city. There are the workers who are oppressed by their punishing work schedules. Little more than extensions of machines, they live underground as robotic figures trudging through their bleak days. The rich, in stark contrast, inhabit a world of sunlight and leisure, leading lives of hedonism far above the grinding monotony of the workers' city. The son of the all-powerful owner of the city is Freder, who one day meets an inhabitant of the workers' city, Mary, who preaches a religion of love to the workers. Freder falls in love with her, and his eyes are opened to the inequality of the existing system. His father, annoyed by his son's liaison, arranges with a mad scientist to kidnap Mary and make a robot in her likeness who in turn preaches violent insurrection to the workers. A carnival of destruction ensues as the workers destroy the machines and flood the underground city where they live. The children of the workers are still in this part of the city. The real Mary escapes and, together with Freder, saves the children from the flood, makes the owner into a more caring person and also appeases the masses. Along with the constant visual referencing of the massed skyscrapers of the city, the narrative themes of technology as source of social discord and of class conflict in a divided city predominate. In the end, however, the classes are united by a religious figure preaching love and reconciliation. Lang drew not only upon Berlin for inspiration but also upon a visit to New York; the verticality of the film's metropolis reflects both the New York City skyline and the skyscraper fad of 1920s Berlin. *Metropolis*'s message is not simple; it presents a sharply divided city that one would think leads to a Marxist reading of society. In fact the film shows the transcendence of class conflict through spirituality. There is no simple reading of the film (Neumann, 1994). An initial revolutionary perspective is blunted by a reformist conclusion. The technology of the machines, the high-rise buildings and indeed the entire city are both celebrated and criticized.

Berlin: Symphony of a City (hereafter *Berlin*), directed by Walter Ruttmann, is a non-fiction representation of a day in the life of Berlin. It begins with a train journey. The city emerges from a sleepy countryside. It is the start of the day; the city is laid out from a bird's eye view with buildings clearly visible but no people yet. The city slowly wakes up, machines start, children go to school, workers go to work, shops open. The movie continues with images of the mass transit under construction, streetwalkers and a wedding, presenting an endless experience of visual stimulation and movement. Trains and trams move thought the city. At noon people have lunch. The film is edited to show the daily rhythms of the city – slow, then fast – periods of languor punctuated by rapidity, people going to the movies, theatre, ice-skating and boxing matches. Fireworks illuminate the sky. The movie ends.

The day in the life of the city is shown more through simulation than representation as both montage and collage effects reveal a spectacle of the modern such as mass transportation with its fleeting exchanges, a process of a new urban subjectivity (Hake, 1994; Gleber, 1999). Compared to *Metropolis*, the plot of which seems to creak with a wooden structure, *Berlin* maintains its zest and vitality. It portrays a city as constant motion, animated by individuals and masses in pursuit of commercial livelihood and pleasure. The film celebrates the sheer variety of the large modern city. The juxtaposition of images does not present an analysis of the city so much as its sensual rendering. Classes and class conflict are especially evident, for those looking for them, but the city is more a collection of individuals bound up in pursuit of both collective enterprises and individual desires. *Berlin*'s modern city is subjectivity in action.

These exactly contemporaneous films' contrasting depictions characterize two very different Berlins. One is embroiled in an economic reorganization of industrial capitalism that brings new social classes into close and antagonistic contact, while the other embraces a social restructuring that enthrones the individual as a dynamic force in the life of the city. The first brings people together; the second pulls them apart, suggesting respectively two dominant theoretical responses to the modern city: the body of writings based in Marxist economics and the sociology of the new individualism. Between these two discourses there is the reformist impulse which combines social investigation with social reform.

The Economic Rupture and the Marxist Response

While the pre-modern city could reach enormous size and complexity, it is only with the modern city that industrial production dominates economic production. From nineteenth-century Britain to twenty-first-century coastal China, the story is the same: rapid urban growth, large-scale economic transformation and wrenching social changes. The modern city is the emergent capitalist city. The first modern cities of this type developed in Britain's early Industrial Revolution. Today they continue to emerge in the rapidly industrializing economies of the Third World. Marxist urban theory is the most sustained attempt to capture this historical moment.

The first cities in this historic transformation arose in Britain in the early nineteenth century. 'From this foul drain the greatest stream of industry flows out to fertilize the whole world': Alexander de Tocqueville wrote these words in 1835 about the city of Manchester, one of the new cities of the nineteenth century that attracted visitors eager to see the brave new world of the Industrial Revolution. In 1760 Manchester had a population of only 17,000; by 1830 this had increased to 180,000 and by 1851 to just over 300,000. Manchester was the eye of the storm, an important laboratory of economic transformation as people and capital were concentrated throughout its urban sites. Factory production replaced household production and industry replaced agriculture as the dominant economic activity, with new social classes finally supplanting the remnants of a tenacious feudalism. The factories of Manchester and other cities in Britain in the early nineteenth century were wonders of the modern world. Indeed, it was the world made modern; centuries-old agricultural dominance crumbled in a sudden seismic economic shift. In 1801 almost 70 per cent of the British population lived in communities smaller than 2,500, but by 1851, over 40 per cent lived in cities with a population greater than 100,000. New cities were built on green field sites, and major cities developed from tiny hamlets.

Britain's new industrializing cities were 'shock cities', not only in the rate of their population growth but also in their impacts. The pace of growth stressed the existing infrastructure. In Glasgow the population increased by a factor of five over the period between 1780 and 1830, but the city infrastructure barely grew. Sanitation, housing and public health were all overwhelmed. The rate of growth exceeded the ability or willingness of government to intervene, resulting in widespread pollution and appalling living conditions for the urban majority. In the decade from 1831 to 1841 death rates rose by 50 per cent in the largest British cities. An American who visited Britain in 1845 noted: 'every day that I live I thank heaven that I am not a poor man with a family in England'. Visitors to today's Chinese cities experience similar shock at the level of seemingly unmanageable growth, rampant pollution, massive rural–urban migration, growing inequality and destruction of traditional social norms. The modern industrial city's emergence has varied widely over the past 200 years, shifting from Europe and North America to Asia, but the same sense remains of them as shocks to the existing social and economic order.

The spectacle of the cities led many to anticipate social revolution. An American, Josiah Strong, noted in 1885, 'The city has become a serious menace to our civilization . . . Here is heaped the social dynamite . . . men who are ready on any pretext to raise riots for the purpose of destruction.' The city was the home of the mob, unconnected to traditional systems of deference, immune to the restrictions of an established social order. De Tocqueville noted in 1835 that 'in cities men cannot be prevented from concerting together and awakening a mutual excitement that prompt, sudden and passionate resolution'.

Shock cities are contexts as well as principal agents for social disorder. While many commentators worried about the insurrectionary possibilities of the modern city, there were others who revelled in the revolutionary possibilities. Marxist writings constitute the most sustained development of this theme. The city had a special place in Marxist thought; it is the built form of the industrial capitalism that Marx devoted so much intellectual effort towards apprehending. His companion-in-arms and principal financial backer, Friedrich Engels, had written extensively on the city in his *The Condition of Working Class in England in 1844*. The book was first published in German in 1845; the first English edition was published in New York in 1887. The year 1844 also saw the publication of the *Manifesto of the Communist Party* and the beginnings of the collaboration between Marx and Engels.

Engels (1820–95) had more than a theoretical interest in capitalism: he was an active participant in one the leading sectors of the era, the textile trade. He worked for an export business in Bremen as a young man and after military service he moved to Manchester in 1842 to work in a branch of the family business as a manager in the Cotton Exchange. Engels led two lives. He was a diligent manager, son and heir to the family business, and also a revolutionary working for the collapse of the system from which he profited. His experiences in Manchester prompted *Condition of the English Working Class*, written between September 1844 and March 1845 and based on his two-year stay in England from 1842 to 1844. Exceptionally well written and supported by official statistics as well as eyewitness accounts, *Condition of the English Working Class* is subtitled 'From Personal Observations and Authentic Sources'. Engels begins with a description of the pre-industrial situation of workers, which he describes as a 'passably comfortable existence'. Next comes the Industrial Revolution prompted by technological changes such as the invention of the spinning jenny in 1764. The rise of the power loom, mechanical power, iron smelting and railways all reinforce the concentration of economic activity. 'Thus arose the great manufacturing commercial cities of the British Empire, in which at least three-fourths of the population belong to the working-class . . . Here the centralization of property has reached the highest point; here the morals and customs of the good old times are most completely obliterated' (Engels, 1973, 55 and 64). In the section entitled 'The Great Towns' he describes the dwellings, clothes, food and working conditions of working people. Engels combines official reports from cities around the country with an in-depth, journalistic account based on his own observations. He documents the dreadful living conditions of English urban working classes, the high death rates, the inadequate food, and the poor housing.

Engels met Marx in August 1844 in Paris. For 10 days they talked and talked, fuelled by red wine and youthful enthusiasms, awakening to their mutual friendship and shared political convictions. Engels, who provided money, friendship, editorial help, constant encouragement and co-authorship of many books and articles marked by vigour and clarity, supported Marx for the rest of his life. He readily admitted the intellectual superiority of Marx, but the ideas did not just go in one direction. In Engels, Marx found someone who had a unique perspective on the capitalist city.

For both Engels and Marx the new industrial city was not something separate from the wider society. This seems an obvious point today, but for many of their contemporary commentators the sheer pace and scale of urban development seemed to have a life of its own; it was a phenomenon outside history and beyond social control, something alien and new and incomprehensible. Even to this day there are social theorists who append the adjective 'urban' as a singular notation, such as 'urban problems', 'urban crime', and so on. This is not just a linguistic convention; it is a form of urban theory that represents the urban as something independent and separate from the encompassing society. Marx and Engels saw the modern city as intimately connected to the new capitalist mode of production; its built form embodied all the paradoxes and revolutionary potential of the capitalist mode. This mutual relationship was a constant theme of subsequent Marxist and neo-Marxist theorizing. Gordon (1984), for example, constructs a general model of urbanization and capitalism in the US to show how the suburbanization of industry was a response to the growing power of labour within cities. Baran and Sweezy (1966) seek to show how investment in the built environment was a way to avoid stagnation within an under-consuming economy. Their model posits how suburbanization staves off the inevitable crisis of capitalism. Harvey (1982) identifies two circuits of capital. The primary circuit involves investment in commodities, while the second circuit involves investments in such fixed capital assets as roads and buildings. In summary, this line of Marxist urban theorizing points to the role of urban development and especially to suburbanization as reasons for the vitality of capitalism, thus accounting for a system that was supposedly doomed to collapse by its own internal contradictions.

Investment in the urban built form, then, offers a way to escape historical inevitability. One recurring problem of this line of theorizing is a tendency to see the urban built form as neatly dovetailing with the needs of capital and with the dictates of capital accumulation. The basic models rarely leave room for the contradictory nature of urban formation and capital investment. The more interesting theories in Marxist-inspired work tend to be the detailed analyses of specific agents operating in real time rather than the general macro-models. Despite such criticisms as can be made regarding Marxist theories, especially those based upon an undue reliance on the under-consumptionist model of capitalist economies, they nevertheless serve well in the identification of the fundamental economic connections between modes of production, patterns of investment and forms of urban organization.

The city for Marx and Engels, and many subsequent Marxists, was pregnant with revolutionary possibilities. In the *Manifesto of the Communist Party*, first written in 1844 and printed in English in 1888, they noted: 'The bourgeoisie has subjected the country to the rule of the towns. It has created enormous cities, has greatly increased the urban population as compared with the rural, and has thus rescued a considerable part of the population from the idiocy of rural life.' For optimistic radicals with a belief in the forward march of history, the city saved people from the impediments of rural life by giving them an experience of their collective strength. Marx made a distinction between classes in themselves and for themselves. While classes could be objective facts, classes in themselves, in order to become agents of history they also needed to become aware of themselves as products of history with an ability to make a new and better future.

The basic Marxist theory declares that rapid industrialization and urbanization lead to class formation and class identity. The testing of this idea is the basis of a major work of historical scholarship, E. P. Thompson's (1963) *The Making of the English Working Class*. This book is one of the first sustained histories from below, and it was influential in establishing the new social history that looked at the workers and the peasants as much as the titled and the wealthy. Thompson helped change the perspective of social history to rescue those marginalized by the 'enormous condescension of posterity'. Class and class relations are pivotal to his analysis of the roles of urbanization and industrialization in the formation of the working class. The title of the book is telling because it implies a double making of the working class as Thompson examines both how the working class became a class in itself *and* for itself. A product of rapid urban industrialization, the English working class also made itself through its sports clubs, burial clubs, political affiliations, religion, civic socialism and trade union organizations.

The connection between city and class becomes more complex as capitalism develops. In the era of primitive capital accumulation of the early industrial cities – the 'Coketowns' of Charles Dickens' *Hard Times* or the *Metropolis* of Fritz Lang, for example – there is a simple two-class division. The city showcases this division. However, as capitalism matures, especially into the era of high mass consumption, less monolithic class divisions begin to appear as residential, racial and ethnic differentiation undermines their former simplicity. The Marxist model of class formation works best in the era of early industrial capitalism's clear class divisions with a working class not yet seduced by the material plenty of an advanced capitalism. However, this seduction is not entirely due to capitalism alone providing more goods and services for the working class. The working class that Thompson identifies demanded and leveraged substantial gain from what was originally a very oppressive system so that its struggle rarely reached that level of revolutionary rupture so beloved by Marx. Indeed, Thompson's working-class dynamic works more as a steady drive towards the improvement of the working and living conditions within an existing system.

Drawing upon the society around them, Engels and Marx developed their urban theory at a time when a revolutionary capitalism swept away much of the premodern world. 'All that is solid melts into air' is the famous phrase that captures their sense of this historical rupture. Urban Britain was a cauldron of the newly emerging working class's concentrated power. As with the city in Lang's *Metropolis,* the cities of early industrial Britain seem ripe for revolution.

Marxist urban theory experienced a revival in the 1970s; we will now consider the work of one of its most influential scholars, David Harvey. Harvey's first book, *Explanation in Geography,* was published in 1969 at a time of intense debate within geography. The book is more concerned with the method of analysis rather than the object of analysis. Harvey's aim is to harness the quantitative model-building approach by formulating criteria for judging the soundness of arguments. He lauds the deductive approach involving the use of models to suggest hypothesis, which can then be verified. *Explanation* is an argument for the adoption of the deductive approach in geography.

Explanation concerned the academic world. The context for Harvey's next book, *Social Justice and the City* (1973), was the wider world of the Vietnam War, the persistence of poverty in the richest countries, intractable racial divisions, and the decline of the long postwar economic boom exposing further inequalities and social discontent. There was also a growing dissatisfaction in the academy with traditional methods of scholarship. In *Social Justice,* Harvey reflects upon and informs the debates surrounding these societal and academic issues. *Social Justice,* then, is really two books. The first part, entitled 'Liberal Formulations', focuses geographical inquiry on socially relevant topics. The second part, 'Social Formulations', marks a distinct epistemological break. Now ideas derive from a particular context, and social justice is less abstract; it is no longer the sort of mental problem that John Rawls favoured, but is instead placed within a wider consideration of society. The concept of the city is radically altered between these two parts: rather than being an independent object of inquiry, it is an important element mediating and expressing social processes. Through considerations of Marxist rent theory and the history of urbanism, the main objective in the second part is to explore the relationship between the city and society from the perspective of historical materialism.

While some see a break between the early Harvey and the Marxist Harvey, with the rift occurring in the middle of *Social Justice,* I would suggest an alternative interpretation. The Harvey of *Explanation* has the same interest in theorizing, model building, and general theories as the Marxist Harvey. 'Liberal Formulations' stands out as the more socially connected. In Harvey's third book, *The Limits to Capital* (1982), the aim is nothing less than to provide an extension of Marx's original analysis of capitalism and rewrite Marx's *Capital*. The exposition of *Limits* mirrors *Capital*: his first chapter, for example, begins just as Marx did, with a discussion of commodities, use values and exchange values. The book is strong on capital; it rarely reveals the limits to capital.

Limits represents the high point of Harvey's confidence in a development of a Marxist urban theory. Subsequent books mark more of a defensive response to mounting criticisms of the Marxist intellectual project. *The Condition of Postmodernity* (1989a) is a sustained response to the postmodernist critique, which states that cultural changes reflect our experience of space and time that in turn is affected by more flexible modes of capital accumulation. The hand of capital, despite what the postmodernists say, is still the dominant motor of cultural expression and production. Cultural changes are mere shifts in surface appearance to the classic rule of capitalist organization. *Justice, Nature and the Geography of Difference* (1996a) again appeals to the basic model of capital to explain the world. Harvey notes that 'I find myself writing *against* an emerging trend' (italics in original). The book is interesting because it is almost a *cri de cœur*. Lambasted as a free-floating intellectual clinging to an increasingly unfashionable theory, Harvey seeks to both defeat and incorporate the ideas of the postmodernists whom he opposes, those involved in the cultural turn and identity politics (the politically committed as well as the intellectually promiscuous). The result is an odd blend of defiance and defeatism embedded in a creative use of criticism and alternative viewpoints.

Spaces of Hope (2000) outlines a dialectical utopianism. In chapter 1 he notes that 'by the early 1990s the intellectual heft of Marxian theory seemed to be terminally in decline'. However, Harvey argues that Marx's writings are more pertinent than ever to an understanding of the contemporary world. All of his books have the same rhetorical flourish of page after page detailing the power of capital and then a few paragraphs of hopeful encouragement at the end for those armed with the appropriate Marxist theory. Like Marx, he is strong on the inner workings of capital but hazy about how to change them. He is at his strongest when developing what he calls a 'historical geographical materialism', noting the connections between the dynamics of capitalist economy and space and time (specifically, how capital accumulation involves production of the built environment over space and across time). Just like an Old Testament prophet who admonishes people not to abandon the true texts, Harvey is a constant reminder of the power and limitation of a Marxist urban theory. He also directly influenced a number of scholars. Andrew Merrifield (2002) draws upon Harvey to resuscitate a Marxist urban theory, and Neil Smith (1996) follows Harvey when he writes about gentrification in the city. Don Mitchell (2003) identifies with both Harvey and Smith when he explicitly adopts a Marxist perspective, but at this late stage his work is more a self-conscious political posturing, more an individual branding in a crowded intellectual market, than a sign of political commitment or intellectual vitality.

While Harvey's intellectual trajectory is unique, his work represents in many ways the general fate of Marxist urban theory. It is primarily based on the experience of early industrial cities in Britain when the primitive accumulation of the capitalist system was particularly readable and brimming with enormous revolutionary potential both in sweeping away the pre-modern and in inaugurating the postcapitalist. Marx and Engels developed a lively account of the economic role of cities, the emergence of antagonistic class divisions and the revolutionary dimensions of the urban conditions of capitalism. The more we move away from this original context, the more Marxist urban theory needs to be tweaked and reshaped.

Capitalist economies continue to function in their broadly original outlines; however, the shift from industrial production to a service economy, the emergence of new classes and the important role of culture in the city do not so much invalidate Marxist urban theory as render it less universal. Harvey's work represents the revival of Marxist social theory in the 1970s and the response to mounting criticism of it in the 1980s and 1990s. His entire body of work maintains a steady commitment to historical geographic materialism in understanding the city as well as responses to, and incorporations of, the critical evaluation of cultural theory, identity politics, the globalization boosters and the postmodern critique. The result is a creative use of Marxist urban theory that remains strong on the power of capital and incredibly weak on the limits to capital. Estranged from any real political moment, Harvey remains at the level of the 'three-mile high' theorist looking down at changing world, adhering to his Marxist ideas yet also developing some valid insights while wrestling with the growing and varied criticism of his intellectual source material. When he descends from the Olympian heights and looks at a particular city, as he does with his 2003 *Paris: Capital of Modernity*, the result is a fascinating, more grounded urban theorizing, to be compared with

Patrice Higonnet's (2002) equally adept rendering of Paris as the capital
of the world.

Socio-economic Change and the Reformist Impulse

There was a counterpoint to the insurrectionary Marxist interpretation.
From the early nineteenth century onwards a reform movement emerged
that combined urban investigation, social reform and political lobbying.
This reformist impulse emerged as a response to the fear of crime, disease
and moral disorder of the modern capitalist city and as a belief that things
could be made better within the framework of existing institutions. Peter
Hall (1988) provides one of the most informative discussions of this
tradition in urban studies. I will identify two main strands: a progressive
force that combined urban investigation with social reform (and here I
include Mayhew, Booth, Riis, Addams and Howard); and a more regressive top-down imposition of grand urban plans that encompasses the
work of Haussmann, Burnham and Le Corbusier.

In the summer of 1849 cholera broke out in London. Almost 13,000
died within three months. In September, a journalist called Henry
Mayhew began a series of articles on the impact of the disease in
Bermondsey, a working-class district in London's East End. He
described the area and its living conditions in graphic detail. Here is a
sample from his first article, published on the 24 September 1849:

> we saw drains and sewers emptying their filthy contents into it; we
> saw a whole tier of doorless privies in the open road, common to men
> and women, built over it; we heard bucket after bucket of filth splash
> into it, and the limbs of the vagrant boys bathing in it seemed by pure
> force of contrast, white as Parian marble.

The article captured the popular imagination and the newspaper
published a series of articles on the urban working class over the next
year. Between October 1849 and December 1850 Mayhew wrote articles,
underneath the byline of 'Metropolitan Correspondent', detailing the life
and living conditions of London's poor and working class. The articles
were published every day for the rest of 1849 and through most of 1850.
The collected articles were published in four volumes as *London Labour
and London Poor* in 1851. Mayhew had a keen eye and a telling turn of
phrase. He was born into a wealthy family but decided upon a journalistic career. In 1841 he co-founded the journal *Punch*. Mayhew's survey

combines a newspaperman's unblinking gaze eye with a journalist's ability to paint a graphic scene with words. Mayhew's book is an early form of urban ethnography, still readable and shocking. It sounds modern as it gives a voice to the poor and marginalized. Mayhew's work was oral history and investigative journalism, as well as social analysis. He distinguished, for example, between those that couldn't work and those that wouldn't work. This is one of the first distinctions between the deserving and undeserving poor. In comparison to Engels, Mayhew focuses more on the consequences of poverty than the causes, and more on the immediate public policy implications than the long-term possibilities for revolution.

While Mayhew's work promoted interest in the world of the slums it did not provoke sustained social legislation. *The Economist* magazine argued, in a common establishment response, that Mayhew encouraged a reliance on public sympathy for help instead of promoting the need for self-exertion. However, as the nineteenth century progressed the scale of the problem grew; crime and disease, which flourished in the slums, were not restricted to those areas but spilled over, making the city unsafe and dangerous for the affluent and wealthy. Some Victorians realized that self-help could not solve all the problems.

In 1883 a Congregationalist minister, Andrew Mearns, published a pamphlet entitled *The Bitter Cry of Outcast London*. The slum was laid bare, with its horrific living conditions and lax morality presented to the middle-class observer. The slums were now seen as both a stain on society and a source of crime and social disorder. The pamphlet reached a wide audience and found a receptive response amongst influential people. A government inquiry was established. The Royal Commission of 1885 proposed more effective use of government powers, including the demolition of slum housing and the building of new housing for the poor. The Housing of the Working Classes Act of 1885 implemented many of the commission's proposals and set the agenda for subsequent social legislation in the UK.

London in the 1880s was a place of turmoil: an economic depression in the middle of the decade increased unemployment and social unrest. Charles Booth, a wealthy shipowner, much influenced by Mearns's pamphlet, established a social survey (one of the first). In a paper presented in 1887 he gave precise numbers to the poor in East London and a simple categorization. He divided the 314,000 of London's East End poor into four categories: the 11,000 barbarians or loafers, criminals, street sellers and performers who were a serious threat to urban order; a large group of permanent poor (around 100,000) who were in chronic need due in part to their shiftlessness; a group of 74,000 who were poor due to their intermittent employment; and 129,000 working poor. Again a distinction is made between the deserving and undeserving poor as a prelude to fashioning ameliorative social legislation. Booth's multivolume *Life and Labour of the People in London* (1892–1903) quantified social problems in the metropolis. Booth's use of social statistics to measure and map urban inequality inaugurated an important strand of urban research in which empirical methods were tied to welfare reform objectives. This strand of urban investigation became a common feature of urban studies in the welfare democracies in the twentieth century. Booth's work played a role in the passing of the Old Age Pension Act of 1908 that laid the basis for the creation of the welfare state.

The combination of social investigation and legislative agendas was an important feature of this urban reform movement. As in London, so also in Berlin, Paris and New York. In New York Jacob Riis's 1890 *How the Other Half Lives* was eerily similar to Mearns's pamphlet. Riis was born in Denmark, but emigrated to the US in 1870. He worked as a labourer before becoming a police reporter for the *New York Tribune*. He used his journalistic position to tell the economically secure how the economically insecure lived. He drew attention to the role that the rich played in the construction of poverty. He constantly argued that the 'poor were the victims rather than the makers of their fate'. In 1888 he worked as a photojournalist for the *New York Evening Sun*. He used flash powder, which enabled him to photograph interiors and exteriors of the slums at night. In 1889 his account of city life, illustrated by photographs, appeared in *Scribner's Magazine*. The following year, a full-length version, *How the Other Half Lives*, was published. Riis was one of the first urban observers to use photography, so now real pictures supplemented words. Riis continued to write and lecture on behalf of the poor for the rest of his life, and his other books included *Children of the Poor* (1892), *Out of Mulberry Street* (1898), *The Battle with the Slum* (1902) and *Children of the Tenement* (1903).

Like Riis, Jane Addams was also a social activist. In 1889 she founded Hull House on Chicago's Near West Side. She worked there until her death in 1935. Jane Addams and the other residents of the settlement provided services for the neighbourhood, such as kindergarten and daycare facilities for children of working mothers, an employment bureau, an art gallery, libraries, and music and art classes. Hull House surveys of the local areas, similar to Booth's survey, led to the construction of maps of household income levels and ethnicity. One interesting feature of Hull House was the important role of women. Eight out of ten of the contributors to the 1895 volume, *Hull House Maps and Papers*, were women. By 1900 Hull House activities had broadened to include the Jane Club (a cooperative residence for working women), the first Little Theater in America, a Labor Museum and a meeting place for trade union groups. The Hull House residents and their supporters forged a powerful reform movement that launched the Immigrants' Protective League, the Juvenile Protective Association, the first juvenile court in the nation and a Juvenile Psychopathic Clinic. They lobbied the Illinois legislature to enact protective legislation for women and children and to pass in 1903 a strong child labour law and an accompanying compulsory education law. The federal child labour law of 1916 was the national result of their efforts. Addams was tireless in her dedication. She wrote many popular books and numerous articles, maintained speaking engagements around the world and played an important role in many local and national organizations, such as the Consumers' League, National Conference of Charities and Corrections (later the National Conference of Social Work), Campfire Girls, National Playground Association, the National Child Labor Committee, the National Association for the Advancement of Colored People and the American Civil Liberties Union. She was awarded the Nobel Peace Prize in 1931.

The size, complexity and danger of the modern city is the context for a particular strain of investigative reporting, the participant observer. The sheer size of the city means that a single person's everyday gaze can not comprehend the variety of the urban condition. And as new urban milieus develop there is both a curiosity about the other as well as a fear of the other. The participant observer gives a close up view into other urban worlds. Olive Malvery, a visitor from India who went to London in 1900 to train as a singer, purposely joined the ranks of the poor and dispossessed. She took a variety of low-paying jobs and lived on sixpence a day. The book of her experiences, *The Soul Market* (1906), was very popular, going through eleven editions, and she became a popular public speaker; although, in an ironic twist for an Indian immigrant, she railed against the influx of foreigners into the city and called for stricter immigration controls. There is straight line between Malvery's work and Barbara Ehrenreich's more recent book, *Nickel and Dimed* (2001). In 1998 Ehrenreich left her middle-class home to take low-paying jobs and live on minimum wages. She details her experiences as a waitress, maid, cleaner and Wal-Mart sales assistant. Her book, very well written, funny and revealing, describes the difficulties and tribulations of the working poor in contemporary America. The Malvery–Ehrenreich tradition is a long and rich one that has exposed many readers to other, less comfortable urban worlds.

For commentators such as Addams, Booth, Mearns and Riis, understanding the city was an important stage in changing the city. All of them wrote with a general audience in mind and sought to influence a broad base of public opinion. They differed in their social activism with the more investigatory Booth at one end of the continuum and the more activist Addams at the other end. To find modern equivalents of Addams and Booth we would need to turn to the pages of investigative journalism, look at certain documentaries or watch some of the better news programmes; we rarely find them in academic journals or books. To a certain extent it is because many of the demands of the urban reformers have been embodied in social welfare programmes that we now take for granted. Their battles have been won and the modern capitalist city is a more liveable, civilized place because of their work. However, the contemporary academic silence is also a mark of the failure of the academy, where too many commentators have swapped social relevance for intellectual fashion, and adopted writing styles only accessible to a narrow specialized audience. There are too few public intellectuals in the academy.

Some of the reformers had the great fortune of seeing their plans turn into physical reality. Ebenezer Howard is arguably one the best examples of a successful reformer. Howard's ideas were enunciated in his 1898 book, *To-morrow: A Peaceful Path to Real Reform*. It was re-issued four years later with a new title, *Garden Cities of Tomorrow*. Howard had a vision of small cooperatives, self-governing settlements. He could see the ills of the big city and the unemployment in the rural areas and suggested a garden city in the countryside where land could be bought cheaply and decent housing made available. It was not a rural retreat. Howard expected that jobs and industry would also leave the big city. The ideal settlement size Howard proposed was 32,000 people at relatively high densities in a city surrounded by a green belt. Once urban growth exceeded this limit a new settlement would be established, and eventually a vast conurbation would emerge of multiple garden cities linked by a mass transit system. The residents would own the land and modest rent levels would be used to fund public services and social welfare programmes. Howard combined the idea of garden cities with communal land ownership and local self-government, all set within a vast urban region.

Howard's ideas were acted upon. Garden cities were built. Letchworth, just north of London, was registered as the first garden city in 1903 with Raymond Unwin and Barry Parker as the main planners. Unwin and Parker went on build more garden cities, garden villages and garden suburbs. The New Town Movement was an important part of post-Second World War urban planning in the UK. Thirty-two New Towns were built and at their height they housed almost 2 million people. The idea also diffused out from Britain. Radburn in New Jersey was the first Garden City in the US, started in 1929 and, just north of the nation's capital, Greenbelt Maryland is a garden city development originating in the New Deal.

Howard's vision was turned into reality but at the cost of his radical social vision. New Towns were built but the cooperative land schemes were rarely implemented. The design elements of garden cities and the garden suburbs became a staple of urban design, but not the physical blueprint of a new social order. The most recent garden cities are private developments, often gated communities built by private interests for private gain, the garden city designs aimed more at the successful marketing of the project than a blueprint for an alternative social order. Howard influenced the layout of the urban fabric but not the structure of society.

There were also urban designers who had visions of new cities but without radical social alternatives or commitments to social reform. These more design-minded urban visionaries included Baron Haussmann, Daniel Burnham and Le Corbusier. They had great visions that bordered on the megalomaniacal. Alas, too many of their schemes were imposed on the urban fabric. The modern city bears the imprint of their visions.

Paris, like many other rapidly growing cities of the nineteenth century, had substandard housing, poor public health and a disenfranchised population that could be a threat to the existing political order. In 1832 almost 40,000 people died in a cholera epidemic, and in 1848–9 another outbreak of the disease killed almost 19,000, including the Prime Minister. The old neighbourhoods, especially in the east of the city, played an important part in the revolutions of 1830 and 1848. Between 1827 and 1849 barricades had been put up eight times in eastern Paris. Disease and social revolution were sources of disorder that the Emperor, Napoleon III, wanted to eradicate. By 1850 the population of the city reached almost one million. Haussmann was charged by the Emperor in 1853 with making Paris a spectacularly beautiful city, a healthy city and a city where the mob was under firm control (Jordan, 1995; Valance, 2000).

Haussmann commissioned a detailed map of Paris at a scale of 1:5,000 that gave the necessary spatial information for his subsequent transformation. To make the city healthier he extended the sewer system, since the old dilapidated one had been a source of disease. To make it safer, he demolished the oldest neighbourhoods in the medieval heart of the city, destroying the homes of 15,000 people. He built boulevards that destroyed the old insurrectionary areas. The wide, straight boulevards made it more difficult to put up barricades and easier to move troops. He effectively moved the centre of Paris to the north west, which was considered a safer part of the city where the rich lived. The Opera House, for example, was moved to Boulevard des Capucines because a bomb was thrown at the imperial carriage in 1858. The new site had wide streets that were more easily guarded. The new boulevards cordoned off neighbourhoods while making it easier to impose public order. The hotbeds of revolution were either demolished or ringed with wide boulevards. Haussmann transformed Paris from a medieval city into a modern city where straight, wide boulevards imposed a new order of public security. Haussmann radically altered the city in strokes that were repeated in many twentieth-century cities as urban renewal schemes demolished old neighbourhoods. Haussmann eventually became unpopular in the city. The middle and upper classes were disturbed by the presence of the thousands of labourers brought in to do the construction work; banks felt the whole project was too expensive; and residents complained that their neighbourhoods were destroyed. Haussmann was sacked in 1870. His plans did not prevent social breakdowns. The next year the Paris Commune lasted for over two months as a revolutionary city government demanded an end to support for religion and the limiting of hours of work. The uprising was brutally quashed, and about 20,000 people were killed. Barricading and insurrection, which had been a relatively easy thing to accomplish in the old medieval street-patterned neighbourhoods, now required more organization and manpower. The Communards were better organized and resisted longer than the revolutionaries of 1848.

Burnham drew upon Haussmann's designs in emphasizing ceremonial long and public vistas ending in neo-classical buildings. Burnham was an architect who designed early skyscrapers and the Columbian Exhibition held in Chicago in 1893, the magical White City on the shore of Lake Michigan. He was one of originators of the City Beautiful Movement that sought to rebuild public spaces with grand designs and imposing processionals. He designed a new civic centre for Cleveland, and in 1909 devised an ambitious plan for Chicago that imposed a classical civic order on the regular grid. By 1925 much of his plan was completed. Peter Hall (1988) shows how the City Beautiful designs spread around the world. They were employed in the imperial capital of New Delhi in India as the British Raj commissioned plans that expressed imperial dominance and racial exclusiveness. A great processional way,

Central Vista, flanked by Queen Victoria Road and King Edward Road, linked the War Memorial with the Viceroy's House in a confident display of British power. In 1912 an American architect, Walter Burley Griffin, also drew upon the iconography of City Beautiful in his plan for Australia's new capital of Canberra. He won the international competition and his design was the template for the construction of central Canberra and its geometry of power and remembrance that links the War Memorial, Parliament House and the downtown Civic Centre. The City Beautiful Movement was the city ceremonial, the celebration of formal power and authority; no surprise, then, that it was also used by European dictators. Albert Speer had a plan for fascist Berlin involving a huge processional with a Triumphal Arch, and Stalin built giant buildings, such as the Palace of the Soviets, all over Moscow. The gigantism of the buildings, completely out of scale with ordinary citizens, is a telling metaphor of a totalitarian system.

Le Corbusier, in his *Vers une Architecture* (1923) and *La Ville Radieuse* (1933), had an architectural vision of a new, high-density city composed of giant towers surrounded by open space and free-flowing motorways. It was a top-down model in which citizens would live in apartments and structures designed by experts and built by the government. What is interesting, and also tragic for the twentieth-century urban experience, is how much of Le Corbusier's vision came to pass because in the period from 1945 to the mid-1970s, governments (in alliance with municipal authorities and various business interests) declared war on city centres throughout much of the world. Governments spent money and marshalled resources to destroy much of the urban fabric, forcibly relocating city-centre inhabitants and aiding the outward movement of jobs and people. One battle plan was unveiled at the World's Fair in 1939 in New York. An exhibit, funded by General Motors, showed a city of high-rise towers and fast, free-flowing motorways; it was a tantalizing vision presented to almost five million visitors. And in large measure this vision brutally reshaped city centres in America and much of the rest of the world.

The plan drew upon a number of foreign and domestic inspirations. Earlier in the twentieth century, the Futurist Felipe Marinette preached the physical annihilation of the traditional city and said, 'we must invent and rebuild *ex novo* our Modern City'. In Germany Walter Gropius of the early Bauhaus School wanted to replace shabby irregularity of the slums with giant blocks of straight lines. Other architectural modernists were equally enthusiastic for a clean, new beginning. Le Corbusier's Radiant City plans of the 1920s, for example, envisioned three million people living in giant skyscrapers surrounded by motorways. These visions of modernity involved the destruction of the past. They transcended political ideology and found a home in Mussolini's Rome, Hitler's Berlin and Stalin's Moscow. Even liberal critics and public housing advocates, saw the benefit of starting over with the city as a blank page. And there were also business interests, such as General Motors, eager to profit from the proposed transformation, with their corporate success tied to the successful incorporation of this future vision.

The bright new future merely implicit in the interwar period was developed fully in the immediate postwar period, supported by revolutionaries and corporate executives alike, liberals as well as conservatives. The demand for a new modernist city decreed a massive transformation of the existing city, effacing its past to make room for its future. The future depended upon the destruction of the past. Postmodern sensibilities grew out of this urban maelstrom.

The Social Rupture

Georg Simmel (1858–1918) spent most his life in the centre of a cosmopolitan Berlin at the heart of elite intellectual life in the city. He retained a love for, and fascination with, the city. His most famous work, *The Metropolis and Mental Life* (1903), is like *Berlin: Symphony of a City*, a partly sympathetic and loving account of the city, which is both a source of personal disquiet as well as of personal liberation. Simmel (1950, 422) notes:

> On the one hand, life is made infinitely easy for the personality in that stimulations, interests, uses of time and consciousness are offered to it from all sides. They carry the person as if in a stream and one needs hardly to swim for oneself. On the other hand, however, life is composed more and more of these impersonal contents and offerings, which tend to displace the genuine personal colorations and incomparabilities. This results in the individual's summoning the utmost in uniqueness and particularization in order to preserve his most personal core. He has to exaggerate this personal element in order to remain audible even to himself.

For Simmel the city was a new opportunity, one fraught with uncertainty but one that marked a break with traditional society, especially the small-scale societies of the predominantly rural past where barter and

exchange rather than monetary transactions guided both economic relations and social identities. The key development was the advent of the
monetarized economy. The roots of modernity, according to Simmel, lay
in the emergence of a money economy because once money becomes the
principal means of exchange, quantitative instrumental perceptions and
attitudes replace qualitative assessments. The city is the centre and home
of the money economy. Simmel concentrates on the everyday life of the
city, and he notes that, especially as cities get bigger and more complex,
more of our daily interaction takes place with anonymous people in fleeting interactions. There are fewer emotional ties involved in most of the
urban contact than in traditional smaller-scale societies where people
tend to interact with people they know more than with people merely
performing roles. The danger of such constant interaction of the nameless
and unknowns is a blasé attitude, a lack of responsiveness and a certain
reserve that acts as a protective shield. The result can be a distancing
between people as they create space between themselves and the rest of
the world. Simmel's work is part of a broad concern with the relationship
between modernity and subjectivity that is found in other fields and
includes such notable figures as Søren Kierkegaard (Garff, 2005).

We can easily summarize Simmel: the money economy dominates the
metropolis, and thus the metropolitan mind becomes ever more calculat-
ing; punctuality, calculability and exactness predominate, and a highly
personal subjectivity (often marked by a blasé reserve and a certain indifference) emerges. As he notes later in his essay: 'The metropolis is the
home of the money economy, individual independence and the elaboration of individuality, [and] reveals itself as one of those great historical
formations in which opposing streams which enclose life unfold, as well
as join one another with equal right.'

While it is easy to summarize Simmel (his famous essay is mercifully
brief and very clearly written), the consequences of his insights continue
to exercise a powerful hold on theories of the city. He was an intellectual
modernist who foreshadowed the academic work on the sociology of
everyday life. The Chicago School of urban research further developed
his ideas, and he had important influences on such thinkers as Walter
Benjamin, Edmund Husserl, Max Weber, Georg Lukács and Max
Horkheimer. In large measure Simmel outlined in his metropolis essay as
well as in his other writings, especially *The Problem of Sociology* (1894)
and *Sociology: Studies of the Forms of Association* (1908), the framework for the academic discipline we now know as sociology. Simmel was
not alone; the other founders of sociology shared similar concerns. Emile
Durkheim (1858–1917) outlines the notion of *anomie* as the pathology of

the modern world. The word literally means 'without law', and Durkheim used the term to refer to the disintegration of accepted normative codes, a breaking of traditional moral strictures. The term has morphed since into a general definition of alienation, the feeling of individual estrangement from the modern world. Max Weber (1864–1920) was also fascinated by the city; his essay, *The City* (written around 1911–13, but only published in 1922), draws attention to the importance of trade, commerce and civic autonomy in the development of the city. Unlike Simmel, Weber sees continuity in the urban story down through the centuries. His aim is to describe the continuities of urban historical evolution. Weber's influence is clear on the magisterial summaries of urban development undertaken by Lewis Mumford (1961) and Peter Hall (1998). But Weber also raises the more disturbing idea that in the modern city there is a compulsion to labour although labour is fundamentally motiveless. He sees a disenchantment at the heart of modern urban life and describes materialism as an iron cage.

Simmel's sociology of everyday urban life continues to be expressed, albeit in new forms and different ways. Walter Benjamin (1889–1940), for example, was writing at the same historical moment that produced *Metropolis* and *Berlin: Symphony of a City,* so his work shares with these films the context of the Weimar Republic's socio-political and aesthetic sensibilities. Benjamin's focus, however, is on nineteenth-century Paris. In *The Arcades Project*, his most telling urban musings are contained in the section 'Paris, Capital of the Nineteenth Century' (Benjamin, 1999). He conceives the city with an emphasis on its crowds, and he is fascinated by world exhibitions, which are described as places of pilgrimage to the commodity fetish. His double concern with the modern as the consecration of the commodity and the intensification of subjective experience especially by means of the mobile gaze, is crystallized in his conception of the *flâneur*, who plays the role of scout of the market place. The *flâneur* is the explorer of the crowd who anticipates the cinematic experience of *Berlin* in his own experience of the city in fragments; the modern city produces the *flâneur* who in turn produces a filmic city. The *flâneur* is a member of the crowd who seeks refuge in the crowd as well as the classifier of the experience, types and people in the crowd. The *flâneur* is the urban sociologist of the nineteenth century but one marked by a nostalgia: the authentic experience of the modern city always eludes the *flâneur* who constantly needs to evoke memory of the past to represent the present. Benjamin draws attention to the role of commodities and commodified experience in the modern city, the importance of the gaze and the crowd and the new subjective experience of the urban.

We can follow Simmel's influence down through the years to more recent urban commentators. In *The Lonely Crowd*, David Riesman outlines the contours of new American character, one in which other-directed characteristics (rather than inner-directed ones) dominate. Spare time is devoting to having fun and the emphasis is on conformity and fitting in, but at the expense of personal autonomy and inner impulses. The result is the paradox of the lonely crowd. Riesman's analysis is on a macro-scale, while Erving Goffman's work is on a more detailed micro-scale. His book, *The Presentation of Self in Everyday Life* (1959), is justifiably seen as a sociological classic. It draws deeply from the sociology of the everyday perspective that Simmel outlines. Goffman develops the notion of social activity as performance. The messages we send to others depend on the performances we enact. Goffman develops the spatial metaphors of 'front stage' and 'back stage'. Front stage is where our roles are played out; back stage is where we can let the mask slip. Goffman first conceived the idea when he noticed how waiters' voices and demeanour changed when they moved from the kitchen into the dining room. In the dining room, they were onstage and had to find the right balance between efficiency, friendliness and deference. Back stage, they could criticize the diner, shout at the chef and gripe about their lives. Front stage is all about making good impressions, fulfilling the roles of good friend, teacher, parent, and wise old person.

The city provides opportunities to play a multiplicity of roles, allowing both anonymity and identification, giving us the opportunity to be both performers and audience in a myriad of fleeting and more sustained social interactions. The characterization of the city as stage has unlocked a whole host of useful metaphors, including plot, script, roles, back/front stage and so on, that have been enormously useful to understanding life in the city. Elijah Anderson, for example, in *Streetwise* (1990), discusses street strategies adopted by different racial-ethnic groups in the neighbourhoods in Philadelphia. His focus is on the Village, an area of gentrification and Northton, a predominantly black area with a vigorous drug trade. The residents of these different types of neighbourhoods often share the same street where different groups adopt different strategies:

> The central strategy in maintaining safety on the streets is to avoid strange black males. The public awareness is color-coded: white skin denotes civility, law-abidingness and trustworthiness, while black skin is strongly associated with poverty, crime, incivility, and distrust. Thus an unknown young black male is readily deferred to, if he asks

for anything, he must be handled quickly and summarily. If he is persistent, help must be summoned. (Anderson, 1990, 208)

Young black males, in contrast, have a sense of both their own vulnerability to being stigmatized as well as a realization of their power to intimidate the white middle class simply by their presence. Anderson draws upon Goffman to inform his fascinating and insightful study of how people of different class, race and age interact in the shared city streets.

Ever since Simmel's essay on the city, some scholars have sought to capture the fleeting existence of the city. Benjamin's urban *flâneur* was both a guide and an example of this fleeting urban experience. The initial idea of the *flâneur* posited an active (male) viewer and a passive city. The emphasis was on the role of the *flâneur* looking at an inert city. However, in recent years the central areas of many globalizing cities have become sites of urban spectaculars of signature architects, festival markets and commodified leisuredomes. The city has been manipulated and restructured to create new consumption modes of urban *flânerie*. There has been a shift from visual to commodity acquisition, a self-conscious transformation of donning the festival mask in globalizing cities and the emergence of new form of urban *flânerie*. Quentin Stevens and Kim Dovey (2004) describe a walk along Southbank, the urban riverfront in Melbourne, drawing attention to the tension between global and local, politics and play, representation and embodied action. Emmanuel Guano (2002) provides us with very good example drawing on a case study of Buenos Aires to show how the new cityscape is used to legitimize inequality.

In *The Practice of Everyday Life* (1984), Michel de Certeau drew attention to the act of walking as well as the more general distinction between strategies and tactics. The city is not just an inert space; rather, it is a range of possibilities that the walker actualizes. The 'chorus of ideal footsteps' brings to life the seemingly endless possibilities of the urban spatial order. Strategy refers to spatial ordering; tactics refer to appropriations and transgressions. Through tactics, the strategies of power can be undermined and appropriated. Life in the city is conceptualized as both reinforcing the spatial strategies of the official city, and also the tactical appropriation and resistance of the everyday resistances. The complex relationships between the two are outlined by Brian Morris (2004), who gives the example of alternative maps of the city, in this case Melbourne, that identify gay and lesbian sites. The spaces of resistance that are mapped and commodified by a commercial publisher suggest practices are 'neither strictly compliant nor resistant'.

De Certeau's work is enormously influential (Ross, 1996; Reynolds and Fitzpatrick, 1999). It points to the need to connect the official and the everyday, the compliance and resistances embodied in the space/time paths we make across the urban built form and the routes we weave across urban social space. The simple dichotomy between resistances and subordination, the official strategies and the everyday tactics, soon breaks down when we consider real people and everyday events. But de Certeau provides us with a useful starting point to producing theories of how 'bodies, power, mobility and urban forms intersect within the contemporary city' (Morris, 2004, 681).

The distinction I made at the beginning of this chapter between Marxist urban theory, which is limited to interrogating social conflict, and an emerging urban sociology dominated by its consideration of the individual, is a useful one but we should be careful of too simple a distinction. Here is Engels, for example, writing about London:

> And still they crowd by one another as though they had nothing in common, nothing to do with one another, and their only agreement is the tacit one, that each keep to his own side of the pavement, so as not to delay the opposing streams of the crowd, while it occurs to no man to honour another with so much as a glance. The brutal indifference, the unfeeling isolation of each in his private interest becomes the more repellent and offensive, the more these individuals are crowded together, within a limited space, And, however, much one may be aware that this isolation of the individual, this narrow self-seeking is the fundamental principle of our society everywhere, it is nowhere so shamelessly barefaced, so self-conscious as just here in the crowding of the great city, the dissolution of mankind into monads, of which each one has a separate principle and a separate purpose, the world of atoms, is here carried out to its most extreme. (Engels, 1973, 64)

This is one of the earliest and still one of the best descriptions of alien-ation and the rise of personal subjectivity in the city. At about the same time, Marx outlines theories of personal alienation in *The Economic and Philosophic Manuscripts* written in Paris in the summer of 1844. And although he draws attention to the rise of individualism in modern soci-ety, Simmel also emphasizes how social conflict could produce group cohesion as well as the personal experiences involved in social gather-ings. He conceives of such social types as the stranger, the poor, the medi-ator and the renegade. Weber is also more attuned to class and class conflict than his critics suggest.

There are other similarities between the two schools of thought that I have presented throughout this chapter. For both, the modern city was something to dissect and analyse. Both presume a distancing, an explicit intellectualism that allows an observer to move away from the swirl of our everyday lives towards making some sense, some order, some theory of that life in the city. The subjectivity of the modern constructs the modern observer. These theories of the modern city provide the huge intellectual leap that makes the study of society possible. The main difference is that Marxist theory has a sense of praxis, a view that the theories not only lead to an understanding of the works but a changing of the worlds. Knowledge is not simply an ability to know the worlds; it is the essential means to change them. In 1989, the world was changing radically, but it was not the works of Marx that were instrumental in knocking down of walls of oppressive governments. In a city beloved by Simmel, represented in two classic silent movies and the capital of Marx's homeland, a new world order was inaugurated when the Berlin Wall was demolished; yet it was the political project of Marxism that was sidelined to the dustbin of history.

3
Theorizing the Postmodern City

For some, the postmodern equivalent to the modern classic of *Metropolis* is *Blade Runner* (1982). The opening shots are overhead vistas of a dense city, cloaked in darkness. Combining *film noir* and science fiction genres, *Blade Runner* depicts a future world of megastructure buildings, corrupt corporations and world-weary citizens, all inhabiting a cosmopolitan yet bleak and polluted city where a perverted science has produced humanoid robots. As in *Metropolis*, there is the same mad scientist, the same reference shots to giant tower blocks, and the same sense that the emotions, even feelings for a non-human, win out in the end. So what makes it postmodern?

Before I answer that question we need to spend some time with the term. As an adjective *postmodern* is a ubiquitous term for all manner of ideas, used in reference to almost anything that is eclectic, multicultural and heterogeneous. *Postmodern* often pertains to the contemporary, the paradoxical, the ambiguous and the strange in various combinations of old and new, universal and vernacular, ancient and modern. The *post* suggests that something has changed in relation to modernism: perhaps a reaction to formalism; a loss of belief in positivism; a resistance to Eurocentrism, patriarchy and 'expertise'; a concern with the past as much as with the future; a resistance to metanarratives, especially those of progress, reason and universal truth. Compared to modernity's categorical certainty, postmodernity is the 'present imperfect' and the 'future uncertain'.

Accepting for the moment at least that there is a rupture between the past and the present that we can comprehend under the general term *postmodern*, what is the role of cities in this divide? The answers revolve around three themes: the postindustrial city, the postmodern look and postmodern urban cultures. I will explore these themes briefly before considering theorizings of the postmodern city and the postcolonial city.

The Postindustrial City

The modern city of Marx and Engels, Simmel and Benjamin was an industrial city producing commodities from raw materials with the application of both science and labour power. Technology triumphant, new classes, new modes of calculation, the rise of consumer culture and subjective individualism were all tied to the creation of an industrial order in and through and by cities. The decline of the industrial economy in First World cities shocked theorists into imagining something so radically different that it broke significantly with tradition. Thus postmodern cities arose from the abandoned factories and empty industrial spaces of mature industrial cities.

'All that is solid melts into air', Karl Marx once wrote about the restless dynamism of the capitalist economic system. Joseph Schumpeter used the term 'creative destruction' to describe the forward drive of capitalism with its repeated waves of technological transformation and innovation, continual striving for market dominance and endless searching for more profits and greater market share. Capitalism's relentlessness modulated significantly in the early 1970s. Three trends are important. The first was the deindustrialization of manufacturing cities in North America and Europe. The creation of a more global economy allowed goods consumed in the rich West to be produced in the lower wage areas of the world. Japan, Korea and more recently China have all experienced waves of industrialization as centres of industrial production were relocated from the West to areas of cheap labour. Standardized production and cheap transport further dispersed industrial production from the old centres of skilled labour. The cotton mills of Engels' Lancashire are long since closed, while textile production is flourishing in Sri Lanka and Vietnam. This global shift in manufacturing production involves a decline of the old industrial working class. The manufacturing cites of North America and Western Europe were the birth places of the organized working class, a class in and for itself in much of Europe, while in the US it is more concerned with seeking to advance into the middle class, and more desirous of benefiting from capitalism than with overthrowing it. The mass affluence of the West was in part a function of the high wages that organized labour could leverage from a capitalism seemingly locked in place.

Even when industrial production remains in place, a post-Fordist, flexible production system restructures it, dispensing with the predictable assembly lines employing full-time and mainly male labour. *Fordism* was the name given to the mass production of commodities on controlled assembly lines, an inflexible system geared towards a constant, standardized production dependent on a highly unionized, stable working class. *Post-Fordism* involves an increasing range of products with shorter production runs, implying more subcontracting, greater vertical integration between firms and just-in-time production. Flexible production is the response to tight markets, finicky consumers and the declining power of labour: it allows firms to adjust quickly to volatile markets by exercising greater control over the deployment of labour and the pacing of work. If Fordism led to the rise of the well-paid working class, Post-Fordism marks its declining power. New labour practices do not lead immediately to changed consciousness, but when large-scale, common working experiences (such as those of the old assembly line factories) are exchanged *en masse* for a more individual contract system, individual positioning does dispatch mass solidarity with relative speed.

Economic globalization at its heart is the increased ability of capital to move across the globe while labour is stuck in place, leading to the decline of the manufacturing sector in the rich capitalist countries, the demise of many industrial cities and a loss of bargaining power and decline in political influence of the working class. This decline had wider political implications as a neo-liberal agenda faced less competition. Reagonomics and Thatcherism were signs of the new tide in the affairs of political economy. As the neo-liberal agenda of marketization and reduced public services now dominates both national and international politics, and as we bid farewell to the working class in the West, the consequent crisis in theory deserves, for some at least, the nomenclature of *post*.

The second trend was the rise of new employment opportunities in the service sector and the high-tech sector. New patterns of employment emerged involving more white-collar work, more female participation in the formal economy, the use of new immigrant groups and demands for very specialized, highly-skilled labour. A more fragmented labour market resulted, polarizing into a core of workers in paid employment, a semi-periphery of contract labour and a periphery of people working on a casual irregular basis. More variety in labour force participation meant that male manual workers no longer dominated the economy. More women, more immigrant groups, and more types of labour all affected a collapse of the neat duality of workers and capitalists into heterogeneous groups with real and perceived differences.

Third, there was also a restructuring of the space economy. Consider the contrasting fortunes of two cities. In 1950 Schenectady, New York, and San José, California, had similar population sizes: 92,061 and 95,280 respectively. At that time Schenectady's economy seemed secured. Over 27,000 people worked for General Electric. The city was flourishing with a vibrant centre and a buoyant job market. Corporations such as the American Locomotive Company provided employment for thousands of workers as well as a way of life. Social clubs and softball teams grew up around the connections workers made in the factory. By 2000 most of those jobs had gone. The Locomotive Company closed in 1968 and General Electric shed over 90 per cent of their jobs in the city. The city's population shrank to just over 61,821; houses lost value and the credit rating of the city has been downgraded to the lowest in the state. The median household income in 2004 was $29,378.

By 2000 San José, in deep contrast, had a population of 894,943 and was one of the larger cities in the US. Decades of spectacular growth, fuelled in particular by the Silicon Valley boom in high technology and computer-related industries, had made San José one of the most prosperous and economically dynamic cities in the country. In 2004 median household income was $70,243. Among the companies headquartered in the city are Adobe, Cisco and eBay. Schenectady and San José, which had been close in population size in 1950, by 2000 were on two different trajectories, one spiralling downwards and the other set on an upwards course.

From 1950 to the early 1970s the urban economies in the West were dominated by the growth of high-wage, unionized jobs. Since then the economy has been marked by cuts in real wages, resistance to union orga-nizing, and the shifting of production to lower-wage sites in the nation and overseas. While capital was more footloose, able to locate in other parts of the county or even the world, labour was caught in place. Deindustrialization has involved the closure of plants, especially in the urban cores and the reduction of workers in existing plants. In vibrant urban economies the loss of manufacturing jobs has been offset in aggre-gate terms by the growth of jobs in other sectors. However, in neighbour-hoods and cities where there has been little alternative employment growth, the loss of manufacturing employment has had devastating effects. Traditional small industrial cities such as Schenectady, Syracuse or Flint have seen the lifeblood of the local economy drained away with-out the transfusion of new jobs.

The Postmodern Look

Buildings, when they are first erected, intimate the future. As they get older they lock up history. Modernist architecture expressed simplicity, honesty in materials and an explicit link between form and function with an accompanying theory of liberation, more honoured in the breach than the practice. In the beginning international modernism drew on the utopian socialist thought of the Bauhaus School, to promote architecture as a revolutionary activity in the design of new built forms for a new social order. But as modernist architecture became the dominant architecture of the second half of the twentieth century, housing communist parties as well as corporate offices, the revolutionary edge was blunted. The 'less is more' mantra of Mies van der Rohe in practice turned out flat-topped, glass-sided, soul-less monotony, often warehousing the poor. The austere beauty of Rohe's classic Seagram Building in New York City was repeated endlessly but without the same sensitivity, quality of materials or design sophistication. Modernist architecture's revolutionary fashion was coopted by capitalist and communist societies, totalitarian and authoritarian regimes around the world. Communist headquarters in Warsaw, government buildings in Brasilia, corporate offices in New York, and public housing in Chicago and London all looked the same; they all had the simple clean lines, the box look and the flat top as the concrete narrative of modernism rewrote the modern city.

Critical commentators began to sense something was happening when one of the archpriests of modernist architecture, Philip Johnson (1906–2004), designed the AT & T Building in New York City. Rather than the usual flat top, the building, which opened in 1978, sported a pediment resembling a Chippendale tallboy. This was the same Philip Johnson who co-wrote *The International Style* in 1932, who built his house in New Canaan, Connecticut in 1949 as a glass box and who co-designed the Seagram Building in 1958. Now this same Philip Johnson was adding ornamentation to an important building on a prestigious site. It was just a taste of things to come, as Corinthian columns, Renaissance palazzos and Georgian façades became the built form for apartment buildings, post offices, office blocks and banks. Architecture's former sobriety gave way to insouciance as brightly coloured pediments topped off buildings to brighten the previously grey-dominated palettes. Even the pretence of a progressive under-girding is dropped as buildings reference the past rather than suggest liberation from it. Postmodern architecture looks forward to the past, reflecting a decline in the metanarrative of modernist confidence; it is an edgy pedimented parody atop a foundation cracked by a fear of the future.

Postmodern architecture is so noticeably different from modernist architecture that the rupture was clearly visible. Beginning in the 1970s this new style took hold in global cities round the world, fuelled in part by growing competition between cities and their increasing need to position themselves as places of cultural heft as well as economic connectivity. Postmodern architecture is now an essential part of the syntax of cities eager to reposition themselves in a changing global economy. The division between modern and postmodern is so apparent that some commentators describe cities themselves as postmodern.

Postmodern Urban Culture

The dominant rendering of culture in the modernist tradition emerges from the importance of class-determined modes of life in the class-dominated cities, or from the decline of community in the rural to urban reorientation, or from the gaze of the *flâneur* as the archetypal modern urban commentator. In the postmodern rendering, the emphasis on urban culture highlights the varieties of experience above, beyond and below these three traditional discourses.

Class is no longer a primary determinant of experience and worldview. Age, gender, sexual orientation, ethnicity, race and a host of other sources of social differentiation are now considered as both reflectors and shapers of urban cultures. The importance of local urban cultures rather than the universal categories of class comes to the fore in a postmodern reading. Much of the cultural analysis of the modern city focuses on the shift from the rural to urban. But urbanization proceeded so far in many advanced capitalist societies that the accommodation of the rural migrants comprises only a small part of the urban cultural mix. The phenomenon of *flânerie* has been subject to critical re-examination in recent years: its former emphasis on the footloose, single white male as the sole source of the gaze has been critiqued as a sexist, partial and incomplete rendering of the subjective experience of the city. In the postmodern turn urban cultures are more heterogeneous confrontations of global and local, universal and particular in new and interesting combinations.

The Postmodern City

The postmodern city is delineated explicitly by what has become known as the LA School. The designation applies to a number of academics who write about Los Angeles, not simply as a case study but as a classic example of the postmodern city. Let us consider three works representing this discursive approach. In 1990 Mike Davis's *City of Quartz* made a dramatic entry into urban studies. Written with a forceful energy that focuses on the new urban forms emerging in Los Angeles, *City of Quartz* contends that Los Angeles 'has come to play the double role of utopia and dystopia for advanced capitalism' (18). The most insightful chapter, entitled 'Fortress L.A.', outlines a privatized city where sadistic street environments, gated communities and bunker architecture destroy public space. Davis achieved a certain fame as his work described a city on the edge of social dislocation just over a year before the LA riots occurred, vindicating his claims. The book has had a tremendous impact on urban studies. With a subversive feel that appealed to a new generation of scholars bored with the pedestrian prose of most urban studies, *City of Quartz* examines a supposedly cool city in a very cool way. The work became popular in wider academic communities, forging links between the cultural theorists and urban scholars. Just as Engels did, Davis combines official data with personal observations. And then there is his implicit claim that somehow LA was the centre of this postmodern storm of change. It was *the* model of utopia and dystopia not just for southern California or the US, but also for advanced capitalism; an audacious claim. Davis seems more of a Marxist than a postmodernist, and his subsequent work mixes a cyberpunk style within a neo-Marxist framework. Staking claims to a working-class background, his book jacket biography states that he is 'a former meat cutter and long-distance truck driver' as well as a 'teacher of urban theory', so he seems the consummate contemporary mix of thoughtful working-class hero and muscular theorist.

In his next book, *Ecology of Fear* (1998), Los Angeles is the product of a vivid apocalyptic imagination, beset by natural disasters of floods, fires, earthquakes and even mountain lion attacks. He argues that there is a conspiracy to hide the 'fact' that LA was a centre for tornado activity. Whether or not it is true that, as he claims, 'no other urban area on the planet so frequently produces large thermal anomalies', it does appear that for Davis, LA is an omphalos of urban id. Such exaggerations say more about Davis's (and indeed the entire LA School's) obsessions with LA than about anything else. For them, LA is not just another city, it is *the* city that reveals the path of the future. And in a remarkably unapologetic mix of civic and academic boosterism, those who study LA are thereby placed at the cutting edge of new urban realities.

Davis is writing less about a postmodern city than explaining how a particular form of modernity is expressed in LA. Davis was more worried about showing how a neo-Marxist analysis could accommodate the new urban realities of postmodern LA than developing a postmodern sensibility. Ed Soja and Michael Dear, in contrast, were more deliberate postmodernists. Through much of the 1980s Soja wrote about the dialectical relationship between space and society in his development of a socio-spatial theory. By the later 1980s he added the term 'postmodern' to his theory and concentrated on the analysis of new socio-spatial forms in LA. *Postmodern Geographies: The Reassertion of Space in Critical Social Theory* (1989) is a work in the transition from geographical theory to urban theory. Again LA is the centre of the world. Space plays a pivotal role in social dynamics, and there is no place like LA 'to illustrate the dynamics of capitalist spatializations' (191). It all comes together for Soja in the southern California metropolis. In *Thirdspace: Journey to Los Angles and Other Real-and-Imagined Places* (1996), Soja muses on the indefinite and constantly shifting spaces of postmodernity. At best, this is a postmodern rendition, a decentred text dealing with a complex, chameleon-like phenomenon of shifting spectral spaces; at worst, it is almost incomprehensible, long on citations, short on genuine analysis. *Postmetropolis* (2000) is a more substantial contribution regarding the spatial dimensions of social theory, which represents a return to Soja's long-standing concern with developing a socio-spatial theory and argues the need for an urban, centred geographical imagination. The long history of the city is presented, leading up to what Soja believes is its contemporary high point; it is a sort of Hegelian view of history with urban history as a forerunner of its current culmination in the city of Los Angeles. Soja identifies six processes of urban transformation in the postmodern city: regional city formation, the development of the post-Fordist city, the rise of the world city, the creation of the dual city of polarized communities, the carceral city of closely controlled urban spaces (including prisons and gated communities), and the simulacrum city of hyper-reality production and consumption. These processes are found outside LA and do in fact constitute the closest thing to a broader description of a postmodern city.

Dear's postmodern theory of urbanism is relatively independent of either Davis's or Soja's. Whereas a lingering neo-Marxism inflects Davis and an enduring concern with the socio-spatial dialectic marks Soja, Dear focuses entirely on the project of developing a truly postmodern urban theory. In *The Postmodern Urban Condition* (2000), Dear contextualizes a domination of edge cities, privatopias, theme park cities, and fortified and policed cities, within a globalizing restructuring. He offers four themes of the postmodern city as *world city*, *dual city*, *hybrid city* and *cyber city*. There is the same breathless LA boosterism:

for example, 'LA is a polycentric, polycultural, polyglot metropolis regarded by many as the prototype of contemporary urbanization' (3). But for Dear, postmodern cities are in part a result of a new postmodern sensibility that seeks to make sense of the complexity of contemporary life. This sensibility involves an interest in peripheries rather than centres, alternative rather than dominant narratives and a multiplicity of ways of knowing. The postmodern urban condition is in part an ongoing process of new socio-spatial practices producing new ways of looking at the world, which in turn shape new socio-spatial practices. Much of the density of postmodern theorizing comes from the difficulty inherent in breaking through this circularity to actual analysis. While Dear has some interesting insights, readers should be warned beforehand to hold on to the book very tightly with both hands. To open the pages is to unlock an enormous cloud of puffery that may lift both book and reader into hyper-space.

The LA School is part hype, part response to LA and part giving a spatial face to the postmodern thought. It still has the open-mouthed wonder of people from colder climes forever in awe, it appears, of a city that is sunny and warm in December. This slack-jawed wonder of people from cooler places (such as New York) or danker regions (such as South Wales) interferes with the more studious gaze of the accomplished academic. The School's output is a mix of personal positioning and political posturing along with serious analysis and honest attempts to make sense of new urban realities. Like the Hollywood movie industry, the LA School has been successful in selling its wares to a more global public although the extent to which the fantasies of southern California capture the complexity of the globe is more the result of successful marketing than a subtle demonstration of correspondence.

There is also the more sober academic analysis as found in *The City: Los Angeles and Urban Theory at the End of the Twentieth Century* (1996), edited by Scott and Soja. It has the usual fan-based rhetoric in places, as in the chapter entitled 'The First American City', which begins, 'Los Angeles is the first consequential American city to separate itself decisively from the European models and to reveal the impulse to priva-tization embedded in the origins of the American revolution' (22). However, other chapters analyse in a more profound manner the relation-ship between spatial processes and built forms in this new wave of glob-alization, hybridization, polarization and privatization.

Postmodern urban theory is not only the coining of the new: there has also been a reevaluation of the past. The work of Henri Lefebvre (1901–91) in particular has been translated and resuscitated to give a new voice to the emerging urban condition. Lefebvre was a French philosopher whose work connected both the modernist and postmodernist theories of the city, just as his writings span the Marxist and post-Marxist phases of social thought. His work was firmly rooted in a Marxist tradition, something he shared with every single French intellectual of his generation, but his attempt to develop a philosophy of the everyday, to spatialize social theories and to identify spatial practices influenced a whole generation of postmodernists from Frederic Jameson to Soja and Dear. He developed ideas about everyday life, modernity and the social production of space that continue to exercise social theorists. His Marxist spin on everydayness, his concern with alienation and the need to hold on to moments of personal revelation as a driving force in self-development mark his work as both interdisciplinary and transdisciplinary. His principal English-speaking interpreter, Rob Shields, describes him as a 'socio-spatial imaginary'. *The Right to the City* was published in France in 1968, the year of the student unrest in Paris; it was a political pamphlet in that Lefebvre suggested experimental urban utopias based on studying what made people happy in the city.

The Production of Space was first published in 1974 and translated into English in 1991, just in time to influence the new wave of postmodern urban theorists. In this book Lefebvre makes a distinction between spatial practices of three urban worlds: the *perceived*, the *conceived* and *the lived*. Perceived spatial practices involve the production and reproduction of the city, conceived the representation of the city while the lived embraces phenomenological representations of the city. Together these practices circumscribe the economic, the social and the imaginative experiences of the city. Lefebvre was a profound thinker able to transcend neat academic divisions of labour and provide tantalizing fragments of insights; he was also an inchoate thinker and unclear writer whose ambitious theorizing (like so much French theorizing) is a Cartesian attempt to impose intellectual Gallic order on an unruly world. French theorists of his stripe have been a source of endless fascination and no small amount of hero-worship for some Anglo-American academics. The lofty French theorists seem more confident, eschewing the messy empirical verification that pervades much of Anglo social sciences, and write as if academic ideas have real political importance. Levebvre's intellectual bravura and his stylistic writing, as much as his concern with socio-spatial processes and developing socio-spatial imaginaries, was a boon to urban theory, influencing both neo-Marxist and postmodern thought.

The Postcolonial City

The term *postcolonial* has a double meaning; it refers to both the resistances to colonialism and its persistence as a discourse and a practice. It refers as much to a time, the era after formal colonialism, as a place, the intersection between colonial and anti-colonial discourses and practices. Let me consider briefly the history of European colonialism and the development of postcolonial theory before considering the postcolonial city.

We live in a post-Columbian global society. The year of Columbus's circumnavigation of the globe,1492, is a convenient place to begin the globalization of the world. There is not a straight line between 1492 and the present day. It is more accurate to consider a series of reglobalizations as different parts of Europe and the rest of the world were bound together in different ways. Globalization is the process whereby local places are incorporated into a global economy and local significations are embedded in global cultures. We can see an emerging global economy by the end of the eighteenth century. The integrated nature of the network is apparent when we consider the first phase of the Industrial Revolution in Britain. By 1775 two-thirds of the value of its trade involved either a source or destination overseas. Between 1780 and 1840 cotton manufacture in Britain was the leading sector in the new forms of manufacturing. Over a half of all Britain's exports during most of this time were cotton goods. The raw material came from plantations in the Caribbean and North America, while three-quarters of cotton manufacturing was exported to Africa, America and Asia. In 1850 India was taking one-quarter of all cotton exports. The global network allowed cheap imports and guaranteed exports. It was Britain's global connections that created the Industrial Revolution.

In Europe, it was apparent that national wealth and security was dependent upon overseas possessions. In the wake of the Columbian encounter, European powers scrambled to gain a piece of the action. Global geopolitics was dominated by an economic nationalism which held the mercantilist belief that it was the business of the state to promote economic interests; the best way to do this was to stimulate foreign trade. Initially the accumulation of gold and silver was considered paramount; then the emphasis changed to the belief that wealth lay in the import of cheap raw materials and the export of expensive manufactured goods. Mercantilism held the world's wealth to be limited and, like a giant cake, it could only be obtained at the expense of others. It became imperative to grab as big a slice as possible.

Another wave of colonial annexation occurred at the end of the nineteenth century. From 1865 to 1914 was an age of imperialism involving the territorial annexation of land and peoples into colonies of European powers and the US. A neo-mercantilist doctrine emerged that argued for protection of home industries and the possession of overseas colonies to ensure cheap raw materials, whilst also supplying a captive market and denying competitors access. National pride and prestige came into play as more of the world was swallowed up and countries sought to claim a piece of the action and avoid global exclusion. There was resistance to imperialism: let us consider just three instances. The Boxer Rebellion of 1898 marked a nationalist response in China to foreign domination. Zulu resistance (in what is now South Africa) which had begun in 1870 continued to simmer, and there were further uprisings in 1888 and 1906. These were defeated and Zulu land was divided into native reserves, Crown land and land given to white farmers. In the Philippines in 1896 a movement of almost 250,000 Tagalog speakers instigated an insurrection against Spanish power. A republic was declared in June 1898. However, Spain ceded the Philippines to the US in December 1898. Filipino resistance continued, albeit moving from armed struggle to political negotiations. It was only in 1946 that the Philippines became a sovereign independent state.

Colonialism was also an empire of cultural signification. The experiences of the colonized were given shape and form and meaning by the metropolitan centre. The production of knowledge was like other manufacturing processes: raw materials were shipped in from the periphery for value added work, then shipped back around the world. Knowledge is produced in place as well as time. The metropolitan centres created a knowledge system from the bias of a certain place. Anthropology, sociology, history and the social sciences and humanities were produced in the context of an imperial system of power. Comparative knowledge systems such as anthropology and sociology created a hierarchy of stages, most often peaking in the imperial centre. The stages of humankind, comparative religions, evolution of society and levels of civilization were all devices used to grade and sift the world into hierarchical classifications. Theory production was part of the imperial project to classify and conquer. It was not just an economic system, but also an empire of signs, a global knowledge system that turned local signification into a worldwide understanding, all from a specific location. The material culture, meaning and significance of the periphery were annexed as well as its raw materials and commodities. There was an intellectual as well as economic appropriation.

A number of writers have laid the foundation of postcolonial theory. Edward Said, especially in his 1978 book *Orientalism*, develops the notion that the West describes and defines the Middle East. The discourse of orientalism is more a product of the Occident than an objective excavation of the facts of the Orient. The Middle East was invented and defined by the West from a position of economic and political dominance. The very definition of the region as well as its broad outlines and precise details were developed in and by and through an imperial Western location. The colonial power relations are reflected and embodied in the ways the world is described, demarcated and explained. We now have a rich body of work that develops the notion of subaltern cultures, otherness as both an identity and a source of difference and hybrid identities in a world marked by inequalities in power and prestige (Spivak, 1987; Bhabha, 1994; Cesaire, 2000). Postcolonial theory is very well developed in literary studies: Said (1993), for example, looks at the inscription of colonial concerns on the literature of the colonial centre, and a host of more detailed studies excavate the inscription of colonial power and resistance on selected texts produced by 'African' writers, 'Asian' writers (Mudimbe, 1988), 'Chicano' writers (Anzaldua, 1987), 'Indian' writers (Suleri, 1992), 'Irish' writers (Lloyd, 1993) and writers in the 'Black Atlantic' of Africa, Britain, the Caribbean and the US (Gilroy, 1993). The quotation marks around these terms are used to imply both signify colonial impositions and subaltern identities as well as anticolonial resistances and communities of resistance. The connections between feminist and postcolonial literary theory are also explored by many writers (Chow, 1991; McClintock, 1992). There have also been alternative theorizings of imperial connections and colonial imaginings. David Cannadine (2001), for example, stresses the construction of affinities as well as difference, and the importance of class and status as much as race and ethnicity.

Postcolonial theory is less developed for an analysis of the city (but see Yeoh, 2001), and yet the city is also a text that embodies and reproduces the colonizing/colonized dialectic. Colonialism is inscribed on the urban landscape in the very construction of colonial cities and the restructuring of urban systems to facilitate colonial control.

Three themes can be identified in a postcolonial urban theory. First, there is the examination of the colonial inscriptions on cities in the imperial centre. Whether it be in the continuing existence of archives of imperial/colonial domination such as botanic gardens that house 'exotic species', museums that contain treasures from 'around the world' and 'international' universities that narrate the world, or in the form of colonial legacies such as the North African population in French cities, Puerto Ricans in New York City or Jamaicans in London, the postmodern city is marked by a postcolonial presence. As more second- and third-generation immigrants from the colonized periphery live and work in the cities of the colonizing centre, new forms of identity, resistances and hybridity emerge. Issues of citizenship, national identity and urban community are at the heart of postcolonial urban studies.

Second, there is the exploration of the construction of postcolonial cities. Kong and Yeoh (2003), for example, look at the creation of postcoloniality in the city-state of Singapore, in the construction of heritage conservation that revalorizes different historic elements in the urban landscape and the changes in place names: Northam Road was changed to Jalan Sultan Ahmad Shah and Western Road became Jalan Utama. These changes were made in a conscious distancing from the colonial past. Garth Myers (2003) plots the trajectory of selected cities in Africa, showing the rebuilding of New Zanzibar after the revolution in 1964 and the construction of the new capital city of Lilongwe in independent Malawi as a conscious break with the colonial past. There are erasures as well as inscriptions. Whelan (2002) highlights the construction of monuments to British Royalty in Dublin and their destruction after Irish independence in 1922. Landscapes of colonial power are transformed and even destroyed in postcolonial cities. While urban studies tend to focus on the production of space, Bevan (2005) reminds us that buildings are damaged and destroyed, and spaces are eradicated. Ethnic cleansing, new forms of national memory, racial marking, terrorist bombs, minor 'police' actions, and 'limited' as well as all-out wars are all part of the forces that destroy cities and buildings. Deliberate acts of destruction are also part of the story of cities. The 'post' of any urban description often contains the eradication of the past as well as the construction of the future.

Third, there are the studies of postcoloniality as a function of time as well as intent. Sanjoy Chakravorty (2000) plots the course of the spatial morphology of Calcutta from colonial to postcolonial city. Colonial Calcutta was deeply divided between colonizers in high amenity enclaves and natives in dense, poor neighbourhoods. There was a place for the English, an Anglo-Indian area and another for the natives. Even after Indian Independence in 1947 the postcolonial city retained the demarcation of the colonial era, as Indian business and political leaders replaced the English in the elite residential area. Residential segregation by income and caste remains a feature of the city. Chakravorty also identifies a more postmodern Calcutta that has emerged since economic reforms in the 1980s and has opened the doors to global competition, foreign investment and new forms of globalization. The most significant development is the development of new cities, such as New Calcutta with a planned population of 100,000 dwelling units to house upper-income residents. New Calcutta is intended to look like other modern cities around the world: clean and well-planned, close to an international airport with a high-tech economic base. New Calcutta will be both post-colonial and postmodern. Anthony King (2003) identifies a new form of postcolonial urbanism in India, also found in much of Asia, that he terms spaces of transnational culture. Residential areas and residences are constructed around notions of 'international', 'global' and 'world class' with a conscious referencing of First World urbanism. A company in Bangalore is building planned residential projects with such names as Oxford Suites, Oxford Manor and Oxford Spires, and individual houses in a series they call 'independent villas'. The developments seek to create an equivalence between luxury developments around the world: the local and the global, the colonial and the postcolonial, the modern and the post-modern intertwined in the built form.

Let us return to the question posed at the beginning of this chapter: is *Blade Runner* a postmodern movie about LA, the postmodern city? Is LA a postmodern city? I contend that it is no more *the* postmodern city than any other large city in the United States, Britain or Australia. I would make a stronger case for Sydney, where a higher proportion of the popu-lation was born outside the country and the city connects with the pre-colonial, colonial and postcolonial in so many complex ways. I am not even sure LA is a truly postmodern city. I would argue it is a city where postmodernity and modernity are still working themselves out. And the movie? *Blade Runner* is set in Los Angeles: it is *Metropolis* done in Los Angeles, a modernist movie updated. I do not see much of a break between *Metropolis* and *Blade Runner*. A much stronger case can be made for *City of Joy* (1992), *Trainspotting* (1995) *Amores Perros* (2000), *City of God* (2002), and *Maria Full of Grace* (2004) These five movies, set respectively in Calcutta, Edinburgh and London, Mexico City, Rio de Janeiro, and a small town in Colombia and New York City, combine a freshness of material with some interesting cinematic representations, including the intertwining stories of *Amores*, the magical realism of *Trainspotting*, and the jagged film editing and dissolved time sequences of *City of God*. Even the more conventional treatments in *City of Joy* and *Maria* have a fresh quality to them, dealing with rural to urban migration in India and Colombia–US. Together they capture urban alienation and joy, a sense of the varied economy and diverse society of cities. They provide new twists to enduring urban stories, from the precarious position of the recent migrant to the city in *City of Joy* and *Maria*, to the alienated youth cultures of *Trainspotting* and *City of God*, the random fleeting encounters of modern life as in *Amores* and the cross-cultural connections exemplified in *City of Joy* and *Maria*.

Taken together, they constitute a fresh urban filmic experience, something different from *Metropolis* or *Blade Runner*; they offer depictions of urban life in all its diversity across the globe from different perspectives, in different languages with multiple points of view. And hereby hangs a moral. It is impossible to understand the postmodern urban condition, one marked by flows and connections, full of hybridities and singularities, embodying globalizations and localizations, if your only case study is just one city on the edge of just one country. And when all the commentators tend to be white, middle-aged Anglo-Saxon males, then the bias is palpable. Let us move on from a sole fascination with *Blade Runner*, a fairly standard reworking of a German classic, and also look at the uplifting and demoralizing stories of people in cities such as Calcutta, Edinburgh, Mexico City, New York City and Rio de Janeiro.

PART II

The City and Theory

4

Globalization and the City

There has long been a connection between globalization and urban development. When Columbus landed in the Caribbean, he inaugurated an exchange between the eastern and western hemispheres that created a truly global world. The splendour of the cities of imperial Spain, especially its ecclesiastical architecture, embodies some of the incredible wealth of this transatlantic exchange, giving urban form and substance to the riches from the Indies, while the colonial cities of the New World represent the urban expression of European power.

Since 1492 there have been a series of pulses of globalization. We will term them *reglobalizations* to refer to the creation of new local–global configurations in an ongoing pattern of globalization. These reglobalizations connect and disconnect cities in different ways. Three significant waves with marked urban manifestations may be identified. The first is the early development of the merchant trading cities that were nodes in an emerging global trade in commodities. We have a marvellous visual record of this network. By the last third of the sixteenth century there was a considerable stock of urban maps and images in a variety of media circulating throughout Europe. Compilations of city maps and prospects were published in 1551 and 1567, but the first city atlas was the *Civitates Orbis Terrarum* by Georg Braun and Frans Hogenberg. One volume was published in 1572 but it became so popular that, by 1617, the work consisted of six volumes with over 363 urban views (Short, 2004b).

The first volume of the *Civitates*, published in Cologne, comprises prospects, bird's eye views and plans of cities from all over the world. *Civitates* provides us with a comprehensive collection of sixteenth-century urban views. In almost all of the images, the city walls figure largely. Cities were often fiercely autonomous, homes to independent power centres, princes and prelates, guilds and town councils. Looking through the atlas at the many pictures of cities, one gains a very strong sense of cities standing apart as separate communities, reinforced by walls and battlements. The images celebrate the grandeur, wealth and power of the city. Many of the urban maps and views were made to evoke civic pride: the atlas rejoices in the urban condition. Collectively, the images provide a comprehensive view of urban life in the Renaissance: its ever-widening range indicates the increasingly global reach of mercantile capitalism and European colonization, forging a world economy among such urban centres as Aden, Peking, Cuzco, Goa, Mombasa and Tangiers, as well as many other cities around the world. While the cities in the *Civitates* are depicted separately, the effect of the compilation is to reveal a global economy of urban nodes and a trading world of connected cities.

Another round of reglobalization occurred between 1880 and 1914 as European powers embarked on the creation of formal empires, and new colonial cities emerged. The typical urban pattern was of a dual city: a western city where the colonial rulers lived and imperial power was made palpable and visible in the built environment, which was separate from the native city of indigenous population and vernacular architecture. The difference between the imperial architecture in the New Delhi of the British Raj and the high-density housing, mosques and temples of old Delhi captures this distinction.

A new round of reglobalization was inaugurated after 1989. In the rest of this chapter I will explore the theorizations of the relationships between this reglobalization and the city. The most important feature of this recent round of reglobalization is the space–time shrinkage of the globe. The world has shrunk with more frequent and cheaper international travel, the Internet and the globalizing of shared images and news reports. Places are closer together, but there are differences in accessibility. Global cities are places of concentrated global accessibility which are different from places just a few hours away. The more the world has become a global village, the more differences within the village matter. Different locales have different ensembles of the same images and goods. While there are shared languages of consumption and exchange, the regional variations are still important. Globalization has created complex hybrids rather than a common standard of homogeneity. Similar goods are consumed differently around the world. People are combining local and national identities with a cosmopolitan identity to produce a rich mosaic of disparate identities rather than one all-encompassing global identity. Globalization breeds hybridity.

'Globalization' is often the catchall phrase for the negative things of the contemporary world. Not all forms of globalization are bad, however; we can identify more benign global discourses of environmentalism, human rights, social justice and economic equity. There are growing senses of a global community and global standards of social justice, environmental quality and political rights. World public opinion created and maintained by global media coverage has often been an important lens through which national dictatorships and local regimes are perceived and evaluated.

Globalization is a super-condensed word from which a variety of many different meanings and interpretations have liquefied from the hot air of discussion. We can make a rough distinction between economic, political and cultural globalization. The distinction is an analytical conceit since in practice the three forms are more linked than separate.

Economic globalization involves the more rapid flows of capital around the world, the lengthening production chains of goods and services that cross borders and the increasing interconnectivity between the economies of different countries. The present round of globalizing capitalism is profoundly transforming. There has been a global shift in manufacturing and a consequent decline of the male working class in Europe and North America and the rise of a new female working class in South and East Asia. National territories have lost their spatial homogeneity as islands of global connectivity or stranded places of global disconnect differ increasingly sharply from the rest of the national space economy. Economic globalization is creating profound differences between sectors of the economy and between parts of the country and the city. There are many studies of economic globalization and the city. Yeong-Hyun Kim (2002, 2004) tells the story of Seoul's transformation in the past 20 years. It is a tale of relentless urban restructuring in the wake of a large increase in manufacturing employment and associated population growth. For many years economic globalization was welcomed as it provided well-paid jobs and new economic opportunities. However, the financial crisis of 1997 and the subsequent International Monetary Fund (IMF) austerity measures blunted the wide support for globalization. Opening up to economic globalization is taking on the tiger, and sometimes it can scratch and claw. Jan Nijman (2002) explores the impact of economic globalization on land values in Mumbai, India. The rapid escalation in urban land prices (in 1996 Mumbai had the highest land values in the world) was not due entirely to the opening-up of the Indian economy: the principal agents were the Indian government and Indian real estate companies, developers and government. The result of this research reminds us that economic globalization is rarely ever a simple impacting of external forces; global, national and local forces all shape urban economies.

Political globalization is evident in such global discourses as trade, aid, security and environmental issues. The world is now organized along more global systems of regulation, monitoring and control. This does not mean the death of the nation state. In fact, distinct elements of the nation state are reinforced by globalization as some parts, especially central banking systems and trade departments, play a pivotal role in managing the global national nexus. New claims are placed on the politically globalized city. Sassen (2002) explores the incipient denationalization of global cities and the creation of openings for such non-state actors in cross-border political dynamics as minorities, immigrants, first nation people and many feminists. Global cities, writes Sassen, are 'a setting for new types of political operations, a new global grid of politics and engagement . . . a strategic terrain for a whole series of conflicts and contradictions' (Sassen, 2002, 20).

Cultural globalization is the degree to which similar cultural forms are found around the world. This has led some to argue for the process of cultural homogenization, which is often portrayed as a form of Americanization. While US popular cultural forms are disseminating much more widely and deeply around the world (more people speak a form of English, eat at McDonald's and watch Hollywood movies), this has not led to an upsurge in pro-American sentiment. There is a subtle difference between the production of cultural forms and their consumption across the world. The consumption of culture is not a passive process of indoctrination, but a more active process of incorporation and creative readings. There is increased difference as new and old, indigenous and exotic cultural forms are tied together in unexpected and creative ways. The process of cultural globalization creates as much difference as similarity. New cultural identities cluster around hybrid forms as well as around invented traditions that often function as a resistance to perceived cultural imperialism.

The city of Amsterdam is a good example of cultural globalization. Terhorst and van de Ven (2003) show how urban social activists won the battle to preserve the existing street patterns, tightly regulate car and truck traffic and maintain social heterogeneity. The building pattern was frozen in time and the central city had a fairly even mix of social housing, rental housing and owner occupation. This distinctive built form, in combination with a liberal social attitude and youth culture, attracted mass tourism. Amsterdam became culturally globalized as tourists from Europe and North America flocked to the city. The large student population of Amsterdam (it is the biggest centre of higher education in the country) acted as a multilingual reservoir of labour able to service a multinational customer base. Amsterdam is now an attractive tourist destination for a wide variety of tourists, including low-budget backpackers as well as more affluent older tourists. Nijman (1999) details the way that the old Calvinist virtues of tolerance have been reshaped to accommodate tourists. The city is thus highly localized and also very globalized as mass tourism intermingles with older traditions in the forging of a unique identity, a product of local identities and global tourism. The connection between mass tourism, cultural globalization and the creation of space is also elucidated by Torres and Momsen (2005) in their study of Cancun. They show how the construction of 'Gringolandia' as a tourist space is shaped by flows of capital, people and tastes into this part of Mexico from around the world. The transnational flows have produced a transitional space in what only 30 years ago was an empty space, and a new space was created marked by 'asymmetrical geometries of power, inequitable social relations and uneven development' (332). Transnational spaces are created by the forces and flows of globalization interacting with the local.

The dominant narrative of globalization tells a story of an integrating world economy, a homogenizing global culture and a coherent global polity. An alternative discourse could focus on globalization as a process that generates fractured economies, splintering cultures and resurgent nation states.

The most recent academic interest in global cities rests upon the work of pioneer scholars and researchers. Hall, Friedmann and Sassen contributed three important foundation studies. Their work is important because they identified strands that, with one exception, can still be seen in recent research.

In the first edition of *The World Cities* (1966), Hall brings attention to cities as centres of political and economic power. He provides a detailed analysis of a selected group of what he termed world cities: London, Paris, Randstadt-Holland, Rhine-Ruhr, Moscow, New York and Tokyo. His focus was on the growth of these cities and the resultant planning issues, especially land-use management. There was little discussion of why these cities were selected, but Hall's work was a genuine innovation. He emphasized the idea of the global city as a planning problem and focused on how to deal with population and economic growth while still maintaining a viable, liveable city. Hall also raised the issue of the global city as an environmental issue. This strand was largely ignored in the subsequent world cities literature.

Friedmann wrote two key articles. Friedmann and Wolff (1982) introduced the notion of a global network of cities as a research agenda: it was a political economy of the global nexus of capitalism and urbanism. The two authors connected patterns of urbanization to the internationalization of capital, and urban restructuring to economic restructuring. They identified a global urban hierarchy with world cities at the apex, characterizing them as the control centres of the global economy with a concentration of producer services, housing a highly mobile, transnational elite and the sites of massive economic, social and physical reorganization. For them, world cities were the source of cultures, of consumerist ideologies and of global integration. Friedmann and Wolff identified the following as world cities: Tokyo, Los Angeles, San Francisco, New York, London, Paris, Randstadt, Frankfurt, Zurich, Cairo, Bangkok, Singapore, Hong Kong, Mexico City and São Paulo. These world cities were asserted rather than demonstrated. In a later paper Friedmann (1986) repeated the notion of world cities as base points of the global economy and identified Tokyo, Los Angeles, Chicago, New York, London, Paris, Zurich, Rotterdam, Zurich and São Paolo as the first-order centres of a global urban hierarchy, a similar but not exact list to their previous one and just as much based on simple assertion rather than careful documentation. Friedmann drew attention to the *global city as command centre* and to the *global network of cities*. His loose definition of these cities remains the hallmark of many subsequent studies.

In *The Global City* (1991), Sassen focuses attention on the big three of London, New York and Tokyo, examining their external connection to the global economy with emphasis on their command functions. She discusses global cities as centres for new systems of coordination and control, and as sites of production of specialized services (especially producer services such as accountancy, financial services and consultancies). Sassen suggests that increasing social and spatial polarization is a feature of the global city. Even though the city is a shared space, it is nonetheless a very differently experienced space. A powerful metaphor resides in the different uses of corporate offices, which during the day house the well connected and well paid making global transactions, but by night are cleaned by immigrant female workers paid minimum wages. Sassen draws attention to two strands, *the global city as command centre* and *the global city as the polarized city*. Her emphasis on the big three of London, New York and Tokyo became a feature of subsequent research.

These three sets of foundation studies created a list of research topics that have persisted; of these, four have retained their interest to researchers:

- the global city as planning issue
- the global city as command centre
- the global network of cities
- the global city as polarized city

The Global City as Planning Issue

While the notion of the city as a planning issue has retained an interest, the notion of what constitutes planning has changed. Hall was writing at a time (at least in the first edition of *World Cities*) and from a tradition that emphasizes the active involvement of national and local governments to improve the liveability of the city. Throughout most of the world, urban planning has become a way to improve economic efficiency and market success rather than a process to improve social welfare and create a fair and just city. Hall's remarks now read like a voice from across a great divide. While the global city as a planning issue remains, the goals and techniques of planning have fundamentally shifted in two main ways: the political context of urban planning, and the changing definition of urban planning.

We can increase our understanding of the global city by extending our understanding of planning beyond the manipulation of the physical environment to the conscious management of signs and symbols. An important element in global city research has been to identify the discursive strategies of global and globalizing cities (Ashworth and Voogd, 1990; Kearns and Philo, 1993; Ward, 1998). Global cities are represented by signs and symbols, advertisements and the hosting of events. Repertoires of city advertising with their emphasis on economic advantages and quality of life factors have been identified (Short and Kim, 1998; Short, 1999). There are also cultural ensembles considered vital to global city status: art galleries, music venues, ethnic restaurants and festivals. Global cities are defined by cultural economics as much as financial economics. There are also constellations of urban spectaculars that include global mega-events and signature architects: the Olympic Games, football's World Cup and music and arts festivals have become a defining feature of global city status. Global cities are enacted, performed and spectacularized.

The Global City as a Command Centre

Global cities are significant locales and embodiments of economic and political power. In the late 1980s and early 1990s there was a plethora of studies that sought to identify global cities. Most of these studies were long on assertion and short on data. Data collection is a vital part of state surveillance and monitoring, so most good quality data tends to be national while good quality international data, such as that collected by the World Bank, United Nations and the IMF tends not to be urban. At a very basic level it is very difficult and time-consuming to provide even a simple table of basic population totals for cities around the world that are comparable in terms of both times of collection and shared definitions of the urban, never mind anything more complicated in the way of sophisticated socio-economic data. There have been two responses to this data problem. The first has been to ignore it. This explains the large number of studies that simply present a list of global cities as given or make claims to global city status based on personal belief. Assertion rather than demonstration has been a major form of explanation in world city research, the so-called dirty little secret discussed by Short *et al.* (1996). The second response has been to identify and generate sources of comparative data. Short *et al.* (1996) and Short and Kim (1999) look at three elements of economic power: stock exchanges, headquarters of major corporations and head offices of major banks. In contrast to most other studies this study examines data trends over time in order to get a feeling for the trajectory of change. While the position of New York, London and Tokyo are confirmed, the data also show the relative decline of London and the relative growth of other European cities, particularly Paris and Frankfurt. London is still dominant and, in terms of producer services, outranks all other cities in the world; but Paris and Frankfurt will compete in the longer term. The great silence, of course, is Berlin which, for obvious reasons, has not filled a peaceful global city role probably since the Olympics of 1936. Over the much longer term, Berlin will be a strong candidate to become Europe's premier global city.

Subsequent analysis leads to two general conclusions: first, despite a slow dispersal over the past 30 years, a large proportion of command functions are still concentrated in just a few cities. Second, rather than a model of competition between global cities for global dominance, it is more accurate to consider a network of global cities with economic control concentrated in only a few cities but with the operation of this power dispersed in the second and third tiers of the global city hierarchy through branch plants and back offices. New York, London and Tokyo continue to exist as centres of concentration of global economic command functions. These three cities account for most of the trading activity in stock exchanges around the world. Together they provide 24-hour coverage, a continuous global coverage of market trading. They do not compete for business in that they complement each other, providing market opportunities for specific time niches.

While London's dominant stock market and global concentration of financial services is without parallel in the short to medium term, over the longer term competition from European global cities such as Paris, Frankfurt and (more realistically over the very long term) Berlin may force a change in the big three. Below the big three, national command centres in individual countries act as the main insertion point for global capital penetration. So while we have the global big three, we also have the national global centres such as Sydney which have few global command centres, in the form of head offices of global banks and corporations, but a large number of regional and local offices of global companies. The third tier of cities, such as Melbourne, to carry on with the Australian example, have smaller global command connectivities but still service regional and local markets. The global urban hierarchy is a network of flows that transmits global command functions across the world.

Studies of cities as economic command centres identify a number of key characteristics: they have articulated infrastructures of market trading involving an agglomeration of demand and supply, an environment of innovation, business support services, pools of highly skilled labour, a proximity of business organizations allowing information to be generated, analysed and disseminated and deals to be struck, and all this set within shared cultures of expertise and of contacts set within an even broader context of a disciplined market, multicurrency trading, and a responsive central bank and governmental system of economic regulation.

A central reason for the concentration of command functions in selected global cities is the need for social relations in global financial business deals. Trust, contact networks and social relations play pivotal roles in the smooth functioning of global business. Spatial propinquity allows these relations to be easily maintained, lubricated and sustained. Global cities are the sites of dense networks of interpersonal contact and centres of the important business/social capital trust vital to the successful operation of international finance.

One important strand in exploring the notion of global cities as command centres of the global economy is the discussion of advanced producer services such as banking, investment, consultancy, insurance and law. These services have globalized, or to be more precise, certain companies have offices in selected cities around the world. There are a number of empirical studies of individual sectors of advanced producer services that highlight their global city bias. Beaverstock *et al.* (2000) have looked at the geographical analysis of the 368 foreign offices of US law firms. Just 15 cities house 73 per cent of the total; London alone accounts for 17 per cent of all offices of US law firms abroad, and 59 per cent are found in just eight cities: London, Hong Kong, Paris, Tokyo, Brussels, Moscow, Singapore and Frankfurt. The US law firms with a global presence are concentrated in New York, Chicago, Washington, Philadelphia, Boston and Los Angeles. The same authors also look at the location of London's law firms (Beaverstock *et al.*, 1999). All but one of the top 30 London law firms has a foreign presence; in total there are 221 foreign branches in 60 cities.

The Global Urban Network

Ranking the command functions of cities is an interesting but limited exercise; it allows us some idea of the relative economic weight of cities and provides an antidote to the mere assertions of previous studies. However, cities not only occupy levels of a hierarchy; they are also part of a network. Intercity linkages take a variety of forms: economic, political and cultural. There are flows of goods and services, capital, ideas and trends, people and information that include foreign investments, overseas remittances, the tour paths of popular movies and pop groups as well as cultural flows including people, films, television, books and events.

As a starting point for a discussion of the contemporary global urban network we can consider the work of Castells (2000) who describes contemporary society as a network society that operates in a 'global space of flows'. Castells argues that the spatial architecture of the world system is based upon the logic of flow, connectivity, networks and nodes. The informational global economy is one where core activities in the economy, in media communication, in science and technology, and in strategic decision-making are linked worldwide in real time. However, Castells stresses that these decentralized networks of interaction require careful management to ensure their commensurability and functionality. The metropolitan nodes of global cities provide the crucial points of articulation in a society where there are possibilities of economic dispersal and distanciation. Two decades ago, the majority of corporate headquarters were located in global cities; now, new communications technologies do not require headquarters functions to be carried out only in the largest cities. In addition, the 1990s witnessed the rising importance of capital flows within so-called 'emerging markets', by-passing the corporate headquarters of the urban West. There is now a space of flows where global cities are no longer defined by the presence of corporate headquarters.

We can build upon the Castells notion of space of flows to examine specific flows in the contemporary global urban network. Again, data are a problem. International migration patterns, to take just one example, are bedevilled by a lack of good quality information. Some data sources have been constructed. Short and Kim (1999), for example, examine airline passenger information to construct flow data based on passenger flows of more than 100,000 persons in either direction between pairs of cities. The overall trend is for the existing channel of flows between North America and Pacific Rim to thicken and deepen, though it is not a global phenomenon. Like globalization itself the process is uneven, with Africa barely registering. Looking at the data for individual cities is revealing. London is clearly the hub of global airline flows. However, a comparison of secondary centres reveals a picture of regional articulations. Los Angeles, for example, despite the protestations of the LA School, is less a global city and more a Pacific Rim world city, while Amsterdam is clearly a European world city. A most interesting pattern emerges from our analysis of Miami. The data clearly reveal the city as the capital of Latin America. Miami is less a North American city and more a Latin American city with connections that make it the hub of flows to the Caribbean, Central and South America. Kingston, Jamaica, is divided into 20 postal districts. Locals use the term 'Kingston 21' to refer to Miami, indicating the degree of connection between the two cities. Miami is the global city of Latin America and the Caribbean.

Migration flows are the human face of globalization. Less than 3 per cent of the world's population are foreign migrants, but in absolute terms that constitutes a significant proportion, close to 180 million people (and this is probably a vast under-estimate since the official counts fail to note illegal migrants). Global cities are home to a variety of different nationalities. Transnational communities of both rich and poor of very different national and ethnic groups are present in global cities. These communities are both the bearers and transmission lines of economic globalization. Much of the literature on economic globalization equates economic globalization with the penetration of local markets by large multinational companies. This gigantist view of economic globalization ignores the extent to which economic globalization occurs in and through transnational communities in cities around the world. Transnational communities are the sites of linkage and flows between, on the one hand, the local and the family and, on the other, the global flows of people, money, capital, goods and services.

Global cities operate as major nodes of reflexivity in global networks through the migration of business elites. As the contemporary international service economy requires specialist professionals to be globally mobile to deliver intelligence, skills and knowledge to the point of demand, the development of a cross-border transnational migrant elite contributes to the production and consumption of the global city. Beaverstock (2002, 2004, 2005) has undertaken extensive research that theoretically and empirically examines the need for face-to-face contact in advanced producer services. In the world of high finance and international corporate law it is essential for international companies providing these services to maintain a tailored personal relationship, built on mutual trust, with clients around the world. This requires global firms to maintain offices in cities in different continents staffed with highly skilled professionals. These elite workers move through the distribution of corporate offices to pass on the corporate culture, to gain knowledge of local markets and to work with specific clients; their career paths trace route through the global urban hierarchy.

A discussion of network flows in the global urban hierarchy would be incomplete without mentioning the work of the Globalization and World Cities (GAWC) researchers who have constructed an invaluable data inventory (GAWC, 2005). To identify a world city network, they looked at the distribution of advanced producer services across a range of cities, generating a data matrix of 316 cities and 100 firms in accountancy, advertising, banking/insurance, law, and management consultancy. They identified firms with at least 15 identifiable separate offices, and also identified connectivity between the 316 cities. Those that had at least one-fifth of the connectivity of the most connected city, which was London, were identified as world cities. They provide us with one of the most sophisticated world city networks produced to date. Peter Taylor (2004) uses this data set as a starting point for an extended essay on the global urban network.

The Global City as Polarized City

In their foundational studies both Friedmann and Sassen draw attention to the social polarization in global cities. A compelling image is of the offices of successful financial services housed in global cities. By day they are full of highly-paid people on life's fast track. At night, low-waged workers (often immigrants) clean them with little job security and few benefits. The offices are like a metaphor for the city: the same place is populated by people with very different life chances and experiences. Capitalism everywhere produces marked social inequalities. Is there something special about global cities that exacerbates social polarization? Deindustrialization in many global cities of the First World reduced the number of relatively highly-paid working-class jobs. Unionized jobs in factories provide steady incomes for many city residents, and the loss of these jobs diminishes the economic opportunities for those people. At the same time the increase in highly-paid financial service jobs leads to groups of workers on the fast track of high incomes and generous benefits. These two trends tend to increase the disparity in economic opportunities for different groups in the cities. Even in the more lucrative financial service sectors, someone has to clean the offices, and office cleaners have never been as well paid as financial analysts or merchant bankers. Global cities can be sites of extreme polarization because the command functions pay well and the basic service sectors pay poorly, while the deindustrialization in many First World cities reduces the job opportunities for many working-class groups. The disparities have been exacerbated in recent years because the shift from the Keynesian to the neo-liberal city has generally resulted in regressive social policies that reduce the social wage of the modest income citizens. The neo-liberal agenda has dismantled much of the welfare state. The notion of dual city or divided city is an important theme of global cities research. Some differences have been noted. The strong welfare programmes in many western European cities compared to cities in the US means a tighter compression of real incomes (wages plus the social wage). But even here the fiscal tax burdens of welfarism have generated some discontent amongst the business community. And the recent rise of an explicit anti-immigration racist political agenda in France, as well as in such historically liberal societies as the Netherlands, that focuses on generous welfare payments to undeserving others is an indication of the depth of popular discontent. Even if they fail to achieve political success, such parties and movements can play a significant role in shaping the public policy response of the political elites.

One argument is that urban politics in global cities may have a slightly different flavour because the sharp polarization in global cities provides for the emergence of new social movements that draw upon the marginalized and dispossessed (Keil, 1998; Sassen, 2000). Purcell (2002) disputes this notion. His work on the rewriting of the city charter of LA finds little evidence of new social movements. New social movements may be more of a hope than an established fact.

New Directions for Global City Research

The globalizing project that is affecting so many cities around the world is the maintaining, securing and increasing of urban economic competitiveness in a global world. This involves many things (as well as counterpoints) including, but not restricted to, global connections (new nationalisms), global identities (new populisms), and a self-conscious global look and feel (the invention of the local and the rise of fundamentalisms). We can identify the modalities of globalizing cities that encapsulate a neo-liberal agenda and urban spatial change signposted by cultural ensembles, designed by signature architects and enacted in global spectaculars. The globalizing project varies in detail by individual city but overall there are recurring features across the world including the reimagining of the city, the rewriting of the city for both internal and external audiences, the construction of new spaces and the hosting of new events. A major goal is the attraction of jobs, and especially favoured are the high-tech and producer service sectors. Global city status is defined by having a range and density of of symbolic analysts. A cosmopolitan lifestyle is also promoted as part of the project complete with settings and performance that synergize the four Cs of culture, consumption, cool and cosmopolitan. The globalizing project also involves a spatial reorientation of the city, the spectacularization of settings, the creation of specifically global (in economic, cultural and political terms) sites and the encouragement of transnational locations.

One important feature of world city research has been the search for world cityness. Many studies have been devoted to identifying whether this or that city is a world city. While the work is interesting up to a point it tends to focus on a narrow range of cities at the top end of the urban hierarchy. This focus tends to ignore how globalization is acting in and through all cities. There is a real need for extending the globalization/city research nexus beyond the restricted and constricting focus on determining which cities are world cities (see Table 4.1). I use the term 'globalizing city' to refer to the fact that almost all cities can act as a gateway for the transmission of economic, political and cultural globalization. The focus on globalizing cities as opposed to world cities shifts the attention away from the question of which cities dominate the global urban hierarchy to how all cities in the hierarchy are affected by globalization. Short (2004a) expounds a number of themes that may help to elucidate the connections between cities and globalization using the notion of globalizing cities, and these include:

- cities and cycles of reglobalization
- competition for global city status

Table 4.1   From world city to globalizing city research

World city research	Globalizing city research
Measuring globalization	Measuring and deconstructing globalization
↓	↓
Globalization	Globalizing
Measures of world 'cityness'	Processes of globalization
City as impacted	City as arena
Being global	Becoming global

- representing the globalizing city
- the globalizing city and global spectacle
- rescaling and globalization
- the city and political globalization
- urban regimes in globalizing cities
- globalization and everyday life

It is important to shift focus from looking for a select band of global cities to looking for evidence for globalization in all cities. Global connectivity measures are dominated by analyses of the well-connected cities and yet it is revealing to consider the black holes and loose connection of the global urban network (Short, 2004a). Much of the literature on exploring the city-globalization nexus has concentrated on economic globalization, yet some revealing findings arise when we look at cultural globalization: for example, the role of immigration and the urban semiotics of signature architects.

While it is important to have an empirical sense of the global urban hierarchy, it is also important to identify the processes of globalization occurring across the range of cities. Globalization is a pervasive force that affects all cities in the urban hierarchy. The main theoretical development of recent years has been the shift from world cities research to globalizing cities research.

Globalizing City Regions

Considerable attention is devoted to identifying world cities. Recent research emphasizes the identification of these cities with the use of corporate organizations, especially advanced producer services (Taylor, 2004); infrastructure such as airline connections (Derudder and Witlox, 2005); and Internet links (Townsend, 2001). While this work is important

in identifying the global urban networks, it is less useful as a way of identifying processes of globalization within urban regions. Work on the
city/globalization nexus is skewed towards external links, with comparatively less attention devoted to the internal processes of change or to the
connections between external links and internal restructuring.

The theorization of the links between the city and globalization is
based on the experience of very few cities. Los Angeles, for example, has
been identified by the LA School as the unique site of new forms of postmodernity and its pattern of development put forward as a model for
other cities. Many of the identifiable trends have yet to be fully tested.
The building of metatheories precariously balanced on a narrow range of
cities, or in this example just one city, is unlikely to lead to a nuanced
understanding of the variation and complexity of urban change around
the world. Grant and Short (2002) have assembled case studies of globalization on the margins, while Gugler (1988, 2004) has done a valuable
job in bringing together case studies of globalization from non-western
cities.

Short (2004a) calls for a shift from the notion world/global city to the
idea of the globalizing city to focus attention on the city as an arena of
globalization, rather than simply as an outcome, and highlights the active
process of globalization rather than the passive impacting of global
forces. Scott (2001) identifies global city regions as the key economic
unit in the global economy. Combining these two observations, we will
use the term 'globalizing city region' (GCR) to refer to large urban
agglomerations that are vital nodes in global networks as well as sites of
complex socio-spatial articulations. These city regions are motors of the
global economy as well as sites of new forms of urban living and spatial
organization.

The uneven development of economic, political and cultural globalization is creating new forms of socio-spatial organization and reorganization within and between GCRs. Amongst the many possible research
themes worth pursuing to both measure and theorize these changes are:
global connectivity; economic restructuring; urban land-use change; the
political fragmentation of metropolitan government; patterns of
ethnic/racial segregation; levels of immigration; new social movements;
issues of scale. Let us review these topics in turn very briefly .

Although there is an over-emphasis on global connectivity measures,
measuring the global connectivity of GCRs is an important element in
any understanding of the relative rank and connectivity of a GCR. While
the data problem is now a well-recognized issue, there is less discussion
about area specification and what should occur when GCRs become the

unit of observation. Standard connectivity studies measure only the connectivity of the individual cities, not the whole region. Using GCRs as the unit of observation rather than the individual city may change the results. At the very least, it would provide a more complex picture of global connectivity.

A significant feature of global markets and the mobility of capital is the deindustrialization of older cities in advanced capitalist countries, and the industrialization of the expansion cities of developing economies. Studies of economic restructuring in a US context, for example, focus on the deconcentration of economic activity from cities and inner suburbs to employment centres dispersed across the outer suburbs. Economic restructuring in China, in contrast, focuses on the impacts of rapid industrialization, subsequent environmental degradation, and the apparent contradiction of a national planning system and adoption of market-oriented tools and values (Friedmann, 2005). The theorizing of economic change based on the experience of only a few GCRs has given us a balkanized understanding of global economic change. Comparative studies of GCRs around the world will provide a more nuanced understanding of the effects of globalization.

There is a bifurcation in urban studies. While racial segregation plays an important part in the research agenda of US and European cities, it plays a less significant role in studies of GCRs in much of the rest of the world. There are exceptions, but the general distinction remains. Much of our undertaking of patterns and consequences of segregation relies on a biased sample of studies. It is time for a broader base of case studies to construct an understanding of established and new patterns of segregation in GCRs.

The past 30 years have seen renewed levels of international migration, both legal and illegal, recorded and unrecorded. GCRs are the main nodal points of this international movement of people. Most GCRs around the world have significant levels of international migration, and yet, patterns of immigration vary among GCRs. Cities such as Tokyo, Shanghai and Beijing have experienced a less significant influx of foreign workers than New York or London. An understanding of the differential levels and the varying implications deserve wider investigation. One hypothesis is that urban politics in GCRs may have distinctive characteristics because of the sharp polarization, the racial-ethnic mix and the larger presence of foreign-born people. Significant analyses of such new social movements remain at the level of bare bones working hypotheses that need to be fleshed out and elaborated.

Any discussion of urban restructuring also requires an analysis of the structure and organization of urban local government. The level of metro-politan fragmentation of local government within GCRs, and to what extent they have regional autonomy from central government, are important factors in understanding the public policy response to managing and promoting globalization. Business and pro-growth coalitions perceive regional cooperation as a means to economic advancement within the global network, while local governments compete and wield power to include or exclude certain groups. An examination of change in GCRs must consider the context and implications of central–regional–local relations and the degree of governmental fragmentation across a unitary economic region.

Identifying GCRs as a unit of observation raises the issue of scale. GCRs exist at different scales, as single points if we measure connections with the rest of the world, as regions with marked economic inequalities, and as a rich mosaic of very different urban social worlds. It is important to be cognizant of the scalar nature of both social processes and our modelling and explanation of these processes. Studies of GCRs need to build scalar sensitivity into their analysis by using a range of scales, both in the form of different spatial scales of analysis as well as in making sure that explanations are scale specific.

We have not exhausted the range of topics that need investigation, but we have outlined a small number of the large range of topics that need to be investigated in order to widen our understanding of GCRs and deepen our analysis of the relationships between the city and globalization.

5
The Immigrant City

Cities attract people. Cities, especially large dynamic cites, are magnets for immigration. The movement of new people into the city is its lifeblood, making it more cosmopolitan, the place of the other, the home of the stranger.

Urban theories of the immigrant city focus on the related issues of how immigrants change and are changed by the city, and they develop in line with changing attitudes to immigration. The late nineteenth-century and early twentieth-century models concentrate on the problems of assimilation. Later models, now being created in a wave of marked cultural globalization, stress the distinctiveness of strangers, shifting the perspective from assimilating the newcomer to understanding the stranger.

In the phase of sustained urban growth since 1800, cities have depended upon immigration. The city could only grow with massive amounts of immigration, especially from rural areas. Death rates in the early industrial cities were so high that without immigration they would have shrivelled in population size. In the early nineteenth century rural to urban migration was not simply a redistribution of the population: it was a change in patterns of social control. Rural migrants were leaving the tight formalized control of rural (often feudal) societies, and entering a much freer society. 'City air makes men free' is an old German expression going back to the time when merchant cities were legally independent from feudal landowners and Church authorities. The sentiments of the phrase resonate still. The relative freedom in the city for recent migrants, especially those without ties of property or family, creates both opportunities and dangers. The cities stand out as beacons of hope for those oppressed, marginalized or just plain bored by life in the countryside and small towns. People move to the city for many reasons, but an important one is the greater freedom the city offers.

This freedom from provincial constraint worried many of the earlier commentators on the city. In the penultimate decade of the nineteenth century Strong (1885, 970) noted with reference to the US:

> The city has become a serious menace to our civilization . . . Here is
> heaped the social dynamite: here toughs, gamblers, thieves, robbers,
> lawless and desperate men of all sorts, congregate: men who are ready
> on any pretext to raise riots for the purpose of destruction and plunder;
> here gather foreigners and wage workers.

The immigrant-filled, nineteenth-century cities were powder kegs full of
flammable material. For Marx and Engels this represented great revolutionary potential; for others, the immigrant city was something to loathe
and fear. For every Marx and Engels there were many more Josiah
Strongs, fearful of the city mob and the urban crowd's influence on traditional society. In an influential essay, the social historian E. P. Thompson
(1971) cast a critical gaze over the workings of the urban crowd. With
reference to the eighteenth-century food riots in England, but clearly
capable of wider applicability, he notes that the riots were not spasms of
hunger but a complex and organized form of social resistance that
defended community rights against the power of the market. The crowd
replaced an unfair and inhuman market economy with a moral economy
that forcefully fixed food prices at an acceptable level. Thompson's
works continue to have great relevance. We can look again at the so-
called urban riots to tease out operations of the moral economy from mere
spasms of anarchy. Martin Luther King once described a riot as 'the
language of the unheard'. Urban riots can be the voice of the dispossessed
clamouring for attention. Thompson has done great service by looking at
the morality of urban rioting.

In the early twentieth century migration to the city was especially high
in the US where urban growth was enormously stimulated by waves of
foreign immigration. One influential theoretical perspective on the role
of immigration developed out of the experience of Chicago in the first
third of the twentieth century. Like many other US cities, Chicago saw
impressive rates of growth fuelled by large amounts of immigration from
both rural America and from Europe. This immigrant city was the backdrop to what has been termed the Chicago School (see Park, Burgess and
McKenzie, 1925). Two of the most celebrated figures in this school are
Robert Park and E. W. Burgess.

Park (1864–1944) had a great love of the city. He was a newspaper
reporter before he became a full-time sociologist, and his writings are
infused with a journalist's acute sense of the city. In his 1916 essay, 'The
City: Suggestions for the Investigation of Human Behavior in the Urban
Environment', he draws upon Simmel's observations but sets them
within the multicultural context of Chicago. At the time of writing he

notes that the city has 19 daily newspapers published in seven foreign languages. The main problem of the city, for Park, is assimilation. This influx of large numbers of foreign others creates problems of social control and assimilation. Park sees the city as a crucible that breaks down traditional forms of social control. As immigrants move into the city the old ties of race, language and culture weaken and occupational success becomes a shaper of residential segregation. Park posits an assimilationist model in which new immigrants provide the dynamic raw material in the creation of a new urban society, conceiving the city as a kind of living organism with successive waves of immigrants creating new social areas. The arrival of recent immigrant groups in an urban industrial society creates a dynamic collection of city areas such as the slum, the ghetto and the affluent sections, all subjects of Chicago School studies. In a remark that foregrounds much later work on globalization, he also notes that the colonies of ethnic enclaves 'are the centre of a more or less vigorous nationalist propaganda' (Park, 1952, 35). New city types are created in the finer divisions of labour found in the city, including 'the shopgirl, the policeman, the peddler, the cabman, the nightwatchman, the clairvoyant, the vaudeville performer, the quack doctor, the bartender, the ward boss, the strikebreaker, the labor agitator, the school teacher, the reporter, the stockbroker, the pawnbroker' (25), accompanied by novel forms of subjectivity. While the small community tolerates eccentricity, the great city rewards it.

In an essay published in the 1925 volume *The City*, Burgess, the other major figure of the School, notes that the transformation from a rural to an urban society is the 'outstanding fact of modern society'. The dynamic of the city was driven by the influx of immigrants. In Burgess's model they move into the cheaper inner-city properties, initiating a process that he describes as invasion and succession. A social ecology underpins much of the Chicago School's conception of the city, again drawing on biological terms to describe the city's organicism. Later critics have accused them of a simple social Darwinism, although I tend to see their biological language as more rhetorical and metaphorical than causal. The new immigrants move into the cheap lodgings while earlier, more assimilated, immigrants move further out, eventually into the larger houses in the suburbs. This process creates concentric rings characterized as:

- business district
- zone in transition
- zone of workingmen's homes
- residential zone
- commuter zone

This model is enormously important in the subsequent development of urban studies. The search for concentric rings of residential differentiation and the uncovering of the dynamics of residential mobility fuelled hundreds of studies of cities in both the US and around the world. In the original model the rings were produced, like a stone dropped into a pond, by immigration to the central city. Overlaying this concentric ring pattern in the original study by Burgess is a mosaic of ethnic areas (the Ghetto, Little Sicily, Greektown, Chinatown) which combine old world habits with new world adaptations. Burgess identifies the competing forces of social disorganization brought about by the mass influx of people into the urban environment with the organizing tendencies of communities. The city's new personality types and social areas arise in the spaces of these competing forces.

For both Burgess and Park, immigration is the driving force of the city. New immigrants were the raw material of the city, helping to create new areas and new types of people in the process of immigrant assimilation. The city is the site of spatial and social reorganization as traditional ties are broken and new ones are forged in a mosaic of emerging residential areas. Underlying the work of the Chicago School is a sense that ultimately there is a move towards an assimilation of immigrants into a new urban order.

In 1963 Nathan Glazer and Daniel Patrick Moynihan published their classic work on ethnicity, *Beyond the Melting Pot*. It was primarily a study of New York City and the extent to which various ethnic groups sturdily maintained their distinctiveness. Their work was a counterargument to the Marxian notion that urbanization leads to class identity, superseding ethnic ties. Their detailed work on different immigrant groups in the city showed that urban living did not diminish the ethnic identities, but reinforced them.

While *Beyond the Melting Pot* highlights the continuing resilience of traditional ethnic identities, more recent work takes a slightly different tack: an investigation of the hybrid identities in the city. Consider the creation of an urban black identity in the US. In 1943 Muddy Waters moved from the Mississippi Delta country to Chicago. A musician well versed in the traditional blues of the rural south, his 1951 recording, *Still a Fool*, marks the beginning of a new urban blues, an electric musical form associated with the streets of Chicago and not the cotton fields of Mississippi. In the 1950s, the rural blues became the urban blues. From then on, black music was associated with the urban experience. The harsh anguish of the marginalized urban dwellers replaced the haunting lament of the rural poor. From Muddy Waters to contemporary rappers, black voices became an important element in the cultural articulation of the US urban experience.

There never really was a melting pot. Ethnic pluralism is the exception rather than the rule. While there has been a slow blend of broadly similar groups, differences persist. Rather than a melting pot, a more appropriate metaphor would be of a lumpy stew, with persistent gristles of meaty singularity within a shared gravy.

There are certain characteristics that make immigrant assimilation easier. If the immigrant group is large, residentially concentrated, speaks a different language, and has different racial, ethnic or religious identity, then assimilation is likely to be slow and often painful. Most British immigrants to the US, for example, share a more similar culture and language than immigrants from Afghanistan or Bangladesh. If the host society is open, with easy social mobility and a tradition of inclusion rather than exclusion, then assimilation is likely to be easier. Thus immigrants to the US find it easier to blend in than, for example, white European Christians moving to Saudi Arabia. The character of immigrant groups and the nature of the host society shape the interaction between the immigrants and identity. Cities play a particular role because even while the society can be closed, homogeneous and intolerant, a city within that society can be more open, heterogeneous and tolerant. Cities tend to be more cosmopolitan than the surrounding rural areas.

While Glazer and Moynihan could still identify ethnic neighbour-hoods and attitudes in their 1963 book, they were writing as the move out of these neighbourhoods to the suburbs was becoming a mythic US jour-ney signalling Americanization, success and integration. It was always tinged, however, with nostalgic regret as a kind of 'invention of tradition' took hold. The old neighbourhoods were soon romanticized as bastions of community and citadels of closeness, their austerity and frugality favourably contrasted in a searing moral judgment with the affluence and conspicuous consumption of life in the suburbs. *The Godfather*, in both the book and the movie trilogy, embodies these tensions as the Corleone family moves from the dense inner-city neighbourhood of the first gener-ation to the Long Island suburbs of the second, then out west to Nevada. The collapse of the family, in both senses of the term, is an arc of Americanization.

Glazer and Moynihan present a picture of the continuing importance of race and ethnicity. The 'melting pot' notion was always something of a fiction, but so is the idea that identities are unchanging and singular. The immigrant experience dramatically transformed the US, for exam-ple, into a pluralistic, multiethnic society. However, while the society has changed, so have the immigrants. They may not have blended into an amorphous, banal mix, although they do not remain unaffected. Second and third immigration immigrants both adopt and add to US ways. There is a complex social interaction as newcomers and natives interact with one another, changing each in turn. Rather than a multicultural society, a condition that implies unchanging groups remaining separate from each other, there are different forms of polyculturalism as various groups interact with and change each other. Rather than thinking of a simple continuum of assimilation, measured from the initial immigrants being different to successive generations becoming more like the rest of the society, we can think of a complex picture with both the immigrant groups and the host society metamorphosing. Thus immigrants moving from southern Italy in the early nineteenth century were not Italians until they came to the US. The construction of an Italian–American identity was not transposed from Italy but created in the US, and the active creation of a new Italian–American identity shaped the US.

Globalization, Immigration and the City

From 1930s to the 1970s cross-border immigration was relatively limited. Since the early 1970s foreign immigration has increased and is now an integral part of the process of globalization. In 1970 the number of foreign-born as a percentage of total population was just under 5 per cent in both the US and UK. By 2000 the respective figures had increased to 11.1 per cent and 8.3 per cent. In the US that means that over 31 million were born outside the nation's borders with significant numbers coming from Mexico, the Philippines, India, China and Vietnam. Substantial numbers of these new immigrants were attracted to the large dynamic metropolitan centres such as New York, Los Angles, Chicago and Washington. We can consider briefly the region of Megalopolis, the urbanized northeastern seaboard stretching north to south from Boston to Washington, and east to west from the Atlantic coast to the Appalachians. In 1980 in Megalopolis the number of foreign-born was around 4 million, constituting 10 per cent of the region's total population. In 2000 the absolute and relative proportions had increased dramatically so that, by the century's end, 10.2 million people in Megalopolis had been born overseas, and they constituted almost 20 per cent of the region's population, almost double the national average. Megalopolis attracted a considerable number, both in absolute and relative terms, of the foreign immigrants into the country. Almost half of all foreign-born migrants admitted to the US since 1960 came to Megalopolis. In 1960 only two counties in the whole region had a foreign-born population greater than 20 per cent, and they were the Bronx (21.5 per cent foreign-born) and New York (22.1 per cent foreign-born). By 2000, some 16 counties had reached this figure, and the type of counties varied from the traditional urban magnets of the Bronx and New York to the more suburban counties such as Fairfax County, VA (25.4 per cent foreign-born). The New York metro region continues to act as a magnet for the foreign-born: the five New York counties of the Bronx, Kings, Nassau, New York and Westchester account for 18.2 per cent of the total population of Megalopolis, yet they house 38.6 per cent of the total foreign-born living in Megalopolis. However, the foreign-born were also living in suburban counties in substantial numbers. In Montgomery County in Maryland, out of a total population of 873,341 more than 26.7 per cent were classified in the 2000 census as foreign-born. The new immigrants to the country live in the suburbs as well as the central cities.

The large economically resilient urban regions (such as New York and Boston) act as powerful magnets for the foreign-born, while more economically challenged cities such as Scranton are bypassed. Scranton had only 3.1 per cent foreign born in 2000, which was less than half the 1960 figure of 6.5 per cent. Baltimore City had 4.2 per cent foreign-born in 1960, but only 4.6 per cent in 2000, which represents an absolute fall from 39,439 to 29,638. The foreign-born are a good barometer of economic growth and decline.

Global cities are points of destination for large numbers of international migrants. Most of the data we have on foreign-born populations is by nation state; data on cities is lacking. Lisa Benton-Short and Marie Price (2006a) have undertaken an extensive survey of foreign-born populations in 150 cities around the world. The top 12 immigrant cities are shown in Table 5.1. This study formed the basis of their immigration index that takes into account the total number of immigrants, the diversity of immigrant origin areas and the relative distance travelled. They identify alpha, beta and gamma cities. The alpha immigrant cites are New York, Toronto, Dubai, Los Angeles, London, Sydney, Miami, Melbourne, Amsterdam and Vancouver. The second-ranked (beta) cities include Riyadh, Geneva, Paris, Tel Aviv, Montreal, Washington, DC, The Hague, Kiev, San Francisco and Perth in Australia. In another paper they identify established gateway cities, unrecognized gateway cities, accidental gateway cities and bypassed gateway cities (Benton-Short and Price, 2006b). Examples of different types are noted in Table 5.2. Unrecognized gateways are found in the Middle East, the accidental

Table 5.1   Immigrant cities

City	Year	Foreign-born as % of total city population
Dubai	2002	82.0
Miami	2000	50.9
Amsterdam	2002	47.2
Toronto	2001	46.9
Muscat	2000	44.6
Vancouver	2001	39.0
Auckland	2001	39.0
Geneva	2002	38.3
Mecca	1996	37.5
The Hague	1995	36.5
Los Angeles	2000	36.2
Tel Aviv	2002	36.0

Source: data from Benton-Short and Price, 2006a.

gateways are particularly numerous in the former eastern bloc, and bypassed gateways (globalized cities with relatively low levels of foreign immigration) are common in Asian cities.

The Benton-Short and Price work is interesting because it gives us a firmer empirical basis for further studies, enriching our understanding. The reliance of Arab cities on foreign labour, the lack of cosmopolitanism amongst Asian cities, the important immigration role of Canadian cities and the gateway status of Miami are all identified by their careful analysis.

Using their data we can begin to make some broader theorizations of the connections between immigration and globalization. The cosy and reassuring notion that immigration leads to greater cosmopolitanism, for example, is undermined by the experience of many cities in the Middle East where very high rates of immigration into cities are marked by cultural xenophobia and religious fundamentalism, rather than cosmopolitanism. In more closed societies large-scale immigration is sometimes considered a threat and one response is to seek greater cultural purity and the comforting messages of revealed religious truth rather than the fuzzy uncertainty of cultural hybridity. In other words, high foreign immigration into Middle East cities is an important context for understanding the rise of Islamic fundamentalism.

The connection between immigration to cities and globalization has two significant aspects. The first is the existence of diasporic communities across the globe, as similar communities are held together by shared identity but separated by thousands of miles. While some popular representations of

Table 5.2   Types of immigrant city

Type	City examples
Established gateways	Miami, Amsterdam, Vancouver, Auckland, Geneva, Los Angeles, New York
Unrecognized gateways	Dubai, Muscat, Mecca, The Hague, Tel Aviv, Medina, Jerusalem, Brussels, Munich
Accidental gateways	Kiev, Tbilisi, Bratislava, St Petersburg
Bypassed cities	Tokyo, Seoul, Taipei, Osaka-Kobe, Pusan

Source: data from Benton-Short and Price, 2006b.

globalization point to the levelling qualities of globalization, the ease of communication allows immigrants to keep in touch with their origin areas. Some globalization trends allow differences to be maintained rather than eradicated. In the nineteenth and early twentieth century immigrants could only return home at enormous expense, and communication was also expensive and sporadic. With the declining cost of international travel and telephone rates as well as the rise of the Internet, videos and text messaging, it is now easier to keep in touch, literally and metaphorically. Immigrants can and do return home, and there are flows of culture across diasporic communities around the globe. DVDs of movies made in Bombay find a ready market in the large Indian communities in the US, UK and Middle East. The links that forge globalization also allow the persistence of difference as immigrant communities can keep in touch with the news and culture of home. And they in turn provide home with information, images, commodities and trends from around the world. The flows of people and the cultural connection that follow in their wake are vital ingredients of globalization. These new diasporic communities enrich and enliven cosmopolitan cultures and resist and contest indigenous cultures.

The creation of new and enlarged diasporic communities has also created a backlash as nativist sentiment arises in many countries around the world. The presence of the stranger, especially one who remains a stranger because of the resilience of local identities in a globalizing world, has prompted worldwide racial, religious and ethnic backlashes. Religious, racial and ethnic identities have not disappeared in the globalizing, and their continued existence threatens those who seek a simpler, more fundamentalist view of the world. The rise of fundamentalism and associated political articulations, apparent in all four of the major religions of Christianity, Hinduism, Islam and Judaism, is just one element of the response to the hybridity and complexity of the contemporary world. Cities have a special place in these debates because they are the destination point for many immigrants. In many countries there is a growing contrast between very cosmopolitan cities and less cosmopolitan parts of the nation. The global cities are both points of cosmopolitanism where new hybrid identities and cultures are emerging, and places of resistant local diasporic identities.

Global connections are also maintained by flows of people. Cities are both the origin and destination points of complex flows of people around the world. There is the flow of cheap labour to fill the spaces of work in the affluent world as Central American nannies look after families in Washington, DC, Filipino maids take care of the domestic arrangements of the rich in Hong Kong, doctors from Egypt provide medical care in Riyadh and young women from Eastern Europe become prostitutes in London. Domestic workers, farm workers and even finance specialists are connecting channels of human movement that link places and cities around the world. The movement reflects and embodies the globalization of the world.

There have been studies of different groups. Transnational corporations, for example, require the international presence of their workers in order to maintain in 'face-to-face' contact between the firm and client and to connect global business and local social networks. Beaverstock (2002, 2004, 2005) studies the role of expatriate workers in globalization processes. He examined 161 firms in London. Surveys showed that in any one year around 65 professional and managerial migrants left London, with 35 per cent destined for New York City, and the others going to Singapore, Hong Kong and Tokyo. This expatriate labour disseminates corporate knowledge throughout the world. London is also home to 'inpatriates', people moving to the city. Expatriates interviewed in Singapore and New York City indicated that once they had left the UK, they experienced feelings of isolation from the company. In Singapore expatriates lived in clusters in specific parts of the city. In New York, however, expatriates integrated much more into the life of the city. This expatriate community is emblematic of much contemporary movement: transient, international and transcultural, affecting both the places visited and the places returned to, as well as the personal identity and economic success of the migrants themselves and the people they work with. It is a process that links people, places, companies and knowledge into a more complex interconnected globalizing space.

The second connection between immigration to cities and globalization is in economic globalization. Urban immigration plays an important role in economic globalization, as the flows of people also become channels of economic transactions. Remittances make up a substantial part of the foreign income in such places as the Philippines, where fully 20 per cent of national income comes from Filipinos working abroad and sending money home. There are connections between gardeners in Los Angeles and the economic lifeblood of Mexican villages, German car factory workers and small villages in Turkey. Remittances from overseas immigrants to families in El Salvador constitute 60 per cent of export earnings and 14 per cent of gross national product. Some countries' roles in the global economy are as providers of human labour as much as suppliers of goods and commodities. In 2003 almost $30 billion in remittances was transferred from the US to Central America (including Mexico). Flows of money do not just take the form of giant trades by currency speculators: they are also made up by a large number of modest amounts of money earned in cities abroad and sent to places back home. The diasporic communities are also conduits of foreign trade as family connections merge into business connections and small import /export companies arise from family and ethnic ties. Foreign trade is not just between giant multinational corporations, but also takes the form of smaller-scale linkages between communities. Immigrants play a key role in the economic development of the city in circulating money from rich to poor places and in identifying possibilities for international trade and exchange.

There are now more transnational families as men and women separate from their families in order to earn money overseas. Visits and transfers of money and information maintain family connections and help to reshape destination cities and host communities. The flows of immigrants to cities around the world create global diasporas and transnational family structures. Individual and group identities are forged against this background of globalizing connections. The Indian movie *Monsoon Wedding* (2001), for example, takes place in Delhi but the foreign connections are always present due to the return of family members from Australia, the Middle East and US; the marriage arrangement itself is between a young woman from an upper-class Punjabi family living in Delhi and the Indian groom who lives in Texas. After the traditional wedding, they will move to the US. The movie also represents multiculturalism in a deeper sense. It is not an 'Indian' film; it was co-financed by India, the US, France, Italy and Spain, and the languages in the movie include Hindu, English, Punjabi and Urdu. *Monsoon Wedding* is an Indian movie made less for a domestic Indian audience and more for an Indian expatriate audience, as well as a broader non-Indian audience.

Theories of immigration into cities in the contemporary world are fashioned against a background of competing forces. It is now possible to assimilate immigrants, but the ease of communication is currently making it simpler for immigrant communities to maintain ties with home. Immigration is a source of creative dynamism as well as social polarization. We have cosmopolitism and fundamentalism emerging as competing views of the world. Few metatheories are likely to emerge from such a complex picture; rather, carefully theorized case studies will provide a sense of the range of contexts, processes and outcomes as the immigrant city condenses the global and the local, the urban and the national, in new and continually restructured assemblages.

Immigrant Niches

A number of scholars have identified immigrant niches in globalizing city regions. In his book *A Piece of the Pie*, Stanley Lieberson used the term special niches to refer to the concentration of recent immigrants in certain jobs (Lieberson, 1980). Wilson and Portes (1980) studied Cubans moving into Miami and found that a significant number worked for co-ethnics. They called these 'ethnic enclaves'. Subsequent research suggested that this was an unusual phenomenon. While immigrant entrepreneurship is very common and found in cities around the world, enclaves of shared ethnicity between workers and powers is much rarer, perhaps even a function of the particularities of Cuban immigration into Miami. More common are immigrant niches where immigrants were over-represented in certain occupations and jobs, and this applies across the range of skills. Immigrant niches are not restricted to low-paid, unskilled jobs but are also found in the higher varying, more skilled occupations. Waldinger (2001) sees their creation in the repeated action of immigrant social networks. He defines a niche as an occupation or industry in which the percentage of workers that are group members is at least one-and-a-half times greater than the group's percentage of all employment (307). In his study of five globalizing city reigns in the US, he showed distinct clustering amongst a whole range of groups including Mexicans, Chinese, Filipinos, Koreans, Cubans and Vietnamese. The clustering in niches occurs for both the better-educated and more entrepreneurial Korean immigrants as well as the less entrepreneurial, less skilled Mexican immigrants, although the particular niches vary. At the bottom of the labour market vacancies tend to be filled by recent immigrants who help to recruit friends and family members. At the higher end of the labour market similar sorts of immigrant network operate as ethnic succession occurs in certain occupations and professions. Once established, an immigrant niche is maintained through the exclusion of other groups and the usurpation of hiring practices. Although Waldinger's work is based in the US, the conclusions are more universal; immigrants secure niches in the urban economies of globalizing city regions and they maintain them through immigrant social networks.

6

The Economic City

The city is many things but one feature attracts particular theoretical attention, and that is its role as a site of economic activity. In this chapter I will look at three scales of theorizing: the wide-angle view given by political economy; the medium-shot vision of work on selected sectors; and the close-ups of particular places.

The Political Economy of the City

To understand the city it is necessary to place it in a wider socio-economic context. The political economy approach yields important, though not complete, insights into the complexity of the city. The obvious starting point is the notion of the mode of production. Karl Marx (1818–83) coined the term and uses it variously: sometimes he refers to the techniques involved in producing a specific good; at other times to the labour process in the capitalist system. In the broadest definition, Marx uses the term in reference to the production, exchange and consumption of relations along with the associated political and social arrangements that reproduce an economic order. It is this broader definition that we will explore in this chapter. Marx suggests that history be seen as the rise and fall of different modes of production; in essence his work identifies the rise of the capitalist mode of production from the feudal mode and examines the contradictions inherent in this.

At the core of Marx's economic analysis of capitalism is the relationship between the capitalists and the workers. In simple terms, the capitalists purchase the labour power of the workers, which is harnessed in a system of production to create commodities. These commodities are sold for profit in a competitive market place. It is the competition and conflict between these two groups that provides the central dynamic of capitalist economies.

The rise of the Marxist and neo-Marxist perspectives in the 1970s provides the necessary intellectual perspective regarding more recent work on the capital–labour dynamic. An interesting body of work now explores the geography of labour relations. Andy Herod (1998, 2001), Ray Hudson (2001, 2005) and Jamie Peck (1996) among many other scholars, extend the early work in this vein by Doreen Massey (1984). Detailed studies include the work of Clark (1981), which shows how spatial decentralization of production and the emergent division of labour are used as bargaining strategies by capital in its dealings with labour. In addition Scott (1988) argues that an understanding of the capital–labour relationship allows us to explain the intra-urban location of different types of industry and the decentralization of much industry towards the periphery. Castree *et al.* (2004) align a number of themes in this new work on the geography of labour. They draw attention to growing segmentation of the labour force, the complexity of capital–labour relations and its variation by space and place, the role of globalization in capital and labour, and the scalar connections between the local, national and global for both capital and labour.

In general, the globalization of production strengthens the hand of capital and weakens the power of organized labour in the developed economies where conditions of work have deteriorated, wages have stagnated and work schedules have increased for many manual workers over the past 30 years. In selected Third World cities, in contrast, the new manufacturing jobs often provide a better economic alternative than traditional agricultural employment, fuelling a massive rural to urban migration that is occurring in countries such as China.

The capitalist system is unstable because the ceaseless pursuit of profit and market share necessitates economic booms and slumps along with periods of social harmony and conflict. At a global scale we can see the disinvestment from the industrial cities of the capitalist core and the investment in factories in such Third World cities as Shanghai. At a national level there is similar socio-economic/spatial reconfiguring: in the US, part of the decline of the Rustbelt and the rise of the Sunbelt is due to capital disinvestment from the cities of the northeast and investment in the cities of the south and west. At a metropolitan level the suburbanization of industry is in part an attempt to move to new sites with weaker labour organizations. There is a link between social changes and economic restructuring. Capital naturally responds to an uneven distribution of investment opportunities. The new investment involves new transport routes and new spatial divisions of labour. The transformed spatial structure in turn guides the flow of successive waves of capital investment. Patterns of fixed capital investment provide the decision-making context for successive waves of investment. Space is not only continually structured but also shapes the basis for subsequent capital restructuring.

One benchmark study that explores the connection between capital flows and the built environment is Baran and Sweezy (1966), which suggests that state stimulation of suburbanization, through the construction of highways and associated infrastructural investment, encouragement of owner occupation, and incentives to new housing construction, plays a vital role in buoying up the economy. Baran and Sweezy point to the stimulating effects of suburbanization on a capitalist economy. Richard Walker (1981) develops this line of argument in a more nuanced form.

The city is the site for the reproduction as well as the production of class and class relationships. The focus on class structure and residential segregation is an important strand of the political economy approach. While cities have provided one of the most consistent points of resistance against the established order, the links between residential differentiation and class formation within the city are more difficult to unravel. In smaller, more 'closed' communities, such as coal-mining towns, local traditions of radicalism may emerge to be sustained and even celebrated. In bigger cities, with a much broader social base, the easy identification of class is more difficult. Sharply differentiated residential areas may produce intra-group cohesion, but the transformation of this cohesion into interclass conflict depends on a whole range of contingent factors, leading to acceptance, accommodation, or the practice of revolt. Detailed case studies reward inquiries into the complications of class in cities. Katznelson (1979), for example, looks at the experience of metropolitan United States and convincingly shows how the strength of residential segregation along ethnic cleavages is one reason behind the lack of class-conscious labour politics. The important point is that there is a complex relationship between society and space, class and locale, city and identity. Untangling these connections can be a significant area of work and a fruitful avenue for further study.

'Mode of production' is a very general concept: it is useful but not specific enough to capture changes in the precise form and organization of capitalist production. The term 'regime of accumulation' refers to the dominant form of securing and accumulating profit, used often with reference to the distinction between Fordism and post-Fordism (Amin, 1994). The name Ford is associated with the mass-production of cars on controlled assembly lines, inflexibly geared towards the constant production of a standardized commodity. Post-Fordism involves greater flexibility of production for an increasing range of products with shorter runs.

This implies more subcontracting, greater vertical integration between firms, and a more 'flexible' use of labour. Flexible production is the response of capital to a tighter market, the declining power of organized labour, and rapid shifts in consumer preferences. It allows firms to adjust quickly to a more volatile market, permits high rates of productivity growth, and reduces employment costs. Flexible production involves a change in the relationship between labour and capital; in effect it gives capital greater control over the deployment of labour, the pacing of work, and the costs of labour. An increasing bifurcation has been noted between a core of highly paid, well-trained employees with good working conditions and generous benefits and a growing number of peripheral workers employed part-time on a more irregular basis and with fewer benefits or advancement opportunities.

Cities and Modes of Consumption

To focus on the relationship between mode of production and city structure is a useful, if very general, first approximation. A major problem, however, is that it lumps together conflated societies as varied as Brazil, the US, the UK, Zaire and Japan. Rio de Janeiro, Detroit, Manchester, Kinshasa and Tokyo have many similarities, but they also have many differences. A distinction is sometimes made between rich and poor cities, referring to their location in so-called rich and poor countries. The problem with this division is that there are rich people in poor countries and cities and poor people in rich countries and cities: New York has some very poor people while Rio de Janeiro has some very rich people. The adjectives rich and poor, when applied to either countries or cities, fail to register these distinctions. A more compelling method is to consider differences in the mode of consumption. We can make a distinction between those countries characterized by high mass consumption and those noted for much lower levels of consumption. This is a rough demarcation, but a useful one.

Capitalism in the nineteenth century was based on the production of commodities. Personal consumption was limited to the rich and the affluent. The majority of people were relatively poor. This began to alter in some countries in the twentieth century, as a capitalism of mass-produced, mass-consumed goods became important. In 1908 Henry Ford (1863–1947) designed his Model T car. By cutting production costs and creating an efficient assembly line Ford was able to build and sell a large number of cars at a relatively low price. Between 1908 and 1928 over 15 million cars were sold. A mass market was created. At the heart of mass consumption is a system of relatively high wages with which people can afford to buy consumer goods, credit systems that enable people to acquire highly priced items and pay back the cost over a long period, and an ideology that sanctions and fosters continued consumption.

The system of mass consumption is based on a whole set of social and political practices. For example, sophisticated credit arrangements promote an ideology of high mass consumption by which people are encouraged to buy and to keep on buying. Recent years have seen an active interest in consumption issues. Jayne (2005), for example, draws out some of the connection between cities and consumption, including the connection between consumption cultures and the development of spectacular spaces within the city. The development of shopping arcades, department stores, out-of-town shopping centres and megamalls all reveal the long history of an urban consumption culture. Furthermore, consumption is part of both individual and collective identity, and patterns of consumption reinforce and undermine racial, ethnic and gender and sexual orientation and categorization in complex ways. An ever more segmented set of spaces of both collective and personal forms of consumption characterize the city. Strategies of bargain basement options at one extreme with the pursuit of high fashion at the other provide two ends of a shopping continuum on which individuals position themselves differentially according to income, persuasion, time, space and event. Consumption informs a repertoire of identities and activities in the city.

The renewed emphasis on consumption has also stimulated work on the role of retail in cities. Wrigley and Lowe (1996, 2002), for example, provide an excellent summary of what they refer to as the 'new retail geography'. They highlight the reconfiguration of the corporate structures of retailing, the role of retail capital in the restructuring of cities, and the development of such consumption spaces as the street, the store, the mall and the home. The home is now a significant site of shopping as online shopping replaces and supplements actual journeys to shops.

The city-centre department store of the 1950s has been replaced by the strip mall along the arteries of the metropolis and by the out-of-town, huge shopping mall in distant greenfield sites. In this competitive market the earlier strip malls and shopping centres are experiencing stiff competition from the newer centres and discount malls. As retailers search for capturing either the bargain-driven or fashion-driven consumers, the middle-of-the road malls in unattractive strips are finding it more difficult to compete. The creative destruction that is the hallmark of the contemporary city also applies to retail. The spatial organization of retailing has experienced a profound transformation in the past 50 years with a decline in downtown dominance and a rise in suburban shopping malls. The competition for fickle consumers involves constant makeovers and new mall developments. It is not only that shopping malls follow the suburbs; now suburbs are following the malls as residential developments on the city's far distant edge are often anchored by a shopping mall.

The mall itself has become a site of competing forces. A place to make money, it must also entice and entertain, enclose without threat, control yet give the appearance of freedom. The shopping experience for fickle sophisticated consumers must always be new but always within the confines of the safely predictable, the comforting repeatable. As Jon Goss (1993, 40) notes:

> The shopping center appears to be everything that it is not. It contrives to be a public civic place even though it is private and run for profit; a place to commune and recreate, while it seeks retail dollars; and it borrows signs of other places and times to obscure its rootedness in contemporary capitalism. The shopping center sells paradoxical experiences to its customers, who can safely experience danger, confront the Other as a familiar, be tourists without going on vacation, go to the beach in the depths of winter, and be outside when in. It is quite literally a fantastic place . . . a space conceptualized, planned scientifically and realized through strict technical control, pretending to be a space imaginatively created by its inhabitants. The alienation of commodity consumption is concealed by the mask of carnival, the patina of nostalgia, and the iconic essences of everywhere.

Lizabeth Cohen (2003) identifies three consequent major effects of the suburban shift to enclosed malls: the commercialization, privatizing, and feminization of public space. The construction of postwar shopping centres is more than just the making of new places to shop: it involves the creation of new public spaces where parking is assured, the weather is controlled and most consumer needs are met. The unpredictability and anarchy of open public street shopping is rendered safe and controlled. In addition, the centres envelop consumers in more than just shopping choices. Restaurants and gyms, banks and movies now sit side by side in specially designed places to keep the customer contentedly entrapped in a totalizing experience. Shopping centres are the new sites of civil society, the new meeting places, the new third space between work and home where consumption is connected to a wider range of leisure activities.

Privately controlled places such as shopping malls have become hubs of a form of public life that is controlled and managed. The privatization of public space entails restricted access and a limited range of behaviour. Unlike public space where open access and free speech is, in theory, allowed, these new commercialized public spaces are restricted. Overt political campaigning is banned from most, and limitations are placed in all on the ability to exercise free speech. Behaviour is monitored. While the shopping centre managers want to make their sites public, they need passive consumers, not active citizens.

The rise of specifically engineered shopping places also comprises the feminization of public space and the encouragement of female orchestrated consumption. Shopping centres are planned and managed with women in mind. Women are often the most active consumers in the typical family households.

Consumption-led urban regeneration schemes, involving new and refurbished shopping centres and orchestrated shopping experiences, are important ways to redevelop and renew parts of cities. This form of urban planning embodies the increasing dominance of consumption in the economic and social life of cities as well as for their citizens.

Urban studies as a subject has moved away from an emphasis on production to a greater appreciation of the role of consumption. In consumer societies mass consumption is not the end point of production, although in some cases it guides and shapes production processes. New forms of consumption are emerging with consequent effects and consequences for the production and representation of personal and group identities. Urban space is being rewritten by the hand of the consumer.

Cities and Modes of Regulation

There is no such thing as a free, unfettered capitalist market. Capitalism has always been regulated. Capitalist economies are embedded in specific societies with different traditions, belief systems, histories and geographies. These characteristics are not incidental to the functioning of the market: they are central. We made one general distinction between cities in terms of the dominant mode of production and another in terms of modes of consumption, but an even further sifting is required if we are to be truly sensitive to the differences between societies within the different types of consumption. There is, for example, wide variation concerning the look, feel, and experience of cities in the United States compared to those in Sweden or the Netherlands, or even Britain. The fact that they are all capitalist societies, marked by high mass consumption, does not allow us to note the differences; to handle these we have to be aware of the mode of regulation of the economic system.

A social regulation school of thought has been developed by Aglietta (1987) and Lipietz (1987; see also Boyer, 1990). Social regulation extends from minimal to interventionist positions and from democratic to dictatorial modes, involving both the institutions for regulation and the mechanisms for regulation. And this form of regulation operates at many levels, from local activities to national economic systems and international regimes of trade to immigration and capital movement. Social regulation is the main institution in the nation state that sets the framework and conditions of much economic activity. The differences in state policies shape the different look, feel and life of cities in different countries. In recent years regulations set by the IMF, World Bank and World Trade Organization have established transnational regimes of trade and capital investment regulation.

A neo-liberal agenda has emerged as the dominant paradigm for city, state and international institutions. This agenda involves a deregulation so that market efficiency is maximized, public goods and services not directly related to capitalist profitability are undercut and capital–labour relations are structured to aid the freedom of capital. There has been a major reregulation of capital–labour relations, and indeed of the entire global–national economy. In this new reregulated political economy, city economies are as closely tied to global regimes as to national systems of regulation. There is a rescaling of social and economic regulation with the local and global becoming as important as the national.

The Economic Role of Cities

A large body of work reveals that the agglomeration of economic activities in cities provides advantages. The clustering of activities in cities makes economic sense. Alfred Marshall (1922) noted that there were three factors behind the external strategies of economic agglomerations: the pools of skilled labour allowing the transfer of information, knowledge and skill; the presence of subsidiary industries providing common goods and services; and the geographic proximity facilitating face-to-face contact, the maintenance of trust and the exchange of information. Marshall's work has influenced much subsequent work and still provides the main theoretical understanding of the continued concentration of producer services in cities.

In the past the economic rationality of cities was transparent. When new industries are locating and new factories are opening in cities, they appear the ideal sites of manufacturing. This is still true today in selected Third World cities such as Shanghai where the economic advantages of cities continue to create agglomerations of industrial enterprises. In scholarship on the city in advanced economies, where the story has been one of manufacturing decline, the main question posed is about the continued viability of the city. As factories close and even services migrate to the suburbs, the economic feasibility of cities comes under scrutiny. Amin (2000) identifies three lines of argument that provide a positive answer: the advantages of urban agglomerating continue to outweigh disadvantages; urban environments play an important role in the sharing, transmission and interrogation of information so vital in today's economy; cities are important basing points of a globalizing economy. Even run-down, inner-city areas have their proponents. Michael Porter (1995), for example, touts four advantages of such areas: strategic location, buoyant demand, regional clusters of competitive advantage, and unique human resources.

Cities are places of knowledge production. In the information age cities continue to provide the opportunity for face-to-face contact. This is an efficient means of communication that helps solve incentive problems, facilitates socialization and learning, and provides psychological motivation. Storper and Venables (2004) write of the positive benefits created by the economic advantages of face-to-face contact in the urban economy.

Cities, especially a select group of large cites, play an important part in the creation and maintenance of the global economy. A large proportion of command functions, such as bank headquarters and head offices of transnational producer/service companies (such as law, advertising, financial services and insurance) are still concentrated in just a few cities. Studies of cities as economic command centres have identified an infrastructure of market trading articulated by demand and supply, an environment of innovation, business support services, a pool of highly skilled labour and the proximity of business organizations. This infrastructure generates, analyses and disseminates information and strikes deals within a shared culture of expertise and a nexus of contacts, which is in turn set within an even broader context of a disciplined market, multicurrency trading, and a responsive central banking and governmental system of economic regulation. The globalizing economy creates lots of information, narrative uncertainty, and economic risk that must be produced, managed, narrated, explained, and acted upon. Global cities are privileged

sites of economic reflexivity (Storper, 1997) and centres of global epistemic communities of surveillance, knowledge production and story-
telling. Nigel Thrift (2005) develops the notion of the cultural circuit of
capitalism. He relates the boom and bust of the so-called new economy to
the rhetorical fabrication of key actors, such as business schools, management consultants and management gurus. Epistemic communities do not
so much uncover reality as create it. Narration has consequences, and
these consequences in turn have further consequences in the self-refer-
encing world of financial epistemic communities.

A central reason for the concentration of command functions in
selected global cities is the need for social interaction in global financial
business deals. Trust, contact networks and social relations play pivotal
roles in the smooth functioning of global business. Spatial propinquity
allows these relations to be easily maintained, lubricated and sustained.
Global cities are the sites of dense networks of interpersonal contact and
centres of the important business/social capital vital to the successful
operation of international finance.

While the exact locational strategies may vary by individual sector
and national category, it is clear that globalizing producer services firms
tend to concentrate in a select range of global cities. The privileged sites
of globalizing producer services are global cities. This tautology is deliberate. Globalizing producer firms create global cities; global cities attract
globalizing producer services. Global service corporations are adept at
producing their own commodities, including new financial products, new
advertising packages, and new forms of multijurisdictional law. The one
thing that all of these developments share is dependence upon specialized
knowledge. The coalescence of a range of expertise produces state-of-
the-art commodities to meet the specific needs of clients. In order to be
able to put together such packages, firms need to be in knowledge-rich
environments. Sassen (1994) suggests that global cities provide such
environments and that face-to-face contacts between experts are facili-
tated by the clustering of knowledge-rich individuals in cities such as
New York, London and Paris. In this way, global cities have become
'privileged sites' housing the 'knowledge elite' that enact the economic
reflexivity crucial for economic success. Reflexivity and networking are
at the heart of understanding global cities as places where people, institutions and 'epistemic communities' work to establish and maintain
contacts. More importantly, these communities act as crucial mediators
and translators of the flows of knowledge, capital, people and goods that
circulate in the world. Doel and Hubbard (2002) reconceptualize global
cities as networked rather than place-bound phenomena. A global city

attends to the heterogeneous global space of flows, lending otherwise incommensurable materials intelligibility and translatability: for example, credit ratings mediate diverse banking systems while global law translates between different jurisdictions.

The Cultural Economy of Cities

In 2004 New York's Museum of Modern Art lent 200 works of art to Berlin's Neue Nationalgalerie. The show cost the German museum almost $11 million. Corporate sponsors included Deutsche Bank and Coca-Cola. The art included paintings by Picasso and van Gogh and, returning to the place of its origin, there was also the German painter Max Beckmann's triptych *Departure*, a commentary on the rise of fascism completed around 1933. The exhibition attracted thousands of visitors, stimulated the urban economy and repositioned Berlin as an international site of art consumption.

The city is now a place where new combinations of culture and economics emerge and develop (Lloyd, 2005; Scott, 2000). Culture is a business for cities, and their cultural economy is now a major urban economic sector. Sharon Zukin (2001) identifies an Artistic Mode of Production that developed in New York between the 1970s and 1980s, consisting of a revalorization of the built environment around cultural consumption and historic preservation, a use of art work to absorb youth unemployment and the creation of a new set of values that valued urban space and labour more for their aesthetic than their productive value.

Art and culture are today integral parts of urban economic development and urban planning. Freestone and Gibson (2004) outline various forms of culture-based planning, including culture-led urban regeneration, the promotion of urban cultural tourism, the creation of cultural districts, and the promotion of cultural industries. Cultural strategies – and these can be defined as attempts to identify, mobilize, market, and commodify a city's cultural assets – are now major elements in urban regeneration and economic stimulation (see Bassett, 1993; Griffiths, 1993; Zukin, 1995).

Strom (2002) shows the connection between cultural institutions and downtown development, while Hamnett and Shoval (2003) examine a specific form, the modern museum as a flagship of urban development. Major metropolitan museums are revenue-generating machines that promote museum shops and restaurants, the hiring out of the museum spaces, corporate sponsorships, the planning of blockbuster exhibitions, and the branding and franchising of the museum's name and reputation. New museums, in particular, are at the nexus of spectacular urban landscapes, signature architects, urban redevelopment and economic promotion. The promotion of urban cultural tourism is a now a feature of many city marketing schemes, especially for former industrial cities seeking to replace the loss of manufacturing. The establishment of the Guggenheim Museum in Bilbao was the result of the international franchising undertaken by the Guggenheim, the search for economic alternatives by the city of Bilbao and the spectacular architecture of Frank Gehry. Not all museums are successful, not all blockbuster exhibitions break attendance records, and not all cultural strategies work. But the success of such institutions as the Guggenheim Bilbao or of Barcelona's self-promotion as a destination for urban cultural tourism provide models for cities round the world.

Getting By

The city is more than an abstract space for anonymous economic transactions: it is the place where people make their living. In order to understand this economic life in cities it is necessary to make some distinctions. With regard to employment, we can make a distinction between the formal and the informal economy. Who we are is a function of what we do. It is one of the first questions asked of people: what do you do? Formal employment connects our private and public selves. Employment in the formal sector involves the sale of labour in the market place, formally recorded in government and official statistics. This employment provides income, status and identity. Unless you are fortunate enough to have inherited large amounts of money, then, like most people, you will need a job to provide an income. The income from employment pays for both the necessities and the luxuries of life. The more money you have the better housing you can afford, the bigger the car you can drive, and the more expensive the clothes you can wear. Differences in income are expressed in modes of life and forms of consumption. Differences in employment income are related to the supply and demand for different types of labour. When and where there is a large demand and limited supply, the price of labour increases. Conversely, when there is limited demand and a big supply the bargaining power of labour is decreased and the resultant income is less.

To this simple model has to be added a number of intervening factors: the state of the general economy, the rate of technological change (which creates new forms of supply and demand), and the ability of labour to control the supply of labour and the work process. Labour lacking skills has a weaker position than labour with skills. The more valuable the skills for employers, the greater the bargaining power of labour. These differences are expressed in the greater income of skilled workers compared with non-skilled workers.

The skills required in the market place are constantly changing. The most important shift in the developed world in recent years has been the deskilling of much manual employment. Flexible production involves a reduction in the demand and hence in the bargaining power of skilled manual workers. More recently, there has also been a reduction in the need for many of the skills of the white-collar workers. Office automation, the greater use of computers, the shift in management practices, and the streamlining of the executive hierarchy have all produced a decline in the need for white-collar labour.

The net effect has been to create a distinct core–periphery structure in the contemporary labour market. The core consists of well-paid workers enjoying employment security, training, and generous fringe benefits. This is the world of the business lunch, the seat in the business section of the aircraft, the keys to the executive suite; this is the world of affluence. There are two kinds of semi-periphery: the first consists of full-time workers with less status, permanence, and prestige, while the second group comprises people on short-term or part-time contracts. The periphery consists of those in self-employment, subcontractors, and those who work from home or through employment agencies. The rise of the semi-periphery and periphery has many implications for the bargaining power of labour and the very experience of work. Flexible systems of employment may allow people to spend more time in the home and with the family. This is in contrast to core workers whose life, especially family life, may be subordinate to their work. Workers in the periphery and semi-periphery are often separated one from another. Consciousness and collective experience increase group solidarity, while atomized, individualized forms of work rarely generate collective solidarity.

Employment is more than just a source of income. It provides meaning and identity. People are defined by the job they perform. Occupations vary in their status and remuneration: some jobs have both high status and high remuneration (for example, medical specialists), while others have high remuneration but less prestige (for example, manual workers earning lots of money through long hours and high performance), while yet others have better status but less money (for example, teachers).

Occupations provide more than just the means of life; they represent success and failure, prestige, relative rank, power and influence. Who fills which positions in the occupational structure is not a random process. Social patterns of differentiation are created and maintained through employment. Gender differences are embodied in patterns of employment: women are over-represented in the part-time, low-paid sector, and even when in the same employment, women in the US are paid less than two-thirds of the male rate. Ethnic differences are also reflected in occupational structure. Recent migrants to a city often fill the role of a reserve army of labour, performing the low-paid jobs that no one else wants. There is also the existence of so-called 'ethnic entrepreneurs'. This term is used with reference to such groups as Koreans in the US and Indians and Pakistanis in Canada and the UK. These groups are over-represented in the small, family-business sector. For ambitious households with strong family ties and obligations, a family business allows sweat equity to be used in a new society in a work environment that maintains and reinforces extended family structures.

Entry into formal employment is controlled by systemic requirements such as educational qualifications, which in turn reflect and reinforce the existing bases of inequality. To become a doctor, for example, it is necessary to go to college, to forgo income in the short to medium term. Some groups, especially the wealthier segments of society, are much more able than others to pursue such a strategy for themselves and their children. There is also a controlling culture that decides who is appropriate for certain types of jobs. Racial, social and gender discrimination act as barriers to certain groups and allow easy entry for others. In an interesting study the British sociologist Paul Willis (1978) posed the question, 'Why do working-class kids get working-class jobs?' Part of the answer, he shows, is in their culture of resistance to the formal education system. By rejecting the ladder of educational attainment as a dominant force in their life they doom themselves to educational mediocrity and hence to limited opportunities. By their rejection they accept a limited horizon of employment opportunity.

Employment is one of the central experiences of our public life. It provides us with money, meaning, identity, social relationships, and a major intersection of shared and private experiences. Because employment is so important the lack of employment can be a devastating blow, entailing not only a loss of income but also a loss of meaning. Long-term unemployment is a profoundly corrosive experience in the modern period because it is experienced individually; it is not a shared predicament but a private grief. An addictive dependency on affluence means the private inability to purchase consumer durables and creates a state of captive dependency rather than the basis for group mobilization.

The informal economy is the unrecorded sector where few, if any, taxes are paid. This sector is just as complex as the formal sector. Based on his work in Latin American cities, Ray Bromley (1988), for example, identifies nine different sectors. These include retail distribution, small-scale transport, personal services, security services, gambling services, recycling enterprises, prostitution, begging, and property crimes involving illegal appropriation through stealth (theft), the threat or use of violence (robbery) or deception (conning). Work conditions vary from short-term wage-work to precarious self-employment. The workers in this sector may be disguised wage-workers (that is, they are paid a wage but it is not recorded), workers on short-term wage-work, dependent workers who may lease a personal transport vehicle from an employer, and the self-employed. In his research on the city of Coli, Bromley found that 40–45 per cent of people who worked in the street were in precarious self-employment, 39–43 per cent were disguised wage-workers, 12–15 per cent were dependent workers, and only 3 per cent were short-term wage-workers.

A great deal has been written about the informal sector (Portes *et al.*, 1989; Cheng and Gereffi, 1994; Cross, 1998). While the emphasis has varied over the years, there has been a consistent concern with the dynamics of the sector. The informal sector can be seen as a sophisticated response to the lack of formal employment opportunities. Nelson (1988), for example, provides a discussion on the sexual division of labour in the informal sector of a squatter settlement in the city of Nairobi. She shows that maize beer brewing and prostitution, although illegal, are rational choices for many women in the area. There is a demand for them and few other employment opportunities. Moreover, the work is done in the home, which enables the women to care for their children.

The divisions between the formal and informal sectors fluctuate according to circumstance. When the formal economy provides many employment opportunities that provide a good living, then the informal sector becomes less significant. However, if the formal sector provides few jobs (or only jobs with low wages), the informal sector can be seen as a sophisticated coping strategy as people use a variety of tactics to make a living.

The informal economy involves transactions that are unrecorded, often because they are illegal. This is the shadowy world of prostitution, selling illegal drugs, racketeering and so on. It is difficult to estimate its full extent. Much of the informal illegal sector consists of the production and distribution of goods and services for which there is a demand, even though they are illegal. The demarcation of legal–illegal varies: alcohol is not illegal in the United States but cocaine is; prostitution is legal and regulated in both Germany and the Netherlands but is illegal in most of the United States; one can buy marijuana in Amsterdam without breaking the law, but the same transaction in New York would be considered criminal. The 'economy' of the illegal informal economy arises because there is a demand for certain goods and services; the 'illegal' comes from the matrix of cultural values and political rhetoric that make some things legal and others illegal.

There is no hard and fast division between the formal and informal sector. The line between legal and illegal is constantly being crossed: police who take bribes; chemical companies that illegally dump waste; corporations that form illegal cartels to charge high prices to the federal government. The distinction between the three sectors – formal, informal and illegal – is at times fuzzy. Rather than look at the differences, a more rewarding strategy may be to look at how transactions transgress the arbitrary lines.

A social economy that consists of not-for-profit activities is also sometimes referred to as the 'third sector'. It includes cooperatives, charities, voluntary groups, trusts and religious organizations. This sphere of economic activity, somewhere between the market and the state, plays an important role in certain parts of the city, as both funding source and employer. While much has been written about its possible transformative role, we have very little hard evidence or detailed case studies.

The communal economy involves the cashless exchange of goods and services. It is common in neighbourhoods and extended family systems. If someone wants a baby-sitter for an evening they have a number of possibilities: they can hire someone and record the transaction and pay taxes (the formal economy); they can hire a teenager and pay them an agreed sum without informing the authorities (the informal sector); or they can ask a neighbour, giving the clear understanding that they will return the favour. The last, and often the most common, response is an example of the communal economy in action. It can range from reciprocal favours, such as baby-sitting, grass-cutting and removal of rubbish, to a host of household chores from building maintenance to car-pooling.

Putnam (2000) writes about the importance of social capital, the interpersonal networks of cooperation that link people in communities. Social capital is the existence and operation of trust-based relationships that play an important role in the life of the city. Social capital is an important resource that shapes group and individual behaviours. The role of social capital in shaping neighbourhoods' fortunes is an important topic that deserves much deeper investigation.

Two competing trends are at work in the communal economy. On the one hand, there is the decline in the traditional communal economy associated with the breakdown of the extended family system in many societies. On the other hand, there is an increase in newer models of the communal economy as many households, especially child-orientated households, are so stretched for time that certain forms of community adaptation have taken place, from informal baby-sitting circles to car pools. This communal economy links households with shared needs and constraints, albeit belonging to different families.

The communal economy both condenses and reflects the strength of community ties. These tend to be strongest when there is a distinct sense of shared identity (and this could be based on family ties, ethnicity, gender, status or income). The communal economy allows informal obligations and rights to be spread in a net of mutual ties and benefits.

The domestic economy is the amount, type, and division of labour within the home. In the affluent world, and throughout much of the rest, a dominant trend has been the commodification of the household economy. More and more goods and services previously undertaken by households themselves are now part of the formal economy. Where households used to preserve their own produce, they now increasingly buy it in. Where households used to decorate their own homes they now employ a professional decorator, and where they used to sit round a fire and sing songs or tell stories, they now cluster around the television screen or a computer game.

This commodification involves a trade-off. It is much easier to use a washing machine than to wash by hand. Domestic appliances 'save' time in one sense. However, they have to be paid for, so time has to be spent at work to pay for them. Time is spent in order to save time.

The division of labour within the household economy has changed over the years. A hundred years ago there was much greater use of paid domestic labour. The increasing cost of labour has meant the decline of mass domestic labour although it still persists amongst the wealthy, and in the rich countries foreign, vulnerable and illegal workers do a high proportion of such work. The division of labour is a source of change, conflict and negotiation within households. As more women have joined the formal labour force, they feel the double demand of work and home because they carry much of the domestic load. The division of domestic labour is not simply an apportionment of necessary work; it involves questions and representations of femininity, masculinity and the family.

There is a range of resources available to households. Income from the formal economy is just one of the resources, and the mix of resources varies. For households with good formal employment there will be less need for the others. In countries with generous state subsidies the quality of household life will not just be a function of private income. Households with few formal opportunities either from the market or the state have to rely on the informal economy. The strategies available to a household will depend on the resources. A household with a large income from the formal economy will not have to sell cigarettes on the street corner. A household with few formal opportunities, in contrast, thus has to look at alternative sources. To get by, households will adopt a variety of coping strategies in order to extend the range of resources available to them.

City Close-ups

Much of the material in this chapter has drawn upon the experience of cities in the developed world. It is thus fitting to end this chapter with some case studies of cities in the developing world.

Consider Africa: a popular view of sub-Saharan and especially of equatorial Africa is that their cities are black holes of global capitalism. There are instances of economic collapse. Michele Wrong (2001) provides a telling account of the rise and fall of Mobutu's Congo. The republic had a heavy colonial legacy inherited from the Belgians, but the postcolonial kleptocracy of Mobutu was kept in power by the World Bank and the CIA. The dictator stole millions as did the rich elite, the *Grosses Legumes* (Big Vegetables), which bankrupted the national treasury and undermined the formal economy. But what Wrong also shows is the adaptive power of the urban poor in Kinshasa as they struggled in a disintegrating formal economy. But economic collapse was not the only economic experience of cities in the region. Richard Grant (in press) examines the case of Accra. The major city in Ghana has a population of 1.7 million, double its population in 1984. Almost 15 per cent of Ghanaians live abroad and their remittances are the third largest sector of the national economy. Foreign investors, often in alliance with expatriate Ghanaians and locals, have poured millions of dollars into the city. There are almost 1,000 foreign companies in the city. The traditional land market has been transformed into a more private market system, elite housing areas of gated communities have emerged and the experience of the teeming slums is producing important urban social movements.

Grant and Nijman (2002) have produced a model of the globalization of cities in the less developed world. They suggest that globalization is the latest in a series of historical phases (the other stages being pre-colonialism, colonialism and nationalism) that are reshaping these cities. With a primary focus on Accra and Mumbai, they show how changes in the urban landscape are linked to global processes through their role as gateways for foreign investment. In both cities liberalization policies encouraged an influx of foreign companies, especially in finance and producer services. They identify the creation of three types of central business district (CBD): a global CBD where there is a concentration of foreign companies and domestic companies with foreign connections, a national CBD and a local CBD.

The Chinese city is the focus of considerable interest as it experiencing major socio-spatial transformation in the wake of rapid capitalist growth. Fulong Wu details some of the major changes in Shanghai, including the marketization of the urban land market, the shift in housing from worker compounds to owner occupation, the increased social differentiation and social polarization, and the frenetic land speculation (Wu, 2005). The Chinese city is the 'shock city' of the early twenty-first century (Logan, 2002; Friedmann, 2005; Ma and Wu, 2005).

Cities in the less developed world are being transformed by the maelstrom of globalization, and national and local forces. In cities as varied as Djakarta (Forbes, 2004), Shanghai (Wu and Yusuf, 2004) and Havana (Rutheiser, 2000), global economic forces are reshaping and restructuring economies and landscapes. We are in the middle of a global urban economic transition that is recreating the nature of urbanization and radically transforming the urban experience.

7

The Competitive City

Cities market themselves to create or change their image with the intended goal of attracting business, tourists and residents. Although urban marketing has been practised since the age of colonial expansion, it undoubtedly has increased in importance and intensity as cities around the world compete in a crowded global market. Indeed, cities' competition has grown so much in recent years that the competition itself is now a focus for theorizing. Discussion centres upon understanding the background to competition, assessing the strategies of urban competitiveness, examining the role of urban representation and analysing the effects of these strategies.

The Competitive Context

Throughout much of the nineteenth century and most of the twentieth there was a relatively crude division of labour; industrial cities of the capitalist core economies supported manufacturing production while the large cities concentrated command functions. In the past 30 years technological developments, leading to the deskilling of labour and the decreasing size of transport costs, have allowed manufacturing production to be undertaken around the world. Labour costs, more than the need to be close to markets or pools of skilled labour, now drive location. The net effect is the relocation of manufacturing, a global shift that fuels the decline of older manufacturing cities in the capitalist core economies and the growth of cities in the newly industrializing countries. New footloose industries also have emerged, especially in the high-tech sectors, with very different locational requirements from those of the older metal-bashing industries. These industries are concerned more with access to information than to a coalfield or other sources of power. These brain-driven, knowledge industries have a high degree of locational flexibility. Service and command functions can also be located away from the previously dominant cities because of technological changes such as email, video-conferencing, cheaper telephone and fax rates. While there is still the pull of personal contact, the push of rising costs allows the relocation of functions previously tied to the very large cities.

There is a greater locational flexibility in the contemporary global economy. The growing pool of mobile capital reinforces this flexibility, as witnessed in the growing number of tourists, conventions and rotating spectacles (such as the Olympic Games) that can be attracted to particular cities with the right mix of incentives and attributes. The perceived mobility of capital, as well as the actual mobility of capital, part of a general trend that features impermanence and change rather than permanence and stability, is an important factor. The implication or potential of hyper-mobility of capital, as much as the actual mobility of capital, promotes entrepreneurialism in contemporary city government. These profound changes have led to a new urban order where jobs and investment move quickly and often around the world, from city to city, up and down the urban hierarchy. In this new chaotic geography cities constantly position and reposition themselves, creating a crisis of urban representation as new images supplant old images in the constantly renewing urban order. Now almost all city governments promote growth aggressively on a scope unimaginable just a decade ago. We live in an era characterized by what Haider (1992) calls 'place wars'.

Making the City Competitive

In the world of hyper-mobile capital and global competition between cities for both fixed investment and circulating capital, global cities no longer have a monopoly of command and control functions, industrial cities in the developed world have to compete with places around the world, and all cities compete for the benefits of the postindustrial economy. The urban shift of command functions, the global shift of manufacturing, and the changing dynamics of a reregulated postindustrial space economy have brought about a new urban order of increased and increasing competition. Let me note just two connected responses to this antagonistic condition. First, there has been a shift in some countries of urban governance from managerialism to entrepreneurialism, as city governments get involved in the competition for scarce and mobile capital. Second, there is the reimagining of the city, as cities seek to represent themselves positively in the new geographies, created and imagined, of late capitalism. It is not accidental, I believe, that a growing literature on urban representation and place promotion accompanies these new realities. Urban rivalries are being fought through advertising campaigns, as cities compete to represent themselves in the best possible (and constantly changing) light.

The new imaginings of the city reflect and embody the new geographies of late capitalism. I will outline four overlapping and interconnected themes in terms of these geographies.

World Cities and Wannabe World Cities

Three dominant world cities can be noted: London, New York and Tokyo. Their positions are relatively stable but not secure. In the case of New York, a series of campaigns have been mounted to secure the city's position as the country's world city. From the hugely successful slogan of 'I ♥ New York' to the more recent '*The* business city that never sleeps' campaigns, the city promotes a positive image. While London lacks a similar formal advertising campaign, the iconography of London Docklands is partially aimed at creating a global-city feel, the tall skyscrapers and large groundscrapers all clad in a postmodern architecture which indicates a city where serious money can be made, monitored, traded and measured. The postmodern referencing of recent building developments in and around the City of London aims to create a more upbeat contemporary business image. All three world cities have been facing competition from what can be referred to as 'wannabe' world cities. These are cities that have some command functions but want more. They include Los Angeles, Atlanta, Chicago, Paris and Birmingham (UK). It is in this level of the world urban hierarchy that extensive campaigns have been launched. A slogan for Atlanta optimistically noted that it was 'Claiming its international destiny'. In some cases there is a conscious attempt to attract formerly big city functions, such as banking. Charlotte, North Carolina, is now one of the largest banking centres in the United States. In other cases, there is an attempt to usurp national urban dominance. In Australia, for example, Sydney and Melbourne have long competed to be Australia's world city, the main connection point with the global economy command structure. The battle was won by Sydney, a victory embodied in the fact that the Sydney Opera House and the Harbour Bridge are now recognizable icons in the international community, while Melbourne still struggles to achieve a distinctive representation.

The wannabe world cities compete for command functions and world spectacles. A good, though not infallible, guide to wannabes used to be those cities that have either hosted or applied to host the Summer Olympic Games. In recent years, however, even the big cities such as

New York, London and Paris have sought to attract the Games. The South Korean Sports Minister, Lee Yeung Ho, noted in 1988: 'Hosting the Olympics gives us international recognition and a psychological boost for our next step to join the advanced countries within the next decade. Look what happened to Japan after the 1964 Olympics' (cited in Maltby, 1989, 206). What happened to Tokyo was not simply the result of the Olympic Games, but the Games aided the internationalization of the city both internally and externally. Olympic Games are not just an opportunity to be the site of a global spectacle, and hence to receive international name recognition: they also provide an opportunity for business and real estate deals, acting as giant urban redevelopment projects.

Wannabe world cities particularly concern themselves with ensuring the most effective international image possible by having all the attributes of a global city. Such prerequisites include an international airport, signature buildings of big name architects (e.g., Michael Graves, Arata Isozaki, Philip Johnson, I. M. Pei, John Portman, Richard Rogers, Aldo Rossi, James Stirling), impressive buildings (the most recently constructed tallest buildings in the world are in Kuala Lumpur, Shanghai, Hong Kong and Taipei), and cultural complexes such as art spaces and symphony halls. Combining these elements is always a useful strategy: hiring a famous architect to design a cultural complex, as in James Stirling's Art Gallery in Stuttgart, Isozaki's Museum of Contemporary Art in Los Angeles, Pei's glass pyramid in front of the Louvre in Paris, or (one of the oldest yet still impressive) Jorn Utzon's Opera House in Sydney. The construction of these complexes involves urban redevelopment schemes through which local developers, landowners, and politicians amass substantial fortunes. Chang, Huang and Savage (2004) consider the case of Singapore's attempts to create urban landscapes that project the city state's global aspirations. The Singapore River Development Zone Project, a river-form multi-land use development to match the waterfront development in Baltimore and Sydney, is intended to project global city status and successfully connect with global flows of capital movement and tourist flows. Both global and local forces are at work and the nature of the development is a negotiated outcome between the perceived need to make global connections with local empowerment and community rights, mediated through debates about national identity.

The rapidly growing cities in the Pacific Rim have recently entered the place wars. The city of Shanghai, for example, has embarked on an ambitious goal of projecting global city status (Wu, 2000; Wu and Yusuf, 2004). Since the early 1990s improvements have been made to the physical infrastructure, including the building of a shiny new town centre of high rise towers and the construction of a new international airport; land-use planning measures have been introduced to encourage the dispersal of industry from central sites and the development of mixed commercial and residential use of prime land; in addition, organizational streamlining has been inaugurated to improve urban management. The project is to make global city that sits alongside New York, London and Tokyo. A self-consciously global city is being created and represented.

Wannabe cities are cities of spectacle, cities of intense urban redevelopment, and cities with powerful growth rhetoric. They also have an edgy insecurity about their roles and position in the world that gives tremendous urgency to their cultural boosterism. The desperate scramble for big name architects, art galleries and cultural events is a fascinating part of the 'place wars' amongst cities aiming for the top of the urban hierarchy.

Look No More Factories

Industrial cities in the developed world have a difficult time in an era of world competition and of the global shift of industry towards much lower cost centres. To be seen as industrial is to be associated with the old, the polluted, the out-of-date. Renovation of the industrial city is a persistent strand of urban representations. The process is described for a range of cities in a variety of ways: reconstructing the image of the industrial city (Short *et al.*, 1993), city makeovers (Holcomb, 1994), selling the industrial town (Barke and Harrop, 1994), and gilding the smokestacks (Watson, 1991). Cities such as Manchester in the UK, Syracuse, Pittsburgh and Milwaukee in the US, and Wollongong in Australia have all been (re)presented in more attractive packages that emphasize the new rather than the old, the fashionable postmodern rather than the merely modern, the postindustrial rather than the industrial, consumption rather than production, spectacle and fun rather than pollution and work. Emblematic of such shifts in meaning was the change in the logo of Syracuse. This city of more than half-a-million people in New York State has an industrial history originally based on salt production and later on a range of manufacturing and metal-based production. One side effect was the pollution of the local lake. Syracuse was a typical Frostbelt industrial city, with an official seal that celebrated its industrial base with images of factories and salt fields. In 1972 the mayor of the city organized a design competition to replace the 100-year-old seal. There was community resistance, and it was only in 1986 that another mayor was able to introduce a new city logo. This logo represents a clean lake and an urban skyline with not a factory chimney to be seen.

Reimagining the industrial city involves the physical reconstruction of the city. The process of deindustrialization sometimes allows opportunities for urban redevelopment as factories are abandoned and new geographies of production and circulation leave old docks and railway lines economically redundant. The urban redevelopments are schemes to make money couched as earnest efforts to revive the city through postmodern architecture and postindustrial economies. Baltimore's Harbor Place and Pittsburgh's downtown developments are good examples. With reference to Birmingham, UK, Hubbard (1996) notes the contribution of spectacular urban landscapes to a new cultural politics of place that legitimates entrepreneurial policies.

The representations of an industrial city also involve internal debate as well as the manipulation of external images. Industrial cities have a culture, an emphasis on manual work, and a collective sense of meaning and significance tied to their industrial and manufacturing bases. Industry provides not only a means of life but also creates a context for individual and collective identities.

Deindustrialization destroys this meaning, and the new representations of the postindustrial city challenge and undermine these identities. Image makeovers are also struggles in which image tends to dominate. Part of this internal debate involves a renegotiation with the physical environment. Old-fashioned industry was very polluting: waste was dumped on the ground and in the rivers and lakes, creating toxic legacies considered to be the necessary evils to the precedence of work. The physical environment was merely a backdrop, a context, and a refuse bin for industry.

Reimagining the industrial city involves restructuring the social–environmental relationship. In the case of Syracuse, the lake was represented in the new logo as pristine and suitable for recreation. The reality was very different, as the lake still holds toxic waste. There are success stories. In Barcelona the urban renewal associated with the Olympic Games involved the opening-up of the old docks to a harbour waterfront with a pedestrianized walkway. Until the mid-1980s, the city had turned its back on the sea, leaving only warehouses and docks at the water's edge. After the makeover the harbour front became a congenial place for leisure consumption rather than for production and storage.

The internal debate also involves the creation of new agendas and the suppression of old ones. In 1988 John Norquist was elected mayor of Milwaukee. The old image of the city was as the beer capital of the nation, an industrial city and a place with a rich socialist tradition. Deindustrialization in the 1970s and 1980s destroyed the old job base of the city, challenged its collective identity, and left a vacuum for new representations. Mayor Norquist led an aggressive campaign to (re)present and restructure the city. He threw out the city's welfare tradition and created a pro-business climate by offering competitive (i.e., low) utility rates and tax rates, initiating a series of lake-front festivals, and promoting public–private downtown construction schemes including a new convention centre. As an avatar of urban reimaginings, Norquist was quoted and celebrated widely in the media. In the current economic climate many local politicians have to present a pro-business image for their cities. However, they also have to get elected. While business has the finance, the people have the votes. The reimaginings of the city thus are a curious mix of pro-business sentiments with shadings of wider social concerns. The extent of these concerns reflects local political cultures. Thus, Glasgow's 'City Vision', launched in January 1996, contains passing reference to quality of life, maximum employment, and a caring social infrastructure. This is in rich contrast to the free market vision enunciated by Mayor Norquist of Milwaukee. The varying forms of urban reimaginings embody differences in community identity, local political culture, and the rhetorics that are most likely to carry the day in particular cities in various countries.

The City for Business

The pro-business message is a standard theme in the reimagining and selling of cities. The hyper-mobility of capital fosters intense competition between cities for both fixed capital investment and a piece of tourism's circulating capital. Conventions, in addition to national and global spectacles, reinforce the age-old basic booster message that this city is the city to do good business. Differences, however, can be noted. Glasgow's City Vision encourages maximum employment as much as technological progress, thus embodying the local political culture while also promoting the city to the wider business community. It stands to reason that local politicians would advocate the Vision for the purposes of re-election in a left-wing city. In the US, by contrast, this left-wing tradition is either lacking or, in the case of Milwaukee, silenced. Moreover, urban promotion in the United States is most often a private-sector activity, the local chambers of commerce being particularly active, either on their own or as the dominant partners in joint public–private initiatives. Thus, urban representation in the United States more totally reflects the needs of business.

Capitalizing Culture

In one of the most sustained analyses of city marketing, Bailey (1989) suggests a three-stage evolution. His model was developed for the US, although I believe it is suitable for wider generalization as it parallels the historical trends in the capitalist economy. In the first phase, *smokestack chasing*, manufacturing jobs are drawn in by enticing companies with subsidies and the promise of low operating costs and higher profits from existing or alternative sites. The poaching of factories from other cities was, and still is, a major element of local job promotion. Urban representation centres on low operating costs and the availability of subsidies. The second stage, *target marketing*, involves the attraction of manufacturing and service jobs in target industries currently experiencing profitable growth. There are still attempts at luring plants from other locations, but the promotion also includes improving the physical infrastructure, vocational training, and stressing good public–private cooperation. Representation continues to mention low operating costs but includes the suitability of the local community for target industries and the more general notion of good quality of life. The third generation, *development*, contains the objectives of the first two stages but includes emphasis on the 'jobs of the future', where representation now includes global competitiveness and human and intellectual resources, as well as low operating costs and quality of life. With each successive stage the message becomes more sophisticated, and urban representation must address quality-of-life issues. Art exhibition spaces, concert halls, museums and festivals are vital to the reimagining of cities, conferring world city status and thus helping to attract and retain the executive classes and skilled workers of present and future high-tech industries.

Urban cultural capital includes more than just traditional elements of so-called high culture. Popular culture in a variety of guises is also important. There is the culture of leisure, for example: cities now represent themselves as fun places where the good life entails both lucrative employment and ample time for leisure. The marketing of the city as a centre for play is tied to dining, shopping, nightclubbing and outdoor pursuits. A number of notable themes include: *the historic feel,* which articulates the historic connections of the city or particular city neighbourhoods, sometimes historicizing whole districts with 'antique signs', 'authentic' landmark sites, and guided historical narratives in the form of routes, maps and brochures. Hewison (1987) refers to this merchandizing of history as 'the heritage industry'. Cities undergo historicization as part of their urban makeovers, upgrading their positive images by highlighting their historical gravitas. *The festival package* emphasizes frivolity, resorts and spas, sporting events, shopping centres and convention centres. Mexico City, Miami and New Orleans use this package to sell themselves in the popular press. *The green and clean theme* situates the city in a postindustrial world with clean air, good beaches, easy access to the 'natural' world, and active recreation such as sailing, fishing, swimming. San Francisco, San Diego, Seattle, Portland, Vancouver and Sydney work this theme into their urban representation. *The package of pluralism* highlights the rich ethnic mix that leads to a varied urban experience, including specialized shopping centres, ethnic restaurants, ethnic carnivals, gay spectacles and so on. New York, Toronto, Los Angeles, Chicago and San Francisco sell this theme. The four themes are not mutually exclusive, and an individual city may use elements of all of them in its representation.

Popular culture also includes spectacles, festivals and sports. Let me just note the increasing importance of professional sports teams in the representation of US cities since this highlights a number of more general ideas about capitalizing culture. Professional sports in the United States, particularly basketball (National Basketball Association or NBA), football (National Football League or NFL), baseball (Major League Baseball or MLB), and, of slightly lesser importance, ice hockey (National Hockey League or NHL), is big business. The franchises are located in cities nationwide. Cities want the franchises for the money they directly generate and for the image they represent. To have an NBA, NFL, MLB or NHL team is to play in the big leagues, to have your city's name mentioned in the extensive sports coverage that saturates the mass media. A successful sports team is great public relations for the city. One city even built its reimagining around professional sports. Indianapolis initiated a new public relations exercise and economic development strategy in 1982 aimed at coordinating development strategies and improving its image. More than $1 million was spent over four years. As a central part of the representation of the city, the NFL Colts were lured from Baltimore in 1983 to begin the 1984 season as the Indianapolis Colts. Professional sports teams provide revenue, taxes, a possible source of civic pride and name recognition.

Marketing the City

There are two broad approaches to understanding city marketing: first, there is a body of work that ties urban marketing to a deeper political economy (Kearns and Philo, 1993); second, there are studies that focus on the range and success of various marketing strategies (Ashworth and Voogd, 1990; Gold and Ward, 1994). The approaches are not mutually exclusive, and many writers use both, often in the same work, but there are differences of orientation: the former emphasizes the transformation in urban governance and the involvement of business coalitions in local economic development, while the latter focuses on the detailed processes and strategies of urban marketing.

The context of the changing space economy of contemporary capitalism shapes urban marketing, often resulting in a crisis of urban representation and the consequent transformation of urban governance towards entrepreneurialism. Reflecting on the current processes of economic restructuring and the accompanying rise of the new urban entrepreneurialism, Paddison (1993, 340) writes, 'the concept of the marketing of cities has gained increasing attention as a means of enhancing their competitiveness'. He also identifies a series of different, but related, objectives of marketing the city: raising the competitiveness, attracting inward investment, improving its image and the well-being of its population. These objectives have been repeated in many other studies on the marketing of cities. According to Kotler, Haider and Rein (1993), the targets of city marketing are business firms, industrial plants, corporate and divisional headquarters, investment capital, sports teams, tourists, conventioneers, residents and so on, all of which promise increased employment, income, trade, investment and growth. The authors argue that strategic, aggressive place marketing is the most adaptive and productive approach to the problems of cities. They even affirm that cities that fail to market themselves successfully face the risk of economic stagnation and decline.

Cities are not merely settings for business activity: they are also commodities packaged, advertised and marketed much as any other product in a capitalist society. This city marketing process consists of several phases. Haider (1992) suggests five activities: analysing marketing opportunities, researching and selecting target markets, designing marketing strategies, planning marketing programmes, and organizing and implementing the market effort. Ashworth and Voogd (1990) provide a broader context: analysis of market, formulation of goals and strategies, determination of geographical marketing mix, and elaboration and evaluation. Kotler, Haider and Rein (1993) focus more on setting attractive incentives and promoting the city's values and image so that potential users are fully aware of the city's distinctive advantages. Image is a critical factor in how buyers enter the market. Thus people's attitudes and actions towards a city are highly conditioned by their beliefs about it gained through depictions and descriptions of it; the image of a city is an important commodity.

The primary goal of the city marketeer is to construct a new and improved image. The status of the city may be improved through an energetic campaign of image-making and place promotion. Images may exist independently of the apparent facts of objective reality.

Image marketing is the most frequently employed approach to city marketing, particularly for traditionally industrial cities whose economies are either declining or stagnant. In the early 1990s Canon ran a very successful advertising campaign with the slogan 'Image is Everything'. With reference to the marketing of cities, the slogan was only half-right, but also half-wrong. It was half-right in that as we increasingly move in a world of signs, symbols and images, our world is image-rich and sign-saturated, so it is important for cities to present a positive image. There is almost a desperate attempt to give the city an image; to do otherwise would be to drown in the limbo of invisibility. Much of city marketing is a frantic attempt to avoid such a fate. But image is only part of the story. For sustained economic development, the brute facts of comparative advantage come into play. While image may be important in getting a city recognized, it does not guarantee economic success (see Wolman, Ford and Hill, 1994).

There are remarkable similarities in the images projected by cities. Most cities are trying to create and project an image reflecting a vibrant, growing place with accessible locations, reconstructed city centres, and sunny business climates. Common features in the promotional texts are appealing quality of life and cultural promotions such as fairs, festivals and sporting events. Postmodern architecture and high-tech industries are also photographically portrayed in splendid clarity by declining industrial cities to represent a revitalized image. Images portrayed by cities tend to be developed by the city's marketing consultancy contracted by the chamber of commerce, economic development association, and the visitors' bureau. Thus, common images mentioned above may be termed the 'official image' of the city. City marketing operations involve the construction or selective tailoring of particular images of the city. Each city selects and authorizes favourable images but the authorization of a particular image, the politics of image-making, is (as yet) rarely studied.

Many studies on marketing the city note an increased attention to quality of life matters, including a healthier, greener environment and cultural, recreational facilities (Goss, 1993). This demonstrates that quality of life has become an important element in the more recent phase of advertising activities. Ward (1994, 58) coins the term 'cultural promotion' to describe cities' appeals to the quality of life. He says this bolsters more than just tourism, because it can be used intentionally to enhance and demonstrate the attractiveness of cities as locations for higher-level economic activities such as conferences and exhibitions.

Advertising has traditionally been the main component of local economic development strategies. After setting attractive incentives and selecting desirable images, cities carry on an advertising campaign to convey these messages to their target audience. There are a variety of advertising packages used by cities: city guides, glossy brochures, fact sheets of industrial commercial information, and advertisements in journals. A study by Short and Kim (1998) analysed magazine advertising by city governments in *Advertising Age, Business Week, Financial World, Forbes, Fortune, Historic Preservation, National Geographic Traveler* and *New Choices for Retirement Living* for the period 1994–5. Two themes were evident in the advertising literature: benefits to business, and quality of life. Many cities use the term 'business' in their slogans to show that they are good for business. Cities marshal a long list of good incentives and images in their advertisements. To attract and retain business, cities advertise that they possess a pro-business political climate, ideal workforce, high-technology industries and research institutes, solid infrastructure and healthy local economy.

Most advertisements used an impressive listing of internationally known companies based in local areas. It is one rhetorical device through which advertisers seek to give credibility to their discourse by referring to their previous successes. The quotations of the opinion of independent surveys on the city are also one of the popular features in the advertisements. For example, Kansas City boasts of its Number 1 ranking workforce in the US by *Fortune* magazine based on skills and availability, and Fairfax County mentions that last year *City and State* magazine proclaimed the county to be the best financially managed in the nation. The testimonial of senior executives of local companies who express their satisfaction with the city is a popular strategy to show how wonderfully the city will work for your business. They also imply that your business can benefit from more economic benefits in their city than in any other. Photo-imagery, including fabulous pictures, is one of the major elements in the advertisements. These pictures capture images of great natural beauty, postmodern architecture, high-tech equipment, gorgeous night scenes of downtown, rich historical and recreational places, festivals, and photos of governors and Chief Executive Officers (CEOs) of major local companies.

There are common features in the design of the advertisements. This is because of the similarity in the projected images between cities and also because of the preferences of the dominant advertising agencies specializing in place marketing such as Leslie Singer Design, which designs the majority of city advertisements in *Forbes*. Despite the similarities, however, there are also numerous examples in magazine advertisements of efforts to distinguish a city from others. To make their cities widely recognized, advertisers create specific symbols or metaphors: Boston's local research institutes with impeccable reputations; Chicago as a world-class financial centre; Fairfax's and Oak Ridge's high-tech aspects; Memphis's distribution advantages; Rochester as a world image centre; Atlantic City's year-round entertainment; Nashville's music; Jacksonville's and Orlando's professional sports teams; and St Augustine's historic heritage. They each claim that its particular individual advantage is globally or nationally recognized. There are also contradictory trends of homogenization (similarity) versus distinctiveness (uniqueness) in urban images projected in advertisements.

In summary, Short and Kim identify a number of themes that run through city marketing in magazine advertisements, as well as other outlets. The two principal ones are the city as a place for profitable business and the city as a good place to live, but there are subthemes: the global city, the green city, the fun city, the culture city, the pluralist city and the postindustrial city. The subthemes condense complex imagery into simple slogans, easily understood images and accessible selling points.

Rewriting the City

Crises of representation occur when systems of meaning are changing rapidly. In recent years the dynamics of capitalism have caused a crisis of urban representation, as cities need to reposition themselves in the reconstruction and reimagining of global capitalism. A variety of representations have been discussed in this chapter: attempts at world city status; the distancing of cities from their industrial past; the presentation of cities as attractive places for footloose business and investment; the city as a place of culture. These (re)presentations are for external presentation and internal consumption.

It is sometimes useful to see the city as text that is constantly being written, reconstructed and deconstructed. The city as text metaphor also raises the notion of authorship and what is left out as well as what is written. Marketing the city is an attempt to both reimagine and represent the city and it bears the mark of power and authority. The dominant images presented in city marketing schemes are not innocent of social authority and political power. The city is written from a particular perspective for a particular audience. The text has its silences. These include the notion of the city as a place of redistributional social policies. Images of social justice are rarely presented; the just city never appears as one of the subthemes in the city as a good place to live. The poor are rarely discussed and never presented. The dominant images represent conflict-free cities, where pluralism leads to a variety of ethnic restaurants rather than competition for scarce resources, where the good life is neither marred nor affected by the presence of the poor and marginalized who are excluded and ignored. The good city is not the fair city, the just city or the equal city, and this is particularly pronounced in the US where social redistributional policies have less appeal than they do in Europe. The images presented of US cities stress individual consumption rather than collective welfare, private attainment rather than social justice and the city as private pleasure rather than collective good.

In the new representations, more is said about the city as a place for business or work, and its attractions for the senior executives and the governing class of the business community, and much less is said about the city as a place of democratic participation, the city as a place of social justice, the city as a place where all citizens can lead dignified and creative lives. Representations of the city are not politically neutral, and neither are they devoid of social implications. In the old radical rhetoric it was important to own the means of production; in the image-conscious world of spatially reorganizing capitalism it seems to be just as important to own the means of representation.

The rise of the new urban entrepreneurialism and the increasing involvement of business coalitions in local politics constitute the framework of contemporary urban marketing. A number of questions remain. First, how can we assess the effectiveness of urban marketing? There is a real need for some assessment of the efficacy of these campaigns. Barke and Harrop (1994) cite an officer's sceptical view: 'We do it because everyone else does it.' They comment that many cities are not really aware of any significant direct gain to their localities from their promotional activities. City governments and chambers of commerce will always assume the most favourable interpretation and thus there is a need for some systematic measurement of these campaigns. Second, there is a connection between changes in the space economy and marketing that goes both ways. We have argued that these marketing campaigns have been conducted because of changes in the space economy, but to what extent can marketing campaigns bring about shifts in the space economy? These questions are related. They pose the difficult issue of measuring the effects and consequences of city marketing. This is an important topic that deserves careful consideration and further work.

8
The Gendered City

In the title of a 1980 paper Dolores Hayden poses the question: 'What would a non-sexist city be like?' The question assumes that the city is gendered. The elaboration of this assumption is at the heart of recent scholarship.

An early intervention is the collective work *Geography and Gender: An Introduction to Feminist Geography* (Women and Geography Study Group, 1984), which explicitly foregrounds the role of women in urban spatial structure. The book points out the lack of a feminist perspective in traditional urban theory by highlighting the field's general indifference to the spatial separation of men's and women's work and its implications as well as to the internal hierarchical structure of power relations in studies of the household. The book was part of a wider interest in the relationship between women and space. Mazey and Lee (1983), for example, show how traditional spatial themes can be enlivened by examining the experience of women.

Geography and Gender also calls attention to the sexist bias in town planning and urban architecture. This theme is developed further in the a multi-authored work that examines women in the man-made environment (Matrix, 1984). The authors show how sexist assumptions about women and family life in general are built into the design of dwelling and cities. They call into the question the traditional assumption that a woman's place is in the home.

Much of previous urban theory concentrates on men's activities to the neglect of women's, due in part to the male bias of the observers. In academia, as in many other professions, women are under-represented. Much of such early feminist work raises themes previously ignored by (male) academics and documents the conditions of women's daily lives in cities. This groundbreaking work not only tells the previously disregarded story of women: it also introduces more general notions of gender, space and power that were to transform urban theory permanently.

Gender and Urban Social Space

Urban space is not only a physical dimension but also has social and symbolic aspects that are particularly relevant to the social construction of gender relations. Space and gender are interconnected as in the differential entrapment and containment of men and women as well as in the opportunities to undermine and transgress rules governing gender segregation. Urban space is an arena where gender roles are inscribed and transgressed, codified and undermined. In traditional Yoruba society, for example, male domination is apparent in the layout of cities, family compounds and even individual dwellings. Urban space is a world of male domination that subordinates women. However, as Helen Callaway (1981) shows, the emphasis on women as independent economic actors allows much greater mobility than the formal spatial patterning would suggest. Women's mobility in the market place and economic agency in part undermine the formal structural gender partitioning of space.

Space is gendered, and so is the ability to move across space. Many traditional societies limit women's mobility. An extreme example is the practice of foot binding of young girls in traditional China. This was the ultimate form of limiting women's freedom to move. Even today, however, women in Saudi Arabia are banned from driving, thus severely limiting their ability to move freely through urban space without a male presence.

Gender partitioning occurs in the formal structuring of urban space, the different abilities and rights to move through space and the timing of place. Space may be shared but at different times. Women's greater fear of urban space limits their timing of space. Urban space embodies the social construction of gender and is the container of gendered experiences of the city. Daphne Spain (1992) gives examples of how geographic and architectural spatial conditions reinforce status and power differences between men and women, while Andrea Spurling (1992) looks in detail at the spaces of education.

The spatial evolution of the city always has been gendered. For example, gender issues are implicit in the process of suburbanization, particularly in terms of the work–home separation typical of the middle-class suburbs where so many women were restricted to the domestic sphere. Other urban structures, such as land-use arrangements and transport systems, also sustain traditional gender roles through reinforcing conventional gender employment opportunities and especially through restricting mobility for women with children (Hanson and Pratt, 1995). As the context of everyday lives, the city is a site for gender-loaded spatial categorizations of domestic and public and therefore is an important focus of feminist work. There is now a considerable body of work on the gendered separation of productive and reproductive spheres, issues of domestic labour, work–home separation, and the overall living and working experience of women (McDowell, 1997, 1999, 2005). Women perform the bulk of domestic labour in addition to carrying out the primary responsibilities for childrearing and childcare. These perceived obligations impose considerable burdens on women who work, both at home and in paid employment. Women are paid less than men and are over-represented in the low-paid, part-time sectors of advanced economies. In the United States, for example, there has been a feminization of poverty.

The design and organization of urban space reinforces the sexual division of labour. The term 'man-made city' is indicative of the social construction of urban space by designs that support gender bias. In a broad historical sweep, Elizabeth Wilson (1991) argues that what is wrong in the design of cities is the masculine desire to control disorder, and especially men's need to control the 'place' of women.

The regulation of urban public space is highly gendered and is used to legitimate gender oppression and regulate sexuality. Duncan (1996) conceptualizes the ideal types of private and public space. As an ideal type the private is associated with the domestic, with family privacy, intimacy and passion; the public with civil society, the market place, the *polis*. Of course the categorizations leak into one another. Not all space is either public or private. There are many privatized public spaces, such as the mall, but in general the public–private distinction is still the most important socio-spatial ordering principle. Public space is controlled as in the spatial marginalization of sex workers or the spatial regulation of homosexuality. Valentine (1996) argues that the heterosexuality of public spaces is maintained by regulatory regimes. She shows how lesbian bodies use lesbian manners and styles to fleetingly produce sexed and gendered spaces through discreet and more overt performances. Longhurst (2001) explores some the links between the body, gender and public space. She shows with reference to three case studies (pregnant bodies in public space, men's bodies in bathrooms and managerial bodies in central business districts) how bodies and spaces are socially constructed and regulated.

There are significant differences in the way women and men experience the city. Women's use of urban space, for example, is more constrained than men's because of the fear of male violence. Women are more sensitive to the fear of sexual violence, and this structures their behaviour in many cities. Strategies of individual safety include avoiding certain places at certain times, going to certain places only when accompanied, or not participating in an entire repertoire of activity, especially at night. Valentine (1989, 386) contends, 'Women are pressurized into a restricted use and occupation of public space.' There is a complex relationship between gender and fear. Elderly women who are statistically least at risk express the highest levels of fear. And while women tend to be fearful of violence from strangers in public spaces, they are more likely to experience violence from people they know in the domestic setting. The connection between space and fear and risk is not simply statistical; it is also performative. How people perform public acts in urban space is itself a reflection and embodiment of changing gender roles. The city is a stage for the performance of gender identities, often with the surveillance of the male gaze. Public space has always been sexed, especially today as more fluid sets of demarcation transgress the formally strict and often legal definitions of the past.

Gender, the City and Social Change

Gendered identities are rarely stable and never fixed. The city is often an important stage for witnessing the unfolding drama of changes in gender relations. We can consider three examples.

First, Christine Stansell (1986) provides careful analysis of changing female identities in the New York City in the first half of the nineteenth century. Because of changing economic conditions there were more jobs for working-class women who shaped new ways of life in the streets, tenements, gin halls and sweatshops. Women now spilled out from the domestic to the public sphere, becoming heads of households, utilizing their children's labour, creating communities of working women and entering into formal politics. This development threatened many middle-class women, unable to work because of cultural norms, who then constituted themselves as moral guardians of the nation. The development of working-class women as an economic, social and political force subverted previously held ideas of the 'proper' place of women and of woman's 'essential nature'. The working-class women created a community that fought for their freedoms; they made a place for themselves in the city. In Stansell's words, they created small freedoms from large oppressions.

Second, Amy Hanser (2005) looks at changing conceptions of gender and sexuality in her survey of new service work regimes in China. Under the Maoist regime strong, physically robust, hard-working women were positively portrayed. In the new market-driven China, other forms of femininity are employed. Hanser looked at the variety of femininities employed in work service regimes. She surveyed three retail outlets in the Chinese city of Harbin in 2001–2. In the state-owned department store there was little attempt at gendered display of the women workers. Uniforms were bulky and unisex. Older rather than younger women worked in the store. The atmosphere echoed the Maoist era. In a wholesale/retail sector providing cheap clothes to recent rural migrants, the selling was done by young, sexily dressed women. There was a hyper-sexualized, undisciplined atmosphere. In the high end, privately-owned department store, the apex of the retail sector, the emphasis was on a youthful but disciplined femininity. The young women were trained in physical deportment and demeanour. They were presented for the discriminating male gaze. Class-coded femininities were employed in the different work regimes.

Third, Moira Munro and Ruth Madigan (1999) look at the way that the space in the western home is being renegotiated. Home is both a physical and social space where ideas of family have shaped domestic architecture as well as how individuals relate to each other in space. In recent years in the West the family has been presented as a more democratic unit with an emphasis on shared activities; yet there is still a marked division within the family home. They looked at how people used this domestic space in a survey of postal questionnaires and extended interviews in Scotland's largest city, Glasgow. They found that while domestic community life, such as shared meals, is idealized it is difficult to organize because of complex timetables. Television provides a more effective collective focus. The design of many family homes is based on the notion of 'companionate marriage'. However, there is tension in the use of the main room with family members often allocated to activities in their bedrooms. The authors found evidence of women finding either little time or space for privacy. Some women used their role as housewife or carer to distance themselves from other family members. Their busyness provided an opportunity to escape from the shared domestic space. Family members negotiated the restriction of domestic space that reflected and embodied gender differences.

Feminist Urban Theory

The work of Munro and Madigan reminds me of the work of the modernist and feminist writer, Virginia Woolf. In *A Room of One's Own*

(1929) she writes, 'a woman must have money and a room of her own if she is going to write'. And while she used the following phrase with respect to literature it is just as pertinent for the city: 'made by men out of their own needs for their own uses'. She went on to separate women as objects of representation and women as authors of representation. In a similar vein we can see women as both prisoners of urban social space and makers of urban social space. This tension is the focus of feminist urban research. Such research connects with other debates in urban studies. For example, an important element of globalization is the large amount of immigration as workers move to other countries in search of employment. The role of female domestic workers is an important issue that links debates on gender, globalization and the construction of transnational communities. Pratt (2004), for example, considers the case of Filipina workers in Canada. Roni Berger (2004) adds a gender lens to the general discussion of global immigration by focusing on the experiences of women. In the course of her interviews with 18 women from around the world who have emigrated she highlights the sense of personal loss, the culture shock and the effects of cultural differences on the women and their families.

Women also play a significant role in resistances to globalization in less developed countries. Maureen Hays-Mitchell (2002) looks at the connections between globalization and women in a study of how poor urban women in Peru both resist and transform the process of economic restructuring brought about by neo-liberal policies and international fiscal regimes. Austerity measures in the country have depressed living conditions and purchasing power. Women are especially vulnerable as they are at the bottom of the occupation hierarchies in both the formal and informal sectors. Hays-Mitchell shows that women producers play an important role in the urban economy providing sustenance to most of the urban poor; they more likely to hire other workers than to invest in machinery, and they invest heavily in family welfare. Economic restrictions are a gendered experience, and resistance is part of the creation of ideologies and identities of gender.

Both empirical and theoretical elaborations of the concept of patriarchy (which can be defined as a system of interrelated social structures, practices and ideologies through which men subordinate women) address the male bias. Through this wide-ranging corpus of feminist urban theory we can identify a number of ways in which the city in advanced capitalist countries embodies the operation of patriarchal power: gender-biased and work–home separations both reflect and strengthen the linkage of femininity to domesticity. Women's responsibilities for domestic labour affect their access to employment opportunities, services and facilities. The work of Hanson and Pratt (1995), for example, shows some of the links between domestic ties, locational restrictions and the occupational segregation of women.

Feminist research illuminates our view of the city, opening up the discourse and uncovering ignored lives and muted voices. The debate is ongoing: a number of points may be noted. First, the notion of patriarchy is in the process of refinement. Crude notions of patriarchy identify its operation in all social structures, behaviours and attitudes that in turn are read off simply from the a priori existence of patriarchy. This is a short circuit to intellectual advancement. It gives the same ideological strait-jacket as structural Marxism, incidentally sharing the same certain, all-encompassing theory and messianic vision. It focuses on grand structure and women as passive victims. More flexible positions emphasize process and struggle and see gender as a site of resistance and contestation as well as a setting for subordination and oppression. Elizabeth Wilson (1991, 2001) suggests that much early feminist writing on the city underscores the construction of women as passive victims in a male urban order by means of their urban containment. She argues for a wider debate that recognizes women's more active agency with cities as platforms for liberation where women widen horizons and escape traditional expectations. This analytical divide of oppression/liberation, containment/appropriation, politics of redistribution/politics of recognition is used by Bondi and Rose (2003) to characterize feminist urban studies since the 1970s.

Second, the concept of a pluralistic feminism increasingly replaces the singular notion of feminism. Subtle and not-so-subtle differences are emerging. Theoretically there are those who link issues of patriarchy to those of class conflict and racial struggle, while there are others who see patriarchy as the primary object of study and as the political adversary. These two sets of coordinates provide a very large graph where current work is widely scattered: postmodern feminisms, Marxist feminisms, and libertarian feminisms. The categories are many.

Third, the simple, undifferentiated notion of 'women' continues to experience revision. Women's experience of the city, for example, is different from men's. This is a useful 'first cut'. But looking in more detail suggests that women of different ages, classes, and races have as many differences as similarities. As with their male colleagues the class and race bias of feminist researchers (predominantly affluent, white and middle-class), unavoidably impacts their work. Less naive conceptions of women that are much more sensitive to differences in age, race and class now prevail (see Katz and Monk, 1993). The contributors to the Katz and Monk edited volume, for example, show how geographies of women vary over the life course. Some of the more interesting work in the future will highlight the tensions, connections and intersections between race, class, ethnicity, age and gender.

Fourth, what strikes most observers of advanced capitalist cities is the changing and unstable nature of gender divisions. More women not only are in paid employment but are also moving up the corporate hierarchy. The so-called glass ceiling may exist, but the trajectories of some women, at least, seem to be upward. Affirmative action in the US, for example, enables more career advancement for white, middle-class women as well as laying the foundations for a larger, black, middle class. This is in stark contrast to the declining employment opportunities of manual workers in the manufacturing sectors. Gender and class are intersecting in some places and diverging in others, producing new and interesting forms of social differentiation. Liz Bondi (1992, 164–5), for example, writes with reference to gentrification:

> In a UK context, the interconnections between class, gender and sexuality are nicely illustrated by the contrasting connotations of the wine bar and the pub: the former is metropolitan, middle-class, sexually integrated and more likely to be tolerant of, or at least not openly hostile towards, 'alternative' expressions of sexuality; the latter is more likely to be local, working-class, sexually segregated and overtly sexist and heterosexist.

Bondi argues that urban social change, such as gentrification, is both a reflection and an embodiment of changing gender and class relations. Deindustrialization, gentrification, impoverishment, the creation of a dual labour market and the decline of urban public services, to name just a few, all have an effect on various ethnic, gender and class groups. Indeed, they help to determine the changing definition and demarcation of these groups.

Finally, the feminist critique will produce, albeit delayed and halting, a masculine response. Feminism places gender on the agenda. The bulk of feminist research, however, has been conducted by and for women with explicit or implicit political agendas tied to the 'women's movement'. Discussion of masculinities receives short shrift within the gender and cities debate. This is a topic that will develop only when men begin to probe fully their individual and collective identities. The city as male space is more assumed than demonstrated: what exactly is the male bias in urban planning? Does it represent only certain forms of maleness? These are questions that will be articulated only when a wide-ranging discussion of masculinities occurs. Gender scholarship tends to be biased towards women, whereas the position of men is taken for granted or subsumed under uncritical and naive notions of maleness masculinity.

There are explorations of male identities. Massey (1995) looks at masculine identities in the high-tech sector and McDowell (2003) explores the relationships between employment change and white-working-class youth. The nuances, depth and coloration of a full understanding of gender and the city will come about only when maleness and masculinity are also a more critical object of analysis. We need to take a reflective view of the social (re)construction and representation of masculinities if we are to round out our understanding of gender and the city.

There are many sources of social differentiation: class, ethnicity, gender and sexual preference. These are some of the most important, though not the only, dimensions of difference; others include age, health, physical and mental abilities and characteristics. The terms themselves are not simple, or easy to use. The problem cannot be solved by a linguistic analysis. The fuzziness of their meaning is an important part of their character; they are textual chameleons, constantly changing, always transforming, suffused with ambiguity and imprecision.

These disputable terms are not only sources of differentiation: they are also sources of subordination. Class, ethnicity, gender and sexual orientation mark people out from one another. But these distinctions are not innocent. To be black in a white city, or working class in a capitalist city, or a woman in a man-made city, or a gay in a predominantly straight town, is to be in a subordinate position that affects your life chances. It is also to be located in a set of cultural values in which some experiences are seen as more important, are used as the standard against which others are measured and evaluated, and are taken as the norm to define deviancy and difference.

Let us return to the question posed by Dolores Hayden at the beginning of this chapter. What would a non-sexist city be like? The answer lies not in academic pronouncements but in the creation of a space for debate and discussion, a place for open negotiation. It implies a full and clear recognition that not all voices are currently heard and not all experiences are validated in the form and function of our cities.

9
The Erotic City

The city is more than just a mute collection of buildings, or the locus of bloodless economic activity. Because it is a place where flesh-and-blood human beings congregate and interact, it is also a site and setting for erotic experiences. The term 'erotic' derives from Eros, the Greek god of love whose chief associates were Pothos and Himeros (Longing and Desire). The eroticized city is the focus of current theorizing about the connections between longing, desire, identity and the built environment. This new theorizing takes place against a transformation in sexual mores and conventions. In this chapter we will explore some of these intriguing connections.

The erotic city is not simply the place of sexual encounter, the dominant theme of contemporary scholarship. We can follow the work of Moore (1998) who writes about cultivating life as an act of love. Updating the work of Renaissance scholars such as Marsilio Ficino, he argues for exploring the erotic possibilities of everyday life. A personal example: I have two routes that I may take to work, the Interstate 95 or the Baltimore–Washington Parkway. The Interstate is a 10-lane highway that is designed to move as many vehicles as possible as quickly as possible to their destinations. It is utilitarian. The parkway is a four-lane road designed to move vehicles less quickly though a green landscape of trees and vegetation. The road is not as direct as the highway, intentionally following a curving sinuous path through the landscape that makes the drive scenic, interesting and sensual. One route simply gets me to work; the other feeds my soul. The city is similarly alive with such erotic possibilities. Places and buildings may evoke pleasure by stimulating our various senses, summoning memories, inciting voyeurism, arousing all manner of desire. The exploration of the possibilities of more erotic cities could improve city life and undoubtedly enliven urban studies. As Moore notes, 'we might build towns cities, buildings, roads, and houses for human beings who have bodies and desires, who need basic pleasure to feel good about themselves and their lives' (1998, 262).

Sex Zones in the City

In her essay, 'The City of Desire; Its Anatomy and Destiny', Pat Califia (1994) writes about the sex zones of the city where sex is a commodity and alternative sexual practices take place. These sex zones can be the red light districts or the topless bar zone as well as the areas of sexual activity superimposed on other types of urban space, such as the inner-city neighbourhood where prostitutes walk the streets along with local residents, or the public park that by night becomes a place for furtive sex and anonymous assignations. There is an interesting urban geography to be written of the rise, fall, extension and restructuring of sex zones. Rather like Burgess's concentric ring model of residential areas, models of sexual desire and practice can also be constructed.

A sex zone of relatively recent vintage is the explicitly gay ghetto. The rise and transformation of gay spaces tells us much about urban development. The inner-city suburb of Paddington in Sydney, for example, used to be a zone of working-men's houses, to use a Burgess term. As the older Anglo-Celtic households began to move in the 1950s and 1960s, they were replaced by new immigrants from southern and Eastern Europe as well as gays attracted to the cheap and accessible housing. The small houses suited the non-nuclear families. The newer suburbs on the fringe of the metropolitan area, in contrast, were places for the more traditional, straight, nuclear-family households. The old suburb became a gay area gradually as pioneers bought and improved housing, and created local spaces such as coffee houses, restaurants, bars, discos and baths that that were gay-friendly. Paddington never became a gay-only suburb, but it became the gay centre of the city as well as a gentrifying neighbourhood.

The existence of sex zones connected to female prostitution has a much longer urban history. Prostitution has been important part of the urban economy for centuries. Today its character is often related to the legal context of sexual practices. In Dutch cities, for example, the legalization of prostitution allows the existence of clearly defined red-light areas where prostitutes sit in windows as potential customers walk past. The persistence of such commodified sex zones is function of economics. Aggregated activity allows customers greater choice and prostitutes access to more potential customers. The economic advantages of clustered behaviour apply to prostitution as well as to much other business activity. By contrast, in most US cities where prostitution is illegal, sex zones have a more liminal quality and are often found in abandoned areas of deteriorating neighbourhoods, shifting spectral urban presences at the edge of the accepted bordering on the dangerous. In cities where prostitution is illegal, and even where it is legal, the zone of street prostitution has a risky feel. In some cases the sex zone shifts to specific sex sites such as a massage parlour or a brothel, sites of commodified sexual activity safely cordoned off into a specific building site that give the advantages of security to the sex workers and a sense of safety to the clients.

Hubbard (1999) gives a general description of the geography of prostitution in western cities. In a more detailed study he shows how a red-light district in the English city of Birmingham was the result of spatial strategies enacted by the state and the everyday tactical behaviour of the sex workers (Hubbard, 2003). The production of this sexual activity space was the outcome of the official strategies of spatial isolation and informal tolerance and the embodied actions of the sex workers. The red-light district was both a place of confinement and transgression, produced 'from above and from below', the boundaries 'fixed both by sex workers as well as police, politicians and protesters' (87).

Recent writings on the eroticized city have spent more time on more general questions of desire, sexual identity and alternative cultures and less time on the economics of the sex industry. Yet the sex industry is an important part of the urban economy, although hard data are difficult to find. But if we were able to calculate the income of every topless bar, gay disco, massage parlour and so on, they would hardly be insignificant. In some parts of some cities the sex industry is the dominant economy. There is an urban erotic economy that connects the object of desire with the desiring gaze. There are a number of studies that look at the creation of an urban entertainment industry centred on the commercialization of sex. Timothy Gilfoyle (1992), for example, examines the development of the commercialization of sex in New York City from 1790 to 1920. He shows that there never was a red-light district as such but that prostitution spread through all city neighbourhoods and could be found in hotels and music halls as well as on the streets and in brothels. Landowners made tremendous profits from the business and helped to corrupt police and politicians; for women, prostitution was a temporary resort in a tight economy; and for a few madams it was a source of considerable wealth. Attempts to stamp out prostitution were continually made and continually failed. Increasing violence against prostitutes, especially by out-of-work immigrant men, led to the rise of the pimp as a source of physical protection. Gilfoyle's careful analysis reveals how much recent urban growth and development in the West is associated with the commercialization of sex.

Desire and the City

The French poststructuralist philosopher, Jean-François Lyotard (1924–98) writes of the libidinal economy. Drawing on Freud's theory of the libido, Lyotard (1993) muses on the unpredictability of events, the things left over and often unsaid in explaining the world. Libidinal energy moves the world. Libidinal energies drive the world, and social systems are created to maintain, channel and hide these energies. There is subtle interplay between libidinal energies and the structures designed to harness them. Extending the work of Lyotard, we can think of libidinal energies at both an individual and group level coursing through the struc- ture of the city, the formal social, economic and political structures as well as the configuration and ensembles of the built form of the city. The interplay between the two is a useful framework for understanding the life force of the city.

Consider the city as a public space. It is the place of social interaction, where people as embodied, gendered and eroticized beings share spaces. The city is the place then of the sexual encounter, ranging from the suggestive gaze, the mildly erotic visual flirtation that we have all expe- rienced with complete strangers (made all the more delicious because of its ethereal transcience), to the full encounter involving the exchange of bodily fluids. In between these two ends of the continuum the city offers endless possibilities for libidinal energies to find objects of desire and longing as well as many permutation of social constructs to harness, curtail and channel these energies. Using Lyotard's notion of libidinal economy opens up a useful language for describing the sexualized nature of everyday urban life. We can then begin to think of the various ways that societies and cities are organized to deal with these libidinal energies. On some level the policing of public space responds to these libidinal forces. There is the regulation of bodies (as in the legality of prostitution and same-sex encounters, rules of dress, and so on) but also in the more prosaic rule of conduct in the work place. We can picture a dynamic rela- tionship between libidinal forces and social structures varying over time and through space. Cities are tension points because they are places where public and private behaviour, public and private spaces, and indi- vidual longings, fantasies and desires operate within community stan- dards, social mores and forms of acceptable behaviours. The city is where libido meets the superego, body competes with the mind, and spatial strategies of confinement and eradication come up against the tactics of gratification and desire.

Communities of Desire

The city is a place where desire is pursued as well as captured. In large cities communities of desire can flourish and grow. One important development in urban theory is the creation of queer city theory. This line of work is tied to two interrelated developments. The first is the emergence of queer theory, a body of critical writings that (amongst other things) deconstructs the binary division of heterosexual and homosexual. The work of Eve Kofosky Sedgwick (1990) is particularly influential. The second is the development of queer politics, which has been linked to responses to the Aids crisis and anti-gay legislation and rhetoric. The term 'queer' has been reappropriated by gays as a label for new ways of writing about and being in the world. Such writing often is characterized as a kind of 'authorial coming out'. Lawrence Knopp (2001), for example, traces an individual but not unique route when he writes of animating queer geographies that are both scholarly and activist, by both being queer and doing queer theory.

There are historical studies of urban gay culture. George Chauncey (1994), for example, writes of the making of a gay male world in New York City from 1890 to 1940. Chauncey recreates the gay world of baths and drag balls and explores the metropolitan character of male gayness. A gay city was superimposed upon the straight city as a gay community and identity was fashioned in both secret and visible practices.

Queer scholarship pays particular attention of the geography of sex. Ingram, Bouthillette and Retter (1997) have edited a useful collection of papers that deals with the spatial context of gayness and gay sex. The discussion of queerscapes and queer sites as well the more general gay community formation open up new ways of looking at the city. David Bell writes in the context of greater visibility of both gay practices and gay scholars. In his 'fragments for a queer city', Bell writes of the gay bar and gay disco as public places that are no longer hidden from view (Bell, 2001). In many cities it is part of a new mixed space in which gay and straight, hetero- and homosexualized identities are connected in a commodified alternative entertainment space.

There is tension between emancipation and commodification. As gays come out of the closet they are being coopted into a more inclusive definition of urban entertainment and urban boosterism. When gay Mardi Gras is both a celebration of gayness and a heavily advertised tourist promotion for the whole city, as in Sydney and San Francisco, then the notion of queer as marginal, secret and liminal is less compelling. Coming out of the closet may mean being seduced into the market place.

There is considerable writing on the relationship between space and sexual dissidence. Bell (2001), for example, writes of the public spaces and gay sex. The formal policing of male toilets in British cities is a particular form of control over gay sexual practices. The city is a place of almost infinite possibilities for sexual encounters from the anonymous passing in the street to the nooks and crannies of the built form. The control and theatrical presentation of sexual identity has also been an important part of queer activism. The right to the city and the freedom of the streets is an integral part of an emancipation and sexual liberation. Some cities now exhibit the theatrical spectacle of queer visibility. Up until now a lot of attention has been lavished upon the erotic possibilities of the marginal, the night, the queer, the furtive, the different. The erotic possibilities of the city have been dominated, it seems to me, by queer scholarship. And while this enlarges our view of the city, there is a lot of room for writing about the erotic possibilities of the centre, the day, the straight, the obvious and the similar. There is a sizeable literature on homosexual urban geographies but paradoxically little about the domi-nant sexual culture of heterosexuality. Hubbard (2000) seeks to right this imbalance when he draws upon ideas of the morality of sexualized iden-tity and the maintenance of Oedipal order to map out the moral contours of heterosexuality in urban social space.

The City and the Body

The sensual revolution that has made the body a more integral part of the presentation of self has led to renewed academic concern with the human body. Following on from Foucault, there has been a tremendous empha-sis on the body as an effect of arrangements of power and as a symbolic system, which produces metaphors for power. Central to any discussion of the erotics of the city is the question of the body. Urban studies for too long have been curiously disembodied. People are routinely analysed as agents, members of classes, economic units and social monads but only rarely are they treated as embodied beings. Elizabeth Grosz (1992) writes of the body as a socio-cultural artefact in relation to the city. She writes of the dominant model of city–body relationships with the city as a reflec-tion and product of bodies. She argues that this model subordinates the body to the mind and presupposes the city as an effect of subjectivity. The relationship between bodies and city is neither causal nor representa-tional; instead, she suggests a two-way linkage, a co-building, in which the city 'is one particular ingredient in the social constitution of the body'. From this position Grosz argues that there is nothing intrinsically unnatural about the city. The city is an active force in constituting bodies.

Longhurst (2001) looks at the social construction of the body with reference to the regulation of pregnant bodies in public space, the relationship between men's bodies and bathrooms and the corporate body images employed by business workers. In her interviews with managers she discovered the importance of bodily presentation in terms of clothing, image, style and grooming as well the desirability of the sculpted, fit body. Bell *et al.* (2001) bring together contributions that explore the connections between bodies, cities and space. While we have a number of general observations, and some highly specific case studies, the full exploration of the relationship between bodies and cities has yet to be achieved (see Sennett, 1994). It remains one of the more alluring possibilities for future urban theorizing.

The Global, the City and the Body

What are some of the connections between this concern with the body as an object of analysis and our understanding of the global and the city? An obvious point, often missed in aggregate economic discourses, is that globalization is not just transference of cultures and beliefs: it is also a movement of human bodies. Increasingly, urban sex industries have a global dimension as workers are recruited from other (often poor) countries. Global flows quite literally involve the juxtaposition of different bodies from around the world in the shared spaces of global and globalizing cities. And the juxtaposition of these bodies becomes the embodied source of division, difference layered with value judgments and systems of power and repression, as well as a powerful source of sexual desire. Colonial and imperial bodies are the loci of emotions and desires denied the urbanizing, industrializing, organizing bodies of the imperial centre. The black man is a site of hyper-masculinity, the female Asian a setting for a hyper-femininity. Black rage and Asian submissiveness are major colonial discourses that have an important legacy in the postcoloniality of many global cities. In many major cities in the US, for example, massage parlours that sexually service male customers frequently tout the Asia connection. The image of submissive and sexually pliant Asian women is a key feature of the promotion, success and growth of massage parlours. The contemporary immigration of women from China, Korea and other Asian countries provides a steady flow of sex workers to fuel these post-colonial bodily imaginings.

The sexual body is now an important part of global flows. The flow of sex workers is an important element of labour migration, while sex tourism is a major component of the international tourist industry. The international migration of sex workers has increased in recent years. The two driving forces are economic incentives, as people try to make a better life for themselves and particularly their families, and brute force. Many women are forced into the sex trade by blackmail and the threat of violence. The flow of sex workers across borders is increasing as Thai women become prostitutes in Tokyo and Chinese women work in massage parlours in Los Angeles.

Global cities now contain a variety of body types; the rich variety of skin colours, body shapes, sizes and weights now form part of the visual texture of a truly global city. Cosmopolitan cities have a variegated stock of bodies. Marketing campaigns that use groups of people now try to display racial diversity. The United Colors of Benetton campaign, with its people of varied skin hue, is just one example of a global advertising imagery that echoes the embodied nature of global cities. Bodily differences are part of the global city, and managers of globalizing cities realize that some degree of cosmopolitanism is an essential ingredient of becoming a truly global place.

Our bodies are sites of globalization. We ingest food from around the world, and wear clothes made and designed around the world. Hairstyles draw on global as well as local and national styles. In some cases our bodies are inscribed by globalization. Tattoos, for example, have become a form of global tribalism drawing on older, different traditions. The flows move up the scales as well as down. Local trends can become more globalized. Islamic fundamentalism, growing out of the dislocation of the Middle East, is a global phenomenon with mosques in cities around the world now focal points for a global movement of religious expression. The dichotomy between cosmopolitan and fundamentalism is embodied in the clothes we wear, the lack or presence of body hair and the food that we eat.

Global cities are important sites for the exchange of flows between the global and the body. Global cities have a range of 'ethnic' restaurants, stores and shops that allow 'exotic' goods and services to be consumed. The cosmopolitan body is more easily sustained and reproduced in the global city, and globalizing cities seek to attract and sustain the cosmopolitan body. Our bodies' movement creates and reinforces hybridity, a recognized feature of a postmodern global world. Immigrants to richer countries can now more easily connect with families and more easily retain their joint status. Keeping in touch across international

boundaries, literally and by voice and email as well as by money transfers, is an important ingredient of cultural hybridity, economic globalization and cosmopolitanism. Bodies are both tethered and untethered by
global connections. It is easier and cheaper for people to move across the
world and yet we are increasingly tied to our means of communication.
Access to the Internet and the telephone is now vital to maintaining our
connections. We have greater mobility but greater reliance on the grid of
international communications. Globalization has both emancipated us
from the heavier constraints of international travel and hard-wired us into
the grid of telecommunication. Global cities are the points in the world
where we can both travel and be connected. Globalization is quite literally embodied and this embodiment is particularly evident in global and
globalizing cities.

The bodies in global and urban space are sexualized. Jon Binnie
(2004), for example, writes of the connections between homosexuality
and globalization. Cities play a particular role as the setting for a queer
cosmopolitanism, centres of gay consumer culture. A cosmopolitanism is
at the 'heart of queer narratives of self and queer consumption practices'
(10). And cosmopolitanism in turn has been partly defined in relation to
an openness to queer spectacles. However, this inclusion is based in part
on the ability to pay and to stay within the (albeit ever-expanding) limits
of acceptable gay public presences and practices. Urban theory would
only be enlivened and enlarged if it grappled with understanding the variations across space and time of the connections between the creation of
transnational queer identities and the construction of cosmopolitan cities.

More generally, urban theory is greatly enriched by the grudging
acceptance that the bodies that inhabit urban space are sexual beings and
that urban social space is an important setting for erotic experiences, in
the widest and deepest sense of the word.

10
The Political City

Politics in the broadest sense takes place in a variety of settings, including the home, the work place, spheres of production, consumption and representation. In this chapter, however, I will restrict my comments to the arena of formal politics and associated informal connections. Theories of urban politics revolve around two fundamental questions of who has power in the city and what they do with this power. The present discussion reviews the main answers to these questions.

The oldest answer is that elites control the city, which was certainly true throughout most of human history. Traditional forms of urban government reinforced this distribution of power. In the Athens of classical Greece only a small, male, minority could vote. Even in the early US slaves and women could not vote under an elaborate system of representation at the state and federal level structured to avoid too much power residing with the unpredictable 'people'. The iron law of oligarchy stipulates that authority is always concentrated at the top of a decision-making hierarchy. Early work on contemporary cities confirmed this finding. Robert and Helen Lynd (1929) studied Muncie, Indiana, in the 1920s and came to the conclusion that a self-conscious elite ran the city. This was further corroborated in Floyd Hunter's (1953) study of Atlanta in the 1940s and 1950s. Hunter asked the influential citizens who the power brokers were. A number of names kept appearing; the most persistent was Robert Woodruff, the Coca-Cola magnate.

Robert Dahl ostensibly challenged this elitist position in his answer to the question posed in the title of his 1961 book, *Who Governs?* In his examination of urban redevelopment, education and party nominations in New Haven, Connecticut, he discovered the involvement of a rich variety of different individuals and pressure groups. There was no tight group of names involved in everything; however, on closer inspection his work did show that despite the plurality of different individuals and separate organizations, the dominant voice was of middle- and upper-income residents and business interests. Nevertheless, Dahl provided a more pluralist answer.

144

In contrast to the elitist position, the pluralist perspective presents power dispersed among a large number of competing interests. The dissimilarity between the two refers to broad differences not only in understanding society but also in approach. The elitist position tends to identify power-holders by reputation. Researchers investigating elitism will often ask a pre-selected group of citizens in the city the question: who wields effective power? The recurrence of specific names helps identify the elite. The pluralist position focuses on identifying the range of interests involved in specific decisions. The attention to reputations highlights a cohesive power elite, while the emphasis on decisions highlights a range of different allegiances. A neo-elitist position, while extending the cruder forms of the elitist position, points to power as lying not so much in the fight over particular decisions but in influencing which decisions come on to the political agenda for discussion.

Lukes (1974) summarizes the differences between the pluralist and the neo-elitist positions. He also proposes a three-dimensional view of power that incorporates behaviour, decision-making and non-decision-making, issues and potential issues, observable as well as latent conflict, and subjective as well as real interests. A study of urban renewal in Oakland by Hayes (1972), for example, discovered business interests promoted urban renewal and that the issues of the destruction of low-income housing and black displacement were never even raised as an item for discussion. Crenson (1971) shows how air pollution was simply not an issue in many US cities in the 1960s. Large companies disputed the scientific findings and successfully linked air pollution in many people's minds with economic growth and job creation. Power resides not only in the control of the formal levers of power but also in the ability to promote, to isolate or to marginalize certain topics and interests for political debate. A more subtle understanding of local political power involves not only the analysis of issues and decisions but also what are non-issues and non-decisions. Power resides in the creation of the political agenda as well as in formal political decision-making.

In recent years the debate on urban regimes has informed the questions of who rules and how they rule. Clarence Stone (1989), drawing on his analysis of the governing of Atlanta from 1946 to 1988, identifies what he calls 'urban regimes' that he defines as the 'informal arrangements that surround and complement the formal workings of governmental authority'. Urban regimes consist of informal governing coalitions that make decisions and get things done in a city. Clarence Stone developed the notion of urban regimes to refer to the informal partnership in Atlanta between City Hall and the city centre business elites. Political questions of maintaining and extending political support and leadership dominate City Hall, while economic issues of profit and loss concern the business elites. The combination of political and economic logic, with all the ensuing tensions, conflicts and ambiguities, constitutes the local urban regime. The options and concerns of urban regimes vary over time and space; they may be inclusionary or exclusionary and will be altered throughout the metropolitan regions (suburban regimes, for example, are more concerned with preserving property values).

Judd and Kantor (1992) identify four cycles of regime politics in the US. In the *entrepreneurial cities* up to the 1870s merchant elites controlled the city. Then, with industrialization and large-scale immigration, business interests had to work with political representatives of the newly organized immigrants. The result was the *city of machine politics*. From the 1930s to the 1970s a *New Deal coalition* prevailed in which federal policies stimulated urban economies and maintained the Democratic power base. This regime collapsed with the internal revolt of the ethnic minorities, who (numerically and politically) became more important. In the contemporary cycle the regime promotes *economic growth and a political inclusiveness*. The ambiguities between these political and economic logics constitute the tension of contemporary urban US.

Stoker and Mossberger (1994) identify three regime types: organic, instrumental, and symbolic. *Organic regimes* occur in small towns and suburban districts with a homogeneous population and a strong sense of place; their chief aim is to maintain the status quo. *Instrumental regimes* focus upon specific targets identified in the political partnership between urban governments and business interests. *Symbolic regimes* occur in cities undergoing rapid changes, including large-scale revitalization, major political change, and image campaigns that try to shift the wider public perception of the city. We should see these three categories as ideal types, with any one city's regime exhibiting characteristics, albeit in different proportions, of each type.

Successful politics is the 'art of the deal', the compromise that works. Sometimes business interests have to work with new political realities. Take the case of the US where the two primary sets of actors are political power brokers and business interests. There has been some change in each set. In many of the large central cities the power brokers now represent African-Americans and Hispanics as well as whites. Business interests now include multinational companies as much as simply local business interests. According to Stone, Atlanta now has a complex, durable urban regime that includes the city centre's business elite and the black middle-class. Business interests managed to incorporate the black elite, who in turn felt that they gained from the deal.

Urban regimes vary over metropolitan space, and three regimes can be identified in the US: central city, suburban and inner suburban. Central city regimes (as in Atlanta) consist of alliances of business interests with the power brokers of the formal political machines. Urban growth issues merge with issues of social inclusiveness, and the need to maintain and extend political support across a coalition of varied political interests tempers the pro-growth lobby. In the suburban regimes, a shared agenda of keeping taxes low and protecting property values unites the population. Here the local regimes exist to maintain the status quo and often to keep out lower income and racially different groups. County governments in the US with suburban regimes tend to minimize the notion of politics as a basis for discussion about compromises between differing interests and instead focus attention on non-political issues of administrative decision-making. Growth interests, especially for realtors, builders and land developers, often attain political priority. Issues of rationality and efficiency trump concerns of equity or social justice.

Occasionally some real politics emerge, and there are cases of anti-growth or no-growth backlashes. One example is Loudon County, Virginia, one of the fastest growing counties in the country. The county increased its population from around 70,000 in 1985 to 235,000 in 2003. During that time just over 300 people were moving into the county every single week. The rate of growth was rapid enough to cause such high levels of traffic congestion and pressure on local schools and services that a slow-growth backlash emerged. In 1999 eight county supervisors were elected on a slow-growth platform, and the newly elected Board of Supervisors consequently cut the number of new houses planned for the county by 80,000. This did not please the local development industry, which successfully bankrolled a number of candidates for the 2003 election. The new pro-growth Board soon created a new plan for the county which, while cutting educational spending by 5 per cent, overturned the previous slow-growth estimates, reversed legislation that would allow localities to charge the developers in order to raise money to offset school construction, revised plans to build new housing, rescheduled historic preservation plans, extended water and sewer lines to aid further development and created fast tracks for businesses seeking county approval. While slow- or no-growth coalitions may occur, in the world of local county politics, developers' dollars can go a huge distance towards influencing opinion and political outcomes.

The political regimes of inner suburbs experiencing decline have yet to be studied in great depth. However, as many inner suburbs begin to share the same economic fate of many central cities, we may be witnessing the dawn of a new form of suburban regime shaped by the facts of economic contraction and population decline.

The concept of urban regimes is an important one in urban theory because it focuses our attention on the linkage between business and politics and the tensions, compromises and deals necessary for democratic politics to work in a capitalist society.

The Urban Political Arena

Any particular issue invokes a range of urban interests. I will restrict my comments to two: household and business interests.

Members of households use the city in a variety of ways: as taxpayers, as users of services and as residents. Taxpayers pay both federal (national) and local taxes. As with all taxpayers around the world, they want to pay the minimum and get the maximum. Below this broad consideration there are a number of other factors. Levels of taxpaying and attitudes to taxpaying vary significantly. In much of Europe, Scandinavian countries in particular, there are much higher levels of taxation than in the United States. In the Netherlands, for example, people seem more willing to shoulder a comparatively higher tax burden to sustain the quality of public services than do households in the US. The results are clear in the different levels of urban public spaces. Households in some countries have a much higher level of taxation tolerance. In all countries, however, there are limits to the taxation load. Households are particularly sensitive to rates of increase and issues of equity. Small and gradual taxation increases attract less notice than sudden hikes. Taxes considered unfair are also unpopular. For example, the Conservative government elected in Britain in 1987 sought to replace local property taxes with a poll tax where every adult, irrespective of income, had to pay the same amount. The tax led to very sudden hikes and obvious anomalies. Resistance to the tax was the background to the overthrow in 1990 of the Prime Minister, Margaret Thatcher, who had committed her government and her reputation to the imposition of the new tax.

There are less dramatic examples of taxpayers' revolts. In California, the passing of Proposition 13 in 1977 on the state ballot was the result of taxpayers' resistance to continual tax increases. The result was a severe reduction in public spending with generally regressive results.

City taxes often are based on property. These are more visible and more direct than taxes based on general consumption (such as sales taxes) or on income tax. City taxes seem more arbitrary and more susceptible to change because they are more local. Moreover, they impinge more directly on the wealthiest members. The net result is that city property taxes are more often fought against because they seem arbitrary and they affect the better organized, the more articulate, the more politically connected. Income tax is a national affair: you cannot escape the net; but local taxes are just that, local, and hence people can move to a nearby location if it is accessible and has a lower tax burden. The net result is that in many countries there are limits placed on city taxes.

Households use a variety of public goods and services. There is a whole range of goods and services that are provided for and by, directly and indirectly, the state. The precise form may vary; in the case of public housing, for example, the government provides a public good that is consumed by individual households. Then there are public goods such as roads and highways that are consumed collectively. We can make a further distinction between goods and services allocated on the basis of need or merit and those more universally available. We have to take care when we use the term 'public goods and services' that we specify which type. Those that are collectively consumed – for example, transport, education, policing – tend to generate more public awareness because they involve the majority of households and especially the wealthier, more articulate groups. Those goods and services that are allocated on the basis of need and generally go to the poorest groups, such as public housing in the US, tend to figure lower on local and national political agendas.

There is often an implied distinction between welfare goods and services and non-welfare goods and services. The former tend to go to the poorer. There is a politics of naming with associated undercurrents of charity and benefits, whereas the public goods and services consumed by the wealthier are rarely seen or discussed as 'welfare' benefits. Both food stamps for the needy and tax concessions to the wealthy are benefits; the difference between them is that one goes to the poor and one goes to the rich. How they are portrayed and described says more about power than about fiscal reality. Over the long term, the range of public goods and services increases, both in cities with a history of social welfarism and even in those that are marked by a commitment to privatism. If we look at cities around the world today compared with 100 years ago, one of the most distinctive changes is in the scale and provision of public goods and services. Whether it be in public housing, public education, public transport, provision of infrastructure, transfer payments or social welfare, the scale of government intervention always expands. In recent years, however, a neo-liberal agenda has promoted policies of privatization, fee-based services and a general rollback of the public sector, social welfare function.

Households are also residents of particular places, which makes them sensitive enough to the politics of location that they actively enter a struggle to reinforce positive externalities and repel negative externalities. The character of a location depends on what is happening around it. The value of a house, for example, partially draws upon the quality of the area in which it is located. We can picture the city as a huge, constantly changing externality surface with households always trying to maximize public goods and repel public bads. Their members will attempt to get those goods and services that generate positive externalities and to resist those that generate negative externalities, especially if they are home-owners. The steady increase in owner occupation throughout North America and much of Western Europe creates a tenure group that is very sensitive to changes in house prices. The purchase of a house is most households' biggest single outlay, their biggest asset, and one of their main sources of wealth and collateral to borrow money. Owner occupiers are thus very sensitive to those factors they can influence that may affect the price of their homes. Most changes in house prices are broad secular trends, but there are also local effects. In a neighbourhood thought to be deteriorating, for whatever reason, house prices will fall. Owner occupiers will resist negative externalities that impinge on house prices.

Although we have used the term 'household', not everyone in the household is equally concerned with the politics of location. In households with a traditional gender division of labour, for example, wives and women are those most sensitive to changes in the local environment because they are the ones who have shouldered much of the responsibilities of the home and childrearing. They therefore have a much more direct experience of such community matters as schooling, levels of traffic flows, quality of local public services, and the intrusion of negative externalities. In the past 30 years we can see a relationship between feminism and community involvement. Women are often mainstays of the kind of successful community action that contributes to the strength, vitality and confidence of the women's movement.

If things deteriorate (for example, taxes rise, the quality of the public city worsens, or a negative externality affects the neighbourhood) households have a choice. The decision is often summarized as exit/voice. It takes a lot, however, before this stark choice is reached. Households vary in their propensity to move. The longer a household is in place, the less likely they are to move. This principle of cumulative inertia means that, especially in stable neighbourhoods, households do not make the decision lightly. Generally, a rather dramatic shift needs to occur before households consider this choice. One of the most dramatic examples of exit is found in the metropolitan US where the white middle-class flight to the suburbs since the 1960s has created 'chocolate cities and vanilla suburbs'. The 'tipping point' was when and where African-American households constituted more than about 10 per cent of the area population. This was enough to set off the out-movement of white middle-class residents. Fear of crime, fear of declining educational standards, and falling house prices are all embodied, for many white households, in the presence of black households.

If households do not move but they still feel aggrieved, then they may articulate their concern. This is the voice strategy. Households, if they are very wealthy, well connected and powerful, can influence events. The power of individuals should not be overlooked in shaping the nature of urban society. The ability of rich families to shape cities for maximum favourable effect is a fact of life. Generally, the less democratic the society and the smaller the city, the greater the power wielded by individuals. However, most individual households have limited influence. They achieve more power to influence outcomes by joining together in groups. These are called resident groups, neighbourhood groups, urban protest movements and sometimes urban social movements. We can identify three general aspects of such group activity: the context, the voicing of concern and outcomes.

We have already discussed some of the reasons for protest: taxes, services and externalities. If taxes are seen to be high, if public goods and services are seen to deteriorate, and if negative externalities are perceived, then there is the context for household discontent and possible group action. In a broad-ranging historical survey of grassroots action in the city Manuel Castells (1983) identifies three major sources of protest, centring on the demand for goods and services, cultural identity and political power. Castells' book is an ambitious attempt at a cross-cultural, transhistorical survey of urban struggles and is a major source of information, ideas, and insights into the city as a site of struggle and social change.

People who perceive that important issues can be addressed by collective action form protest groups. This implies that there are those with the time, commitment and belief to mobilize and organize the local community. Such people are few and far between, although a previously marginalized group may move from political exclusion to rioting for, as the English politician Charles Fox noted in 1777, people 'who have no hope and nothing to lose will always be dangerous'.

The outcomes of collective action form a continuum from success through partial success to failure. The result will depend on a variety of factors, but of prime importance is the relative degree of power wielded by the group compared with the authorities. Although the group may have limited resources and power, if it shares the same interests as the authorities then some measure of success may be expected. Success is most likely when a group has effective power and a congruence of interest with the relevant authorities. Success is least likely when weak groups are pitted against authorities that do not share the group's interests or concerns.

In some case workers and residents can combine to create successful urban social movements. In Brazil in 1980, the Workers' Party – Partido dos Trabalhadores (PT) – was formed. In 1988 the PT won the city government election of São Paulo and began a policy of encouraging citizen participation (see Alves, 2004).

Business interests vary in size, type, location and long-term strategy. There is a big difference between General Motors and the family-run corner store. There is also a big difference between General Motors, Dow Chemical and Microsoft. The term 'business', therefore, is a loose, generalized expression covering a variety of different interests, but a number of more specific points can be noted regarding key elements of business strategy as built into the dominant ideologies of capitalist societies.

Reducing costs, making profits, and retaining and increasing market share are the primary concerns of business interests in the city as political arena. Businesses, especially big business, have advantages: they provide employment for the population and revenue for city and state governments. Business interests can be politically represented by specific parties and individuals, or indirectly represented through the interconnections between business and political elites, or else through the fiscal realities imposed on local communities and city governments. The lack of a business presence does not mean a lack of political representation. Over the years, business leaders have become less directly involved in local urban politics. They rarely need to be, because their interests are already at the top of the agenda. A sound local economy is essential for good employment opportunities and a solid taxation base. The subculture of senior business people reinforces the active role of leadership, authority, and hierarchy. This experience clashes with the more face-to-face confrontation and open discussion traditionally associated with the democratic political process.

Certain constraints do impose themselves upon business despite its role as a major player in the urban arena. Although business has economic clout it does not have votes, although it may buy votes, directly and indirectly, formally and informally, legally and illegally; politicians need to appear responsive to public opinion to get re-elected. When there is a win–win situation politicians can appease both business and the electorate, but when conflicts between business and community arise, then politicians have to decide. Thus business has power, but not unlimited power. In some localities political representation may even embody a political culture that responds as much to labour as to capital.

What is clear is that business interests play an important role in shaping urban policies, often directly through the interlocking personal and business connections between the business elite and the political elite. Even where there is a more formal separation between business people and politicians, business interests shape the boundaries and nature of local political debate.

Logan and Molotch (1987) document the economic-growth lobby formed through a consensus on stimulating investment and economic growth while limiting the redistributional function of the state among the leading players in US cities. Realtors, local banks, influential politicians, corporate chairs and chambers of commerce all help to define the city's goal and main function as an economic growth machine. They all are eager to promote a pro-business agenda for their particular city. The increasing competition between cities as previously outlined strengthens this growth machine. The urban growth machine exerts subtle and sometime not so subtle political direction over the city's over-riding political concerns. Jonas and Wilson (1999) provide a more recent assessment of the urban growth machine.

The Crisis of the State

The state is subject to various kinds of pressure. Elsewhere, drawing upon the work of Jürgen Habermas, I describe these pressures as a series of crises (Short, 1984, 1993) and employ the term 'crisis' in the double sense that it has in Chinese, where two ideograms represent it respectively as danger and opportunity. An *economic crisis* occurs when the economy fails to meet popular expectations. Lack of jobs, decline in living standards, and reduction in purchasing power are all perceived in a negative manner. If these factors affect more than a permanent underclass, they create the conditions for a *legitimation crisis*, in which the state loses its ability to reflect the popular will of the country. *Rationality crises* result from the failure to make the necessary amount of correct decisions. Two subtypes can be noted. Type 1 occurs when economic policies are incorrect, and Type 2 occurs when the state fails to provide the necessary education programmes and so on. *Fiscal crises* occur when expenditures exceed revenues.

Crises express themselves in different ways at the different levels of government. This is most evident in the case of fiscal crises. There is often a distinction between government taxation and spending. Central governments pass some of the responsibilities for spending on to city governments while keeping a large proportion of tax revenue for themselves . The effect is to shift the burden of the fiscal crisis on to the cities, especially the poorer cities where there are more demands for different types of welfare spending.

The urban fiscal crisis in the US fluctuates in line with general economic and political conditions. From the 1950s through the 1960s and into the early 1970s city government revenues grew from local sources, as well as from federal and state aid. An expanding economy was the tide that raised all government revenues, but by the mid-1970s a sluggish economy led to a crisis as expenditures went beyond revenue. This municipal crisis was most vividly demonstrated in the case of New York City.

From the 1930s to the mid-1970s the city government of New York had an ambitious social agenda, reflected in public health, education and social services spending that increased by between 4 and 5 per cent every year from 1945 to 1975. However, in the same time period, the tax base weakened due to the out-migration of people and jobs to the suburbs. Municipal revenues declined because of the erosion of the tax base, and by the early 1970s city politicians were borrowing heavily in order to hold the line on tax increases, to maintain services and to preserve the jobs of city workers. The city was deep in debt, and after a six-month period from October 1974 to March 1975 during which the banks sold city securities, the city was unable to borrow any more money. A fiscal crisis was declared, and budgeting was taken out of the hands of the electoral process. Almost 40,000 workers were laid off, and there was a freeze of the city's budget and a state takeover of city finances.

The fiscal crisis of New York City marks a turning point in urban politics in the US and, to some extent, for many other capitalist cities. From 1945 to 1975 city governments could and did pursue more redistribution policies by spending money on welfare, public health and education if they had the political will. After 1975 the fiscal realities precluded such ambitious social spending. The tax base declined in most cities and the reliance on raising money meant a greater reliance on obtaining and keeping a strong credit rating. Since most cities now need to borrow money, their credit rating determines the ease and cost of borrowing money. Credit ratings are based not only on the basic financial health of a city's finances but also on the policies they are pursuing. Pursue policies considered too radical by the credit agencies, and a city's credit rating drops. Credit rating agencies have been much more stringent in rating cities after the New York City fiscal crisis, which they failed to predict. All the major credit rating agencies gave the city a good rating right up until the crisis was made public. Subsequently, the agencies assess all cities with a much more critical eye. The policies of cities are structured more by the generally conservative opinions of credit agencies than the needs, demands or political will of their citizens.

The Decline of the Keynesian–New Deal City and the Rise of the Entrepreneurial City

The Keynesian city is named after the English economist, John Maynard Keynes (1883–1946), who argued that government had a major role to play in stimulating effective demand in the economy. While Keynes mapped out the theory of an activist government in capitalist societies, Roosevelt's New Deal put it into practice. Faced with massive unemployment, Roosevelt's Administration began in 1933 to use government spending to get the economy working at a higher capacity in order to soak up unemployment and secure social stability. The Keynesian–New Deal city lasted from the 1930s to the 1980s.

The period from 1933 through to the 1980s marks the high point of the Keynesian–New Deal city when there was a consensus between capital and labour on the role of government. Government spending stimulated demand so that unemployment would be limited and controlled. Government spending on programmes which ensured that the majority of the population had access to relatively affordable health, housing, education and social welfare softened the social consequences of business downturns. In the US business interests held a stronger hand in comparison to Northwest Europe where organized labour was more powerful and where social welfare programmes were not so curtailed by the greater resistance to taxes and to the role of government in general. Military spending sustained the US's global reach but restricted social welfare spending. On both sides of the North Atlantic, however, the economic muscle of organized labour had an effect, forcing concessions out of business and government. Life in the Keynesian–New Deal city took away the rough edges of a capitalist economy.

From the 1980s onwards the Keynesian–New Deal city began to disappear. There were many factors at work that have been widely documented: the persistence of stagflation that seemed to disrupt the balancing act of government spending which could minimize unemployment while avoiding inflation; and growing resistance to government taxation as programmes were funded by deepening and widening the income tax and local property tax base. However, what especially underlay the seismic shift was the declining power of organized labour. The loss of manufacturing jobs and the consequent decline in the size and importance of organized labour meant that business interests gained. Beginning in the 1980s a new metanarrative takes over that limits government spending, especially on welfare programmes, reduces social subsidies, frees up markets, globalizes economies and imposes limits on tax increases, all resulting in a massive redirection of government spending and a dramatic reorientation in the nature of the city (Hall and Hubbard, 1998).

As the federal government reduces social spending and the tax base declines in many formerly buoyant industrial cities, the entrepreneurial city replaces the Keynesian–New Deal city. Today city authorities are more concerned with generating money than with spending, and even the spending is now orientated more towards creating fertile climates for business. The social welfare of citizens no longer constructs the political discourse of the city so much as the competitiveness of local business and the consolidation of footloose capital. This shift involves specific strategies, such as looking at the development opportunities of plots of publicly owned land and creating public–private partnerships in which business and local governments pursue joint developments. The city is seen less as a place of residence and more as a site of business.

The shift from Keynesian–New Deal to entrepreneurial city also entails a shift in political culture that gives rise to a less caring city. People as residents and citizens convert into people as workers and consumers. Being poor becomes less a condition and more of a moral failing. To be economically marginal in the entrepreneurial city is to be at best a social cipher, and at worst a social threat.

The decline in communal public spaces and the rise of commodified, semi-public, semi-private spaces (such as malls) distances those less able to consume and buy. General urban public spaces are segmented into income groups and the marginals disappear as citizens and reappear as threats. And the more people hide behind gated communities, live in segregated suburbs and patronize socially segmented sites, the more urban public space becomes less a site of regular interaction and more one of a scary encounter. The higher the walls go up, the lower feelings of safety and security sink. As middle- and upper-income groups retreat from urban public space, it increasingly becomes a place of threat and danger to be disciplined, policed, controlled and avoided.

A substantial number of studies have focused theoretically and empirically on the transformation in urban governance from the welfare state model towards an economic-development model in the European and North American context (Harvey, 1989b; Gaffikin and Warf, 1993). Although the focus and methods of these studies vary, there is a widespread agreement that what lies behind the shift in urban governance is the growing competition between cities for local economic growth. Globalization of markets, production, technology and finance, global economic restructuring and the high mobility of capital is the broader context of the increased competition between cities. US cities, in particular, have suffered due to the loss of federal funds in the postfederal period. To cope, city governments have been attempting to solve fiscal problems by chasing local economic development. Severe competition to attract and retain business forces city governments to introduce a range of policy initiatives, such as enterprise zones, urban development corporations, urban subsidies and public–private partnerships. These programmes are intended to make the city more attractive to investors.

Many scholars inquire into who are the main beneficiaries of this shift. There are competing interpretations. One, most often proffered by Peterson (1980), argues that the growth of cities is to the benefit of all residents because any development project has only positive consequences for the city overall. Contrary to this argument, a group of scholars point out that local economic growth does not necessarily promote the public good (Peck and Tickell, 1995).

The ideology and policies of post-Keynesian administrations encourage the institutionalization of the business interests of regional entrepreneurs (Lowe, 1993). Their 'growth ethic' – growth is good – is used to eliminate any alternative visions of the purpose of local urban government or the meaning of community, and thus civic pride in the growth and loyalty cuts across class lines. The coalition draws on local histories, culture and images to underpin its activities. Peck and Tickell (1995) summarize the contribution of growth coalitions, first, to the subordination of welfarist goals to the over-riding imperatives of local competitiveness and growth; second, to an acceleration in place-based competition for both public and private investment; and third, to the formation of a new layer of business political actors at the local level. Business interests are established as political phenomena and subsequently institutionalized.

City government has become less concerned with controlling or regulating local business and rather more concerned with promoting local economic growth; marketing the city has become an important and growing force in contemporary urban economic development.

Such terms as *the bottom line, fiscal realities* and the *new urban realism* are all phrases that seek not so much to identify fiscal constraints as to close off an alternative discourse about other fiscal priorities and different spending choices. The constant use of natural, and especially body, analogies in urban boosterism (for instance, the notion of revitalizing the heart of the city centre for reconstructing the area) does not so much dramatize the endeavour as present it as the work of a wise doctor tending the sick (see Wilson, 1996). Who could possibly argue with such an image? Only someone who was unreasonable, and beyond the reach of everyday common sense.

The End of Urban Politics?

Given the severe fiscal constraints on many of the world's largest cities, it is legitimate to ask the question: has real politics, the politics of debating different alternative strategies, been abolished? Has the overwhelming power of finance and the relentless logic of competition for scarce resources embroiled cities in the politics of the unpolitical? Gottdiener's provocatively entitled 1987 book, *The Decline of Urban Politics*, argues that cities, hemmed in by the power of banks and financial institutions and federal and state failure to provide the necessary revenue, have seen the 'eclipse of the polity'.

There are some countervailing trends to this bleak view. Let us return to New York City. Lynne Weikart (2003) follows expenditure policies in New York City since the mid-1970s fiscal crisis. Examining the policies of Koch, Dinkins and Giuliani, she finds that while the mayors' amount of money to spend was restricted by outside forces, they had some measure of autonomy in what to spend it on. Koch increased the number of city employees, and Dinkins increased the amount of spending on social services, while Giuliani reduced both social services and health services and spent more on law and order. The results of this careful study reveal two things: first, that urban politics is primarily and fundamentally shaped by the external fiscal reality. The credit rating agencies play a huge role in threatening negative ratings if taxes are raised or more money is borrowed, and they are particularly critical of more liberal mayors such as Dinkins. Second, the mayors did have some measure of relative autonomy in affecting policies. There was an urban politics at work, but one which was severely shaped by external forces. The need to concentrate on economic development and supporting business interests squatted so forcefully on the agenda of city government that everything else was pushed to the periphery.

A real urban politics does continue to exist, but it is heavily constrained by fiscal realities and economic pressures. In the late 1990s the city of Toledo, for example, gave DaimlerChrysler exemption from property taxes and moved 83 households and 16 businesses so that the company could expand. This is a typical example of the incentives cities offer to companies and corporations. And as each city offers incentives, the results are more generous tax breaks and fiscal incentives; a growing public subsidy of private interests. Cities have to compete but, the more they compete, the less the prize is worth.

The decline of urban politics seems more appropriate in the developed world where the organized working class has declined in political power and a neo-liberal agenda has swept all before it. In cities in the less developed world the same forces of globalization are generating new sources of democratic mobilization: squatter movements are extending the question of citizenship, the new working class is beginning to flex its muscle and the small (though rapidly expanding) middle class is demanding more political participation, especially in formerly authoritarian and totalitarian. states. It would be naive to see a wave of democratization occurring in globalizing cities, but it would also be wrong to ignore the democratic possibilities occurring in these cities.

11
The Designed City

Cities are physical and social constructs. They are designed. The questions that interest urban theorists regarding the designed city fall into three main areas. Who is designing, what are the dominant designs, and what are their consequences?

Who is Designing the City?

We live in cities made in large part by other people. The more cities are designed, the more we are living in other people's vision of the city. There is something inherently authoritarian about architecture and totalitarian about urban planning.

The deskilling of labour is a dominant trend in capitalist society. Capital's drive to reduce labour costs and to control the labour process has resulted in the automation of whole areas of work. There remain, however, some occupational groups who create or maintain strong positions in the work place. These are the traditional professionals, such as doctors and lawyers, and emerging groups, such as financial consultants. Their power lies in their ability to influence our perception of the world. Their codes and rationalities govern our lives and affect our cities.

A 'profession' is a group that claims expertise and that can enforce its status through regulation of individual members. Most professions have the traits of assertion and integration. Assertion springs from the need to claim legitimacy. The establishment of the position of expert involves the notion of superior judgment. Doctors, for example, are very persuasive that they are experts on other people's health. Professional groups claim to have more and better knowledge. The integrative element springs from a need to tie their actions and existence to wider social concerns. Few professions say that they are in it for the money. Thus, lawyers argue that theirs is not simply a highly paid profession, but rather they are the pillars of a system that ensures justice and fairness; similarly, doctors portray themselves as barriers to sickness and death. According to lawyers and doctors, therefore, only the highly paid legal and medical professions prevent us from returning to some kind of neolithic medical barbarism. Every professional group seems to go through a life cycle in its relationship with the wider public. Stage one involves the establishment of the profession. Stage two is a 'trust-the-expert' phase, with the corporate body maintaining its reputation. Stage three is opposition. The medical profession, for example, in recent years has come under severe criticism from consumers and the alternative medicine movement; their response has been to reiterate their expertise, with reference to its 'scientific' basis, and to question the value of alternative health therapies.

Two professional groups have a particular importance for the city: architects and planners. Each has a specific story but they are part of that broader history, the emergence of the expert in urban design.

In the past, there was a dominant image of God as architect. Today it has almost been replaced by the myth of architect as God. It is impossible to identify the architects of Chartres or of Wells cathedrals. Their design and construction involved collective endeavours over long periods of time, with a variety of builders and masons working towards a common purpose and a shared objective. There was no such thing as 'the architect'. The profession only began to develop with the division of building labour, and it was only in the nineteenth and twentieth centuries that architects made a sustained attempt at professionalizing. The Institute of British Architects was established in 1834 and received its royal charter in 1837.

On the integrative side, architects began to see themselves as creators of a better way of life. For the Romantics, such as John Ruskin, the architect's job encompassed moral uplift and social purpose. For some of the Socialists, architecture was a vehicle for radical social change. Twentieth-century modernist architects, such as Walter Gropius, saw themselves as designers, not just of buildings but also of a utopian society.

On the assertive side, architects began to see themselves as arbiters between mere building and 'architecture'. In 1927 Le Corbusier (1887–1965), one of the most influential of modern architects, decreed that 'Architecture is the masterly correct and magnificent play of masses brought together in light'. Notice that architecture is now art, and the architect by implication an artist, free from the brute demands of an untutored populace. The twentieth century saw the attempted enthronement of the architect as artist, visionary and guru. Le Corbusier's real name was Charles-Edouard Jeanneret. Any profession whose guru's pseudonym dispenses with the familiarity of a forename while arrogating a definite article must be treated with great caution.

Architects grew in status with the growing separation between the users of buildings and the people who commissioned them. Renaissance princes generally lived in the buildings they commissioned, often supervising much of the building work. The modern, bureaucratic princes, in contrast, yield to building committees, with architects often given a prominent place. In the private sector, especially since the Second World War, there has been the growth of speculative office blocks, built with no specific client in mind. They were built according to general design considerations, with the voice of the architect becoming more important than the eventual users of the buildings. Discussions tend to consider aesthetic and budget considerations, rather than the preferences of the users. As the emphasis has shifted away from client preferences to architectural fashion, the architectural profession has become increasingly arrogant, a posture best summed up in the lecture by Philip Johnson, 'The Seven Crutches of Modern Architecture', given to architectural students at Harvard in 1954, which parodies Ruskin's *The Seven* Lamps *of Architecture* (1849). Johnson attacked seven needless crutches of architecture: history, pretty drawing, utility, comfort, cheapness, structure and serving the client. 'It's got to be clear', he told the young students, and a generation of important architects, 'that serving the client is one thing and the art of architecture is another'.

Taking Johnson's advice to heart, modernist architecture is strong on commissions, individual reputations and international competitions amongst the cosy few. It is weaker on user needs, appropriate human scales, social credibility and compassion. A dramatic indication of its social failings was the demolition, in 1972, of the high-rise housing towers of the Pruitt–Igoe scheme in St Louis. The complex had become uninhabitable and no one wanted to live there. The scheme, which incorporated much of Le Corbusier's design principles, had won an architectural award in 1951. In British cities similar types of high-rise housing were demolished in the 1980s and 1990s as local authorities blew up buildings less than 20 years old because they were unpopular and uninhabitable. It may seem harsh to blame architecture for what are problems of wider social significance, but architects must shoulder some of the responsibility for the production of an alienating urban environment and ultimately an alienated urban population. To be sure, Le Corbusier's vision of residential blocks with communal facilities was realized ultimately as tower blocks without the facilities. Some of the blame must lie with others, but he and other modern architects had the arrogance to assume that they knew best, and that they could design cities and dwellings without reference to citizens and inhabitants.

On Wednesday, 30 May 1984, Prince Charles spoke at a gala dinner of the Royal Institute of British Architects (RIBA). Royalty in Britain are often called upon to say a few words at such occasions: 'Delighted to be here. What a wonderful institution. Keep up the good work.' The usual kind of thing is expected and usually given, but on this particular night Prince Charles did not say the usual kind of thing. He lambasted modern architects for their lack of interest in ordinary people and their concern to design buildings to please other architects rather than the tenants. He criticized the assembled heavies of British architecture for what they had done to the skyline of London. He described the extension to the National Gallery in Trafalgar Square as a 'monstrous carbuncle on the face of a much-loved and elegant friend' and referred to a building in the Mansion House Square as 'another glass giant stump'.

He struck a resonant chord with most of his future subjects. Most non-architects consider modernist architecture as something of a joke. Most buildings given architectural awards are monstrous failures for a wider populace: too hot in summer, too cold in winter, sometimes leaking and always inconvenient. It is a common belief that buildings which win architectural awards begin to fall apart after two years and drive their occupants crazy after four. Sadly, the response of many architects is to go further into their over-designed shells. Seeing themselves as artists and visionaries, they treat criticism as merely an outburst of philistinism from the ill-informed mob. They like to compare themselves to nineteenth-century artists found wanting by their contemporaries but lauded by later generations. If you have the arrogance to believe that history is on your side, then present criticism can safely be ignored.

Popular contempt for architects also springs from perceptions of hypocrisy. Gropius, a leading light in the German Bauhaus movement, and later a professor of architecture at Harvard and one of the founding fathers of modern architecture, made his reputation designing high-density worker housing consisting of large blocks. This was good enough for the workers, but when it came to his own house, Gropius built a low-slung building nestling on a 30-acre site in the New England countryside. More recently, in an interview with a journalist, Michael Manser, one-time president of the Royal Institute of British Architects, and the defender and designer of flat-roofed, high-rise residential blocks, claimed that it was a myth that people didn't like living in them. The interviewer went on: 'I asked him why, if he was such a defender of modern high-rise, he himself lived in a nice traditional Georgian house in London. He said, his wife was a passionate gardener, otherwise he might' (Davie, 1983). Like most professions, architecture it is a modern priesthood; entry is granted only after initiation rites, and critics are damned for their audacity or patronized with mild contempt. Architecture separated from its consumers has taken on a life of its own. Modernists' claims and counterclaims and the various voices of postmodernism develop and decline within a hermetically sealed debating chamber. The design of places reflects changing professional considerations more than the varied needs of consumers.

The most recent development in architecture is postmodernism. Modernism was the international style of flat-roofed glass boxes, high-rise towers elegant in simplicity, boring in repetition, often lacking any sensitivity to site, location or older buildings. For the architects they were the symbol of a new aesthetic, true to society's needs and honest in relation to materials. For the consumers they came to represent the 'fashionism' of architecture, devoid of any real community involvement in building design.

Postmodernism can be identified by strong primary colours, arches, tubular decorations, pediments, and the downright whimsy of rococo façades covering factories and baroque entrances to post offices. It is an improvement on the austere asceticism of modernism and some fine buildings have been produced, but it is still a game just for architects, where they can play at spotting the references and identifying the influences; at best, it is a return to a vernacular tradition, and at worst, a camp wallow in bad taste, kitsch replacing culture. The simple conclusion is that the design of buildings and cities is too important to be left only to the architects. Their mistakes endure long after they have passed on to the next lucrative contract, the next architects' conference or the next showing of their designs to a small, select band of fellow architects. Our cities are the graveyards of outdated architectural theories. The giant glass towers, once the buildings of the future, are now the tombstones of architectural modernism.

Urban planning has a long history, from the Egyptians to the Aztecs and from Imperial Rome to Renaissance Europe. As a profession, urban planning's roots lie in the massive urbanization of the nineteenth century when villages became towns, towns became cities and cities became major urban regions. In 1800 there were no cities in Europe with a population greater than a million, but by 1900 there were nine, four of them in Britain: London, Manchester, Birmingham and Glasgow. The demand for planning came from several sources: there were the civic authorities, who wanted cleaner, safer, more efficient cities; there were the business groups, who wanted to off-load on to the state some of the costs of production and reproduction, such as housing for the workers and transport for people and goods; and there were the reformers, who condemned the urban squalor. For them, the city was the cause of social unrest, and planning was more than just a technical exercise: it was a platform for improving life chances and ensuring social stability. The drive for efficiency, material interest, fear of social conflict and the desire for social reform all shaped the early development of planning and continue to exercise their influence.

Several factors strengthened the adoption of various urban planning measures in North America and Western Europe. There was growing recognition that the state could and should become involved in the urban arena. The development of planning reflected and marked the acceptance of the need to regulate property rights. In addition, various urban planning experiments set an example. Robert Owen's New Lanark in Scotland at the end of the eighteenth century was one of the best-known examples of a planned community for factory workers, attracting visitors from all over Europe. Similar schemes were established in North America, with Alexander Hamilton and the Society for Establishing Useful Manufactures founding the model town of Paterson in New Jersey. Later schemes (such as Port Sunlight on Merseyside, Bourneville outside Birmingham and Pullman, near Chicago) confirmed the economic benefits of a well-housed labour force; they showed what planned towns could do for social harmony and return on investment.

The planning reformers successfully lobbied governments and the ensuing legislative measures created a demand for planners. The British Town Planning Institute was established in 1914, five years after the 1909 Housing and Town Planning Act, which gave planning powers to local authorities; the American City Planning Institute was formed in 1917 after several cities had developed zoning ordinances regulating land use.

Early urban planning theorists had radical roots and utopian visions as well as pragmatic policies. To achieve their goals they used the state. Consequently, planning always has been linked closely to the requirements of the state. The bureaucratic system of government practice enmeshed the growth of the profession from its beginnings, and the general tendency has long been for plans combining social reform and civic design to be shorn of their radicalism and, if implemented, restricted to physical design. Governments have, in most cases, evaporated the radical ideas of social change leaving behind the residue of civic design.

End-point master plans, by which preferred land-use configurations inform policy decisions, dominated urban planning in theory and practice until the 1960s. The planner's role involved designing a physical plan for the city and coordinating the decisions of the various public bodies (such as electricity, gas and water services, education and social services) so that the plan was achieved. Since the 1960s, the concept of the master plan has come under criticism. Rosy assumptions about economic growth, population projections, family size and fuel costs proved to be wildly inaccurate, and there was mounting criticism about top-down, non-participatory forms of planning. With their master plans taken away from them, the planners sought, chameleon-like, to maintain a role for themselves by changing their ideas to suit the changing circumstances. In the 1960s redistributing economic growth was the planners' main concern; by the 1980s they had smoothly made the transition towards generating growth. Powerful critiques emerged arguing that planning benefited those who were already powerful, and that urban planning was not an innocent activity devoid of social meaning and redistributional consequences (Sandercock, 1998, 2003).

Planning and social justice connected with a Keynesian city are fast disappearing, to be replaced, it appears, by market-led, market-dominated planning. Some theorists began to question the role and purpose of planning. Mike Douglas and John Friedmann (1998) call for planning to be more concerned with democratization, multiculturalism and human flourishing. Planners are reimagined less as state functionaries and more as handmaidens to emancipation. It is all heady stuff, especially if you are in the planning profession, or (to be more accurate) the teaching of the planning profession. While this call to arms is exciting, the practical meaning never really is outlined. Planning as everything quickly becomes nothing: planning unspecified by time or space is a banal, sterile topic kept alive only by people who teach planning theory.

The attack on traditional planning did a valuable job of demystifying planning, but could do little more than criticize the status quo. Now we have a practice firmly rooted in routine government action and radical theories weak on praxis. Planners, who guide the infrastructure necessary to attract employment, do not ask about the quality of jobs, and the radical theorists do little more than criticize the establishment bias towards current planning practice. Both groups lack a vision of planning and have failed to inform the debate about what makes good and fair cities where people can lead creative and dignified lives.

Dominant Urban Designs

The two most significant issues impacting recent urban design are the rise and fall of modernist architecture, and the decline of large-scale public master plans.

Modernist architecture is the dominant urban signature of the twenti-eth century. It developed against the ornamentation of the nineteenth-century city and promised a new, rational, minimal look to cities. The sleek skyscrapers became part of the urban semiotics of modernity throughout the world, a globalization of urban form at home in capitalist and communist economies, rich and poor countries, small and large cities. It marked a distancing from the past and a belief in the future. In theory it was the shape of the future; in practice, the shell of failed dreams. Postmodern architecture was a reaction to the monotony and the failure of architectural modernism. A new aesthetic marked a return to ornamentation, a referencing of the past and the explicit use of vernacu-lar motifs. The shift marked a loss of belief in the future bias of the modernist project. The future no longer promised a brave new world. The new architectural fashion also allowed people, places and cities to repo-sition themselves as postmodern buildings now marked the edge of fash-ion. In the twenty-first century modernist buildings are now part of the past, with a smell of failure and sense of decline.

The twentieth century also saw the rise and fall of large-scale public master plans. Public health concerns and questions of social stability advanced the development of urban planning. The extent and scope varied by country, with European countries having a heavier public inter-vention than the US. Visionaries such as Le Corbusier and Howard, with such contrasting urban visions, identified new solutions to urban prob-lems. Le Corbusier envisioned a high-density city with 3 million people housed in high-rise tower blocks. In 1899 Howard published *Garden Cities of To-morrow*, reissued four years later as *To-morrow: A Peaceful Path to Real Reform*. He suggested that the advantages of urban and rural environments could be combined in garden cities, new towns where the fresh air of the countryside could be mingled with the job opportunities of the city. The community held the land so that any increase in value, and hence rents, could be used for the provision of municipal services.

Howard sought to turn his ideas into reality. In 1902 he founded the Garden City Pioneer Company, which bought 4,000 acres in Hertfordshire in the UK. The first new town was Letchworth. In 1920 the second town of Welwyn Garden City was founded. Howard's ideas were taken up by various people, such as F.J. Osborn and Lewis Mumford, and given institutional form in the Town and Country Planning Association (TCPA). For those who see no role for idealistic pressure groups the TCPA is a salutary reminder of their periodic success. During the inter-war period they lobbied for new towns in the UK, and in 1946 the New Towns Act established 14 new towns between 1946 and 1950. Another

18 were set up after 1950. The success, unfortunately, was limited to design matters. The community control of land, as envisaged by Howard, was watered down. New towns in the UK are examples of civic design that did not become social experiments. Almost 2 million people were housed in the UK New Towns, but it did not lead to an alternative system of land ownership. State power can turn dreams into reality, but often at a cost to the radicalism of the original visions.

In many cities around the world elements and fragments of both Le Corbusier's and Howard's visions persist. However, by the late twentieth century such plans fell out of favour. There was criticism of public sector urban planning. The dreary tower blocks and the new towns with depressing environments and unsuitable economies gave ammunition to those who argued that the state got it wrong most of the time, and cost a great deal of money all of the time. A developing neo-liberal agenda under-cut the justification and funding for state planning. The withdrawal of public support for building urban utopias probably saved us from some dreadful mistakes, but also eradicated the sense that the public sector could provide the good life. Planning refashioned itself as a tool for generating urban growth. Rather than promising us the good life, planning theory posited vague notions of planning as argumentative and communicative.

Large-scale end-point planning did not disappear. Motorways and airports still need to be built, urban spectaculars such as the Olympic Games are still constructed and staged, and major investments continue to endow transport, new technologies and urban megastructure; but now these projects are less the visions of a better world and more adjuncts to private sector investments. It is not so much that large-scale end-point planning has disappeared, but that it serves private rather than public interests.

Even though cities are still planned, specific private sector needs trump notions of the public good. Indeed, the value of the public good depends upon its animation of the private sector. Day-to-day planning also continues; land-use planning continues to guide developments and investment decisions; impact assessments continue to be made of proposed urban developments. But all this urban planning is tied less to public end-point plans and geared more to meeting the immediate needs of private sector investments. The private sector continues to rely heavily on a planned city. The real issue is not whether urban planning is a good thing, but who is planning, for whom, and who benefits.

For example, the fine-tuning of retail space design now maximizes our spending. A newly emergent 'science' of shopping makes us buy more things more often (Gladwell, 1996). Tables placed in the centre of such stores as The Gap and Banana Republic assist customers in touching the sweaters and shirts (because the more we are able to touch merchandise, the more we are likely to buy). Chocolates and other sweets placed near the checkout induce impromptu purchases with less guilt due to children's annoying and usually successful pleas to their parents. The makers of cereals pay the stores extra to have their produce located at eye level where they are more visible and more likely to be bought than those cereals languishing on the bottom shelf.

The Effects of Urban Design

The city is a human construct. A major question concerns the effects of this construction. The answer resides at a variety of scales and from various perspectives. On a larger scale, a well-planned city actually does help economic activity. Chaotic traffic layouts, for example, lead to traffic jams that increase the cost of doing business. In a highly competitive world, poorly designed cities are uncompetitive. There is a pressing market need for well-planned transport systems and up-to-date communication technologies. An efficient spatial organization is vital for a city's competitive advantage. Yet between the idea of an efficient city and its practice lies a great deal of rhetoric. General arguments mask narrow interests, and there are always competing claims. An international airport is vital for a city's success, but it cannot be located too close to a city because of noise and pollution. Locate it too far out, and it adds time and money for travellers. Cities are balanced precariously between competing forces, such as the need to organize themselves for business while also being liveable places for people. Constantly changing compromises are embodied in the design of cities.

The design of cities affects people's lives in numerous ways. One of the more obvious areas is the issue of public health. The surrounding environment affects the health of individuals and communities. Place, in its entire myriad dimensions, plays an important role in influencing health outcomes. There have been a number of explorations of the relationship between the built urban environment and health (MacIntyre and Ellaway, 2000; Kawachi and Berkman, 2003). Early social epidemiological work in this area includes Engels, who noted the association between decrepit living conditions and poorer health among the British working class in the nineteenth century and the detailed work of John Snow in 1850 that mapped cholera cases and identified a contaminated urban water pump. In recent years there has been a renewed concern with how the organization of our social space can affect a range of health outcomes such as heightened risk of obesity (Vandegrift and Yoked, 2004), greater risk of mortality (Kennedy *et al.*, 1999), functional decline (Glass and Balfour, 2003), and the prevalence of specific health conditions such as asthma (Etzel, 2003). While the built environment is the setting for a number of epidemiological studies, little theoretical or conceptual work exists linking the features of the urban setting to public health outcomes. Much of the existing literature focuses on the measurement of the phenomena rather than the conceptualization. Thus, this line of inquiry is limited to significant correlations with little or no critical analysis of *why* these phenomena may be related. For example, D. Cohen *et al.* (2000) demonstrate that rates of gonorrhea were significantly higher in neigh-bourhoods that have abandoned cars, graffiti, litter, and deterioration, but they offer no explanation linking these neighbourhood characteristics to disease risk.

An exemplary work linking built environment to health is Klinenberg (2002), which looks at the mortality levels in different Chicago neigh-bourhoods related to the heat wave of 1995. He held class and income constant and yet still found significant differences between neighbour-hoods. A higher level of mortality was found amongst older people in an area where there was little street life and a greater fear of crime. The older adults tended to stay indoors, thus putting themselves at greater risk from heat exposure and isolation. In the higher-density, more vibrant commu-nity, such people felt able to go outside and maintained contact with others. Strong social networks in the neighbourhood helped older people avoid heat-related mortality by reducing social isolation and encouraging them to leave their over-heated apartments. In other words, the social and physical fabric of the neighbourhood had a direct impact on mortality levels. It is clear that the effects of the built environment on health must be teased out more meaningfully at this detailed level, but that requires substantial investigation and conceptualization of the causal factors.

There are many ways in which health can be linked to the quality of the urban environment: for example, once touted for its accessibility to exercise and fresh air, suburban life is now associated with an *increase* in the risk of obesity (Vandegrift and Yoked, 2004). Much of this excess risk may be attributed to the distance separating shopping centres, health care and homes, which has made car usage a necessity beyond the city limits. As caloric intake increases and exercise declines, the result is higher levels of obesity. In areas with more public transport, people tend to walk more, both as a mode of transport and at either end of mass tran-sit systems. The significant difference in obesity between US and

European countries has also been explained in part by the greater use of mass transit in European countries and hence the greater degree of informal exercise though walking. Suburban sprawl also has led to an increase in automobile fatalities and emissions-related health problems in all nations.

In general, work to date has been successful in establishing associations between the built environment and health, but not causality or exact estimates of risk to individuals or populations.

The effects of urban design on individual behaviour are also apparent at the more detailed level of place. Take the example of Oscar Newman's theory of defensible space. In his 1972 book of the same name, Newman identified a connection between high crime rates and design. He found that crime rates are highest in poorly maintained spaces isolated from public scrutiny. Places that have a greater degree of local surveillance and a feeling of territoriality have lower crime rates. If we assume that crime is not caused by design then Newman's work suggests that certain designs can reduce crime rates. In 1991 the Five Oaks community in Dayton had very high crime rates and many people stayed in their homes at night because they were frightened by the threat of violence. Newman applied the principles of defensible space. The area was reorganized into smaller mini-neighbourhoods of cul-de-sac streets with gates to block through traffic. According to the city's Office of Management and Budget, crime fell by 25 per cent and violent crime by 50 per cent (Newman, 1996).

Urban environments play a role in shaping attitudes and behaviour. One contentious theory is the broken window hypothesis. In a famous article in *Atlantic Monthly* in March 1982, entitled 'Broken Windows: The Police and Neighborhood Safety', James Q. Wilson and George L. Killing maintained that small-scale neglect, such as leaving a broken window unrepaired, sends a message of decay and indifference that encourages even more anti-social behaviour and leads ultimately to greater crime. The thesis was simple and the prescription clear: mend the broken windows and crime will decrease. The interesting thing is not whether the theory is correct or not, but the fact that it was believed to be correct and became a staple of strategic policing in many US cities. Mayor Rudy Giuliani in New York City implemented a Broken Windows policing policy of 'zero tolerance' for minor civil infractions such as panhandling and jaywalking. Crime in New York dropped dramatically in the 1990s but the extent of the role of broken windows policing is difficult to ascertain. The crack cocaine epidemic subsided and a rising economy reduced unemployment. The New York Police Department never in fact mended any broken windows. More detailed assessment of crime in neighbourhoods finds that social cohesion among neighbours is the greatest predictor of neighbourhood crime: their willingness to intervene on behalf of the common good could be considered a form of social capital (Sampson, Raudenbush and Felton, 1997; see also http://www.ambiguous. org/robin/word/brokenwindows.html.

There is also work on an even smaller urban scale. William H. Whyte's classic 1980 book, *The Social Life of Small Urban Spaces*, is a gem. Whyte reports on detailed work in urban public spaces. His general concern is with the liveability of cities, and his particular focus is on the social use of urban public spaces. He found that the main attraction of urban spaces for people is other people. Using time-lapse photography as well as ethnographic methods, he shows that people prefer places where other people are. The findings of Whyte's work condemns the bunker architecture and fortress mentality of some places in cities and reminds us again of the conviviality of cities and sociability of urban places.

Moses versus Jane Jacobs

Let me end this chapter with a story taken from the planning and design of a US city (Short, 2006), which is of much wider significance as it condenses many of the themes in the planning and design of the modern city and the rise of the postmodern city.

Robert Moses (1888–1981) was the master builder of the New York metropolis for over 40 years (Caro, 1974). He started off as a civic reformer passionately committed to public service and the notion of efficient government. From 1924 until 1968, he held immense, unelected power. He held a variety of non-elected positions, including Park Commissioner, Construction Coordinator, member of the City Planning Board, chair of the Slum Clearance Committee and also of the Housing Committee. At one time he held twelve official posts. His control of the bridge and tunnel toll charges in the city gave him a never-ending supply of money and power. Over a 40-year period he built parkways, expressways, roads, parks, playgrounds and housing. He was a leading force in the building of Lincoln Center, the New York Coliseum, the United Nations Headquarters, the Shea Stadium and Co-op City. His road-building projects sweep around the entire metropolitan region and include the Long Island Expressway, the Staten Island Expressway, the New England Throughway and the Henry Hudson Parkway. He built the Triborough, Verrazano, Henry Hudson and Throgs Neck bridges. He constructed 95 blocks of public housing on eastern Manhattan that housed almost 150,000 people, and was responsible for the building of apartments housing over half-a-million tenants. It has been estimated that, in 1968 dollars, he built $27 billion of public works.

In his earlier years Moses was on the side of the angels. He constructed parks and playgrounds. He was the leading force in the creation of numerous city and state parks, including Rockaway Park, Jones Beach State Park, Battery Park and, of course, Robert Moses State Park. As well as the park, he also had a parkway, a causeway and a dam named after him. But by the 1950s, massive road construction was the dominant Moses imprint on the city.

Moses rammed numerous expressways through the city, including the Bruckner Expressway, the Staten Island Expressway, the Cross-Bronx Expressway, the Long Island Expressway, the Major Deegan Expressway and the Brooklyn–Queens Expressway. To make way for the fast moving car lanes he evicted between 250,000 and 500,000 people. It was a massive urban renewal project that destroyed neighbourhoods, creating apartments for the wealthy and bleak sterile blocks for the poor.

One of his projects was the 7-mile-long Cross-Bronx Expressway. The first eviction letters came on 4 December 1952. Local residents were told to move to make way for a new expressway that lay across the path of 113 streets, one subway line, three railroads and five elevated rapid transit lines. They were given 90 days to leave. Local groups tried to stop the project but their opposition was unsuccessful. Construction began in the summer of 1955. It took twelve years and it cost $10 million per mile. The human costs were even more staggering. The Bronx, once a vibrant neighbourhood, was blasted into dilapidation and decline. Moses said in a television interview at the time that, when building in a metropolis, 'you have to hack your way with a meat ax'. As a young boy, the social critic Marshall Berman witnessed the axe. 'I can remember', he recalls, 'standing above the construction site for the Cross-Bronx Expressway, weeping for my neighborhood' (Berman, 1982, 295). For Berman it was an early experience of modernity. In his 1982 book, *All That is Solid Melts into Air*, he extends the experience into a very sophisticated analysis that draws upon Dickens, Baudelaire and Dostoevsky as well as Walter Benjamin and Goethe to describe the creative destructiveness at the heart of modernity. The book draws widely on sources across the world, but its origins lie with a young boy looking at the destruction of his community. The title of this book is a quote from Marx's *Communist Manifesto* that tries to capture the restless, ceaseless destruction of the past to create the future. Urban renewal and highway construction were the axes of modernity. 'As

I saw one of the loveliest of these buildings being wrecked for the road',
Berman noted, 'I felt a grief that, I can now see, is endemic to modern
life'.

Moses blasted almost 130 miles of urban expressways through 20
neighbourhoods and almost 500,000 people were forcibly relocated.
Underlying the vision was a basic contempt for the city with its crowded
neighbourhoods and its slow-moving traffic routes. The density and
depth of urban living was to be replaced by sharp, clean lines, straight and
fast transport routes; a world of organic neighbourhoods was to be
replaced by a cold, modern aesthetic, a promise of something new writ
large on the blank page of obliterated communities, whose destruction
was justified by their designation of 'blighted' or 'slums' or 'transitional'. The city was reimagined as a modern space to replace outdated
places, a city of easy flows to replace the city of living communities.
There was a fear and contempt for the existing city in all its messiness and
heterogeneity and a burning desire for a remade city. Beneath the vision
there was a hard core of material interests. Land conversion, development
and renewal were all sources of business and profit for builders, developers and real estate people.

Moses had plans for more urban expressways. He had long held a
vision of three expressways that would carry traffic east to west across
Manhattan: a Lower Manhattan Expressway that would have swept
through Greenwich village, an elevated Midtown Expressway at 30th
Street and an Upper Manhattan Expressway at 125th Street. When his
plans surfaced for the Lower Manhattan Expressway in the mid-1950s,
Moses collided with Jane Jacobs.

Jane Jacobs was born in 1916 in Scranton, a town on the anthracite
coalfield of northeastern Pennsylvania. She had an early interest in journalism and, after high school, worked unpaid on the local newspaper. In
the middle of the Depression she went to New York City where she found
occasional writing work. She lived at 555 Hudson Street in Greenwich
Village until she moved to Toronto in 1968 so that her sons would not be
drafted. She wrote for a metals trade paper and freelanced for the *Herald
Tribune* and *Vogue*. After the Second World War she wrote for
Architectural Forum.

Jane Jacobs had no formal training in architecture or urban planning.
Her most famous book, *The Death and Life of Great American Cities,*
owes less to academic theories or architectural visions than to her everyday life on the streets of Lower Manhattan in Greenwich Village (Jacobs,
1961). It combined her now honed writing skills with her experience of
city living. 'This book', begins the first line of the opening chapter, 'is an

attack on current city planning and rebuilding'. Writing at the height of the war against the cities and in a New York lacerated by Moses expressways, Jane Jacobs enunciates a new vision. She revels in the density, heterogeneity, diversity, complexity and messiness of city life. She sees the regular use of sidewalks as essential to the safety of a city, social interaction, and the socialization of children. She extols the importance of small blocks and aged buildings. She encourages diversity of land uses, the recycling of older buildings and the nurturing of communities rather than their destruction.

Moses and Jacobs embodied two opposing visions of the city. Where Moses saw routes, Jacobs saw neighbourhoods. When he reached for the axe, she suggested holistic care. Where he saw giant new projects that prioritized the car and the journey, she saw small-scale places for congenial social interaction.

Jacobs' book can only be understood as a riposte to Moses, his vision and his methods. It was written at a time when, and in a city where, Moses was rebuilding in a bankrupt modernist fashion. When she criticizes 'promenades that go from noplace to nowhere' or 'expressways that eviscerate great cities' she is criticizing Moses. And when she writes of urban renewal as 'the sacking of cities', she is lambasting Moses. The book offers the counterpoint to the Moses city. It is the product of a particular context but, like all great books, it transcends the specific. To read Jacobs today is to see the emergence of an alternative conception of the city that speaks to recycling, community, human scale and public participation. The book revels in the role of the corner, the importance of the block and the necessity of neighbourhood. The sense of community, the feeling of urban congeniality runs through her book. It is the city as being, lived memory, the setting for social interaction. The Moses city, on the other hand, is the city of grand visions, the city as becoming, the blank page for sweeping motorways and grand ensembles. Jacobs and Moses represent two contrasting visions of the city. One is a close connection to lived experience with a profound sense of community and a palpable feeling of history. The other is the city as centrally planned vision, a concern with mobility and the destruction of history. The Jacobs city is diverse, organic, spontaneous. The Moses city is uniform, imposed, planned.

Moses planned an eight-lane elevated highway from the East River to the Hudson River that would have cut a 225-foot swathe though Soho, Greenwich Village and parts of Little Italy and Chinatown. It would have involved the forcible relocation of 10,000 workers and residents. The plan surfaced in 1961. Jacobs led the community opposition to the project. There were rallies and demonstrations. She was arrested and charged with riot and public mischief. People wore badges and carried signs that read 'Moses Madness' and 'Kill the Expressway'. A coalition of Jews, Chinese, Italians and Anglos resisted the Moses wrecking ball. At a Board of Estimates meeting in December 1962 the Moses plan was rejected. The Expressway was cancelled. Jacobs had won and Moses had lost. He would continue in power for another six years, but his influence was on the wane. The defeat of the Lower Manhattan Expressway was the beginning of the end for Moses' restructuring of New York City.

Jacobs and Moses are remembered in very different ways. Moses is now seen as an idealist turned to addled old man, who was unable to learn from his mistakes, arrogant, undemocratic and deeply flawed in his vision of the city. Since his death, his name has become synonymous with everything wrong about urban planning and urban renewal. Caro's majestic biography, *The Power Broker* (1974), did not paint a flattering picture, and subsequent writers have carried on the remorseless criticism of what and how Moses built. Jane Jacobs, in contrast, is seen as the patron saint of a humane urban vision. Her words and ideas, written from the margins of power and influence, have now become the standard orthodoxy. Her ideas of small scale, recycling buildings and congenial places have become the mantra of the New Urbanism.

Moses and Jacobs have become archetypes: Apollo and Earth Mother; power-crazed old man and the wise, kindly woman. They have become opposite poles: the bloodless, rational, modernist versus the feeling, sensitive, nurturer. Moses left a legacy of bitterness and regret, while Jacobs was midwife to a more sensitive postmodern urbanism.

12

The City and Nature

Over 5,000 years ago a sophisticated urban culture emerged in Mesopotamia. In cities such as Lagash, Ur and Uruk, irrigation, writing and the understanding of the stars were first developed on a systematic basis. Around 4,300 years ago the cities were organized into the world's first empire centred on the city of Akkhad. Standardized rules, weights and measures were introduced and artistic expression flourished. A complex urban culture was created. And then suddenly the empire collapsed. The once proud cities were laid low and eventually abandoned to the desert winds. Recent research suggests the cause was a severe drought. A mighty urban empire was brought to its knees by climate change: this gives us a reminder that the city, the most human of inventions, is precariously predicated upon ecological systems of water circulation and climate change.

Cities provide inevitable contrast with the 'natural'. A consistent strand of thought has sought to place the city as a human invention in opposition to the 'natural', the 'pristine', the 'wilderness'. Cities have been described and understood as somehow separate from the so-called 'natural' world. This has been reinforced by the increasing separation of life in the city from the wider environmental context. When food is more available in a supermarket aisle and less in a field outside our homes, and when we can turn up the heating to keep out the cold and/or turn on the air conditioning to keep out the oppressive heat, there is a tendency to see the city as somehow apart from the physical world.

Urban theorizing has for a long time been conducted on a flat, featureless plain. For too long urban studies have ignored the physical nature of cities, the emphasis having been on the social rather than the ecological. And yet cities are ecological systems which are predicated upon the physical world mediated through the complex prism of social and economic power. In recent years there has been a renewal of interest in the city as ecological system. The emphasis has been on the complex relationships between environmental issues and urban concerns, between social networks and ecosystem flows. The starting point is the assertion that the

177

cities are as much natural as wilderness, and the environment is as much social as the city. We can examine the range and focus of this research through a brief consideration of the work of William Cronon, Mike Davis, Erik Swyngedouw and Martin Gandy.

Reorientations

In his 1991 book, *Nature's Metropolis*, Cronon examines the relationship between Chicago and its hinterland from 1850 to 1890. He shows how the physical world was turned into a commodified human landscape as grain, lumber and meat production transformed prairies and woodlands into the physical basis for the city's growth and development. Merchants, railway owners and primary producers transformed the 'wilderness' into a humanized landscape that was the basis for the city's impressive economic growth. Cronon's work demonstrates that urban economic growth draws heavily on a physical world.

In *The Ecology of Fear* (1998), Davis continues his work on Los Angeles by looking at the 'natural disasters' that continually threaten the metropolitan reign. From the storms that sweep across the basin from the Pacific, to the wildfires of summer and the landslides that push expensive houses into the valley or sea below, Davis presents a picture of a city in an ecological disaster zone. While enormously exaggerated (a common feature of the LA School) and marvellously overwritten, Davis' does point to the often-fragile presence cities have on the surface of the earth. They are subject to droughts and floods, heat waves and biting cold. Everyone will remember those images from the tsunami in Southeast Asia, as waves full of debris and mud swept people up and away in a deadly torrent. The images were a cruel reminder of the unforeseen physical forces that can wreak havoc on our cities and our lives.

We need to make the point that 'natural' disasters are, on closer inspection, much more closely connected to social processes than their name would suggest. Wildfires are less a pure ecological phenomenon than one deeply affected by land-use patterns and burning practices, and the death and destruction is in part less a fault of nature and more a result of social practices. When people build on eroding hillsides or locate houses in earthquake zones, then the natural disaster turns out to be in part a social construction. And the term 'natural' disaster also hides the social implication of their effect. Poor countries are more affected by floods and storms because they do not have expensive technology to provide as much early warning or as rapid evacuation as richer countries. The same level of storm would have vastly different human consequence in different places.

On closer inspection the natural appears more social, and the social life of cities is more accurately seen as implicated in natural processes. The city is the centre of a social–nature dialectic. This dialectic is the focus of Gandy's (2002) book *Concrete and Clay: Reworking Nature in New York City*. Gandy looks at the urbanization of nature in New York City and explores a series of relationships between nature, the city and social power in his consideration of the creation of the city's water supply, Central Park, the construction of urban parkways, a radical Puerto Rican environmental group in the 1960s and 1970s, and an anti-waste campaign in the Green Point–Williamsburg district of Brooklyn. The final two sections deal with the issue of the environmental justice movement in a city where toxic facilities and land use are consistently concentrated in minority-dominated areas of the city, and major infra-structure projects, such as the Cross-Bronx Expressway, have destroyed viable neighbourhoods. He also points to the privatization dynamic and the current danger of corporate, non-democratic takeover of water supply, waste disposal, and other environmental services.

The interconnecting relationships between 'natural and 'social' is at the heart of Swyngedouw's (2004) book, *Social Power and the Urbanization of Water*. He focuses on water in cities and in particular the city of Guayaquil in Ecuador, where 600,000 people lack easy access to potable water. He shows that flows of water are deeply bound up with flows of power and influence; water provision is not simply about connecting supply and demand but about the interconnections between the physical and the social, the environmental and the political. He concludes with a call for a more progressive water politics. The role of water in the historical geography of cities is also explored in a more general way by Maria Kaika (2005).

Even this relatively brief review of these contrasting works reveals a similarity in theoretical outlook; the city is implicated with the 'natural' world in connections that embody and reflect social, economic and polit-ical power. The city is an integral part of nature and nature is intimately interwoven into the social life of cities.

The City as Ecosystem

The physical geographer Ian Douglas (1981) suggests that the city itself can be seen as an ecosystem with inputs of energy and water and outputs of noise, climate change, sewage, rubbish and air pollutants. Another way to consider the city–nature dialectic, then, is to consider the city as an ecological system with a measurable amount of environmental inputs and outputs. Amongst the most obvious inputs are energy and water.

Human activity in the city is dependent on large and regular inputs of energy. When we leave heated buildings to drive in cars to purchase goods, we use energy. The commercial activities we pursue, the micro-climates we create, heating in winter, cooling in summer, all use energy. In seeking to overthrow the tyranny of nature, cities use prodigious amounts of energy. Despite improvements in energy efficiency, cities are deeply dependent on energy sources. In some countries the structure of cities is a function of energy costs. In the US, where petroleum has tradi-tionally been very cheap, cities sprawl across the landscape. In countries where energy is more expensive, cities tend to be higher density and more reliant on public transport. Large-scale suburban sprawl is a function of cheap energy. It is tempting to theorize the impact of a long-term, sustained increase in energy prices on suburban sprawl and urban struc-ture.

Water is an essential ingredient of life. Both the people and the commerce of cities are utterly dependent upon water. One of the largest urban differences in the world is between cities with clean, easily acces-sible water and others where it is expensive, inaccessible and polluted. In order to provide cheap, clean water immense engineering projects have been undertaken. And as cities have grown, the catchment areas have extended outwards and the engineering sophistication of piping in water has grown and deepened. In poorer cities in the world polluted urban water is a major source of disease and illness, especially for children.

Even in rich countries the availability of fresh water is a determinant of the limits of urban growth. In the arid west of the US, for example, urban growth has been predicated upon massive federal subsidies and expensive engineering projects that have provided fresh water at low cost to the consumers. The ecological limits are always more flexible than the environmental determinists suggest, but neither are they infinitely extendable. We may be reaching the 'water' limits of urban growth in the arid US.

Cities also modify the environment. The most obvious example is the urban heat island. Cities tend to be warmer because of the amount of extra heat produced in the city and the heat absorption of tarmac and concrete. Heat is absorbed by these surfaces during the day and released at night. The net result is for the air around cities to be warmer than surrounding rural areas. One side effect is to reduce the need for heating in the winter but to increase the need for air-conditioning in the summer. The heat island means you can turn the heating down in London in December but need to increase the air conditioning in Washington, DC, in August. The extra heat leads to the thermally induced upward movement of air, and an increase in cloud and raindrop formation. Cities are cloudier, more prone to thunder and slightly warmer than rural areas.

Human activity in the city also produces pollutants. Industrial processes and vehicle engines all emit substances that include carbon oxides, sulphur oxides, hydrocarbons, dust, soot and lead. The air in cities has traditionally been very unhealthy, which is part of the reason for the higher urban death rate throughout most of human history. The pall of smog that hangs over many cities is a visible reminder of the effects of concentrated human activity on the environment. The pollutants of cities are not only injurious to the health of individuals, but they also cause more general damage; cities are in part a major cause of global warming and ozone depletion.

A major output of cities is waste. High mass consumption in association with elaborate packaging has created a rising tide of rubbish in cities. Burning it causes air pollution, while hiding it leads to massive landfills. The environmental justice literature shows that these are generally located in more weakly organized communities. As in so many cases, issues of environmental management are tied into wider issues of equity and social justice. Patterns of environmental racism are clear when we note that most noxious facilities are located in lower-income, more marginal communities.

Cities also emit noise. Cities are noisy places and those who inhabit busy urban streets for more than 15 years are on average likely to experience a 50 per cent reduction in hearing capacity. The effects of noise pollution vary from annoyance through to deterioration in hearing. A high backroom noise level leads to a general increase in stress and a lessening of the quality of urban life.

Cities often develop along rivers, water frontages and coastal locations, and are therefore an integral part of the hydrological cycle. Cities modify the flow and direction of rivers in order to increase commercial activity. Cities impact the daily and seasonal flows of water. The large amount of impermeable surfaces, for example, means that when it rains, run-off levels spike dramatically. Cities thus need to create modified flows through channels and conduits that can cope with the irregular high flow rates. As urbanization increases, so does the over-loading of the hydrological cycle. Cities tend to pollute water systems, reducing the amount of fresh water and in some cases posing major health hazards.

In *The Los Angeles River*, Blake Gumprecht (1999) tells the story of the relationship between one city and one river. Before western invasion, the river system supported a dense network of Native American settlements. Later it proved the main reason for the location of a new city. The river provided drinking water and irrigation for farms. Orange groves were watered with river water. As urbanization extended along the riverbank the seasonal floods caused more and more damage. A series of winter storm floods in the late nineteenth and early twentieth centuries led to calls for greater river management. The river was channelled into 51 miles of concrete culverts. Now it is a completely urban river, occasionally running through an entirely human-made channel system, but little more than a small trickle of water flowing through a wide concrete scar through the city. Gumprecht's book is subtitled *The Life, Death and Possible Rebirth*. He suggests that the exhumation of the river and the greening of its riverbank could become important goals of ecological restoration, environmental improvement and urban renewal. In this regard Los Angeles is like many other cities around the world that see the greening of the city as a possible focus of urban makeovers. Urban environmental improvements are now often the centrepiece of urban renewal projects. Former industrial cities now see the cleaning-up of industrial pollution as a vital stage in creating both a new city and a new image of the city. Improving the urban environment has become an important trend and goal in urban reimagineering. The Sydney Olympic Games of 2000, for example, took place at Homebush Bay, a former toxic waste site; after the Games, part of the site was developed as a new suburb.

To theorize the city as an ecological unit is to open new possibilities for understanding the environmental inputs necessary for urban growth and the environmental impacts of urban growth.

An Urban Environmental Story

As one example consider the giant urban region of Megalopolis that extends along the northeastern seaboard of the US. In his classic 1961 study, Jean Gottmann identified this region and explored major social trends. He said very little, however, about the environmental impacts. In a follow-up study I updated the work. Megalopolis now consists of 52,310 square miles stretching across 12 states, one district (the District of Columbia) and 117 counties. In 1950 the population of Megalopolis was almost 32 million. By 2000 it had increased to almost 49 million. In absolute terms the area saw an increase in population of almost 17 million people. While the Megalopolis share of the total US population fell from almost 21 per cent to just over 17 per cent, this change can be read in a number of ways. On the one hand, it does indicate a relative shift in national population away from Megalopolis. The rise of the Sunbelt and the postwar growth across the country, especially in California and the West, has shrunk the relative share of the population of Megalopolis. On the other hand, this small area of just over 52,000 square miles with only 1.4 per cent of the national land surface still contains over 17.3 per cent of the population. Despite the redistribution of the US population to the south and west, Megalopolis continues to remain a significant centre for the nation's population, with almost 1 in 6 of all the US population in this one giant urban region. In 1950 the average population density was 610 persons per square mile, but by 2000 it had increased to 931 persons per square mile. While Megalopolis has lost some of its dominance, it continues to be the home of a significant population concentration at densities much higher than the national average. Megalopolis is still the largest single concentration of population in the US.

The environmental impact of this population is enormous. More people driving more cars in ever more journeys; more people running dishwashers, flushing toilets and showers; more people in more and bigger houses. It is arguably the most environmentally impacted region of the country subject to the constant and growing stress of a rising population with an ever-growing list of needs and desires.

Consider automobiles: using the standard estimates of one car for every 5 people in 1950 and 1 car for every 2 people in 2000 gives us a total of 6.4 million cars in 1950 and 24.25 million cars in 2000. In the same surface area, the number of cars has almost quadrupled. And this total does not include the buses, cars and trucks that pass through this region from outside. There are now, at the very lowest estimate, over 24 million vehicles releasing exhaust, needing roads and requiring parking spaces. The landscape has had to be completely rewritten to give these cars the space and freedom to move throughout the region.

Turning to water usage, the figures are as follows. In 1950 daily per capita water withdrawals for the US were around 1,027 gallons, and by 1995 (the latest available statistic) this figure had increased to 1,500 gallons per capita per day. In Megalopolis, not only had the population increased but the daily withdrawal had increased by 50 per cent per head. These statistics need to be treated with some care since using national statistics will tend to over-estimate rates of withdrawal since per capita water usage is lower in urban areas than rural areas. However, while the absolute amounts are only very rough estimates, their direction is clear.

Total water withdrawal increased in the region by over 150 per cent from 1950 to 2000.

A similar picture emerges for municipal rubbish generation. The figures only go as far back as 1980 when 151.5 lb was generated per person per day. By 2000 it was 231.9 lb per person per day. By the end of the twentieth century the population of Megalopolis was generating approximately *5,600 tons of rubbish per day.*

Whatever the measure, it is the same story of increasing population in association with increased affluence and spiralling consumption, producing greater environmental impacts and increased strain on the natural systems that sustain and nurture life. An incredible environmental transformation has been wrought across the region as rural land has been subdivided into suburbia and more population (with a greater environmental impact) has been crammed into the region. Close to 50 million people, with the greatest environmental impact per head in the history of the world, now live in Megalopolis.

Urban Sustainability

A central notion in the city and nature debate is urban sustainability, which is the idea that cities should environmentally sustainable over the longer term. There is a widely shared belief that many cities impose such heavy environmental costs that the long-term future of the city may be undermined; the heavy reliance on fossil fuels, for example, and the increasing use of the private car as the main urban transport mode tend to degrade the environment. The problems are particularly acute in rapidly growing cities and cities in poor countries where environmental regulation is weaker and environmental improvement may not be an important political issue (see Panayotou, 2001). In China, for example, the rapid and often unregulated economic growth of the past 20 years has been purchased with the severe degradation of air, water and land. We can picture a three-stage model of the relationship between cities and environmental sensitivity: in the early stages urban growth is small and environmental impacts, while strong, are very localized. As we move into a more industrialized mode of production, environmental degradation is more severe as the environmental impacts are heavier and longer lasting. As the economy matures and people become more affluent, a greater premium is placed on the quality of the urban environment. Chinese cities are at this second stage of development. However, it is also apparent that in cities around the world, rich and poor, developed and less developed, the struggle to live in a better urban environment, one with clean water, fresh air and pleasant conditions, is a fundamental source of mobilization and action (Evans, 2002).

Questions of environmental quality are intimately connected to issues of social justice; the worst environmental conditions are imposed on the lower-income, most marginal urban residents. Poverty and environmental degradation tend to go hand in hand in a web of multiple deprivation and social exclusion. Haughton (1999) presents principles of sustainable development that also are aware of social justice: intergenerational equity, geographic equity, procedural equity and interspecies equity. He also goes on to suggest approaches to achieving sustained development including the creating more self-reliant cities that reduce the environmental impact on the wider bioregion and redesigning cities so that land is used more effectively and rationally. Hough (2004) also lays out a road map for urban sustainability that recognizes the importance of maintaining the integrity of urban ecosystems. One oft-touted example of a more suitable city development is Curtiba in Brazil. This city of 1.6 million people developed a master plan in 1965 that limited central city growth and guided development to two north–south running corridors. The concentrated growth allowed the more effective use of public transport. There are now 1,100 buses that carry 1.4 million passengers a day, and a network of pedestrian routes that allow people to travel by foot in the central business area. The net result is less demand for private car usage so that there is less pollution and a more pleasant urban environment. Many cities in the developed world could learn from Curtiba. Sustainable development practices can flow from poor to rich countries as well as from rich to poor countries. In many poor countries, the need to husband scarce resources, recycle goods and reimagine the city provides a rich context for new urban practices.

Nature and the City

Cities also reference nature. Since the nineteenth century there has been an explicit urban park movement and landscape architects such as Frederick Law Olmsted have left a permanent legacy on cities. It is difficult to imagine New York without Central Park or Washington without the Mall. The modern park movement is more closely tied into active participation than the environmental contemplation so beloved of the early park movement. Now city parks are developed as much for their recreational opportunities as their aesthetic appeal. Successful cities realize that the successful referencing of nature is an important element in creating the right atmosphere. Whether it is in the beaches of southern California, the lakeside shore of Chicago, or the parks of London and Paris, a commonly accepted attractive feature of urban life is the successful incorporation of nature into the urban lifestyle, the city's image and the metropolitan experience.

Nature is present in cities in often unforeseen and unplanned ways. Wildlife in a variety of forms continues to find ecological niches in the city. Urban tensions can be written through the narration of the relationship between cities and wildlife. Urban animal geographies can tell us much about the city–nature dialectic, whether it is in the stories of rats in cities or the story of hawks in the city. Consider the case of Pale Male and Lola, the two red-tailed hawks that made their nest in the façade of an exclusive high-rise apartment block in New York City's Fifth Avenue. Hawks have been noticed in the area since 1998 and every year the birds would return to nest, breed and feed their young. Birdwatchers followed their progress through binoculars, cameras and websites. There is something heroic about the capacity of hawks to thrive in the city. Some residents of the apartment block thought otherwise. The president of the coop board, the wealthy real estate developer Richard Cohen, unilaterally ordered the nest removed in December 2004. Residents had complained that the hawks were causing a mess on the sidewalk. Red-tailed hawks are rare enough to have been protected by a treaty signed in 1918 between several nations, including the US, Canada and Russia. An earlier attempt to evict the birds was blocked when their defenders invoked this international agreement. Under one provision, a red-tailed hawk nest could be removed if it contained no eggs or chicks. The coop board used this loophole. Their decision sparked off a major protest. Protesters dressed as birds mounted a vigil across the street from the building. The media got the story. One subtext was resistance to the notion that the power of the wealthy could rewrite the ecology of the city. Apartments at 927 Fifth Avenue can sell for as much as $18 million, and residents include the wealthy and the famous. The image of very rich residents evicting hawks from their perch was too delicious to ignore. The extremely negative publicity for the apartment building and its residents eventually led to a reversal of the eviction. Pale Male and Lola still nest on the building. You can follow the urban saga of Pale Male and Lola at their own website, www.palemale.com.

Not all wildlife that shares the urban environment is as welcome as Pale Male and Lola. Rats, for example, have managed to find a home in the most cities. They inhabit the dark tunnels and the hidden recesses of the city, and have become symbols of disease and decay; they bring out fear and loathing rather than love and respect. And yet, like the cuddlier animals or the more photogenic birds, they too are urban survivors.

Theorizing the city–nature dialectic is possible through careful case studies that explore the different and myriad ways in which cities are ecosystems, how the city embodies nature while nature is an integral part of urban life. Our cities are more environmental than traditional urban studies suggest, while nature is more urbanized than most environmental studies credit. We can only try to improve our understanding of the physical environment by considering its many and subtle links with the city and we can only enhance our understanding of the city by exploring its relationship to the physical world.

13
The City of Difference

In his magisterial work *Labour and Life of London* (1902–3), Charles Booth identified different parts of the city. He produced a colour-coded map of individual streets. He used a seven-colour classification which showed the 'lowest class' in black, the 'very poor' in blue, 'mixed populations' in purple, 'fairly comfortable' in pink, the 'middle class' in red, and the 'wealthy upper class' in yellow. The main variable used to distinguish the areas was the percentage of poverty. Booth also drew wider descriptions. The areas of black were, 'lowest class, vicious, semi-criminal'. Booth's work was based on the experience of the rapidly expanding cities growing in size and complexity. The mapping of different areas of the Victorian city was like the mapping of colonial territories in Africa and Asia; it was an attempt at understanding and controlling new spaces.

The identification of different areas of the city has been a consistent element of urban study. Three themes predominate: what are the different areas of a city; what do they represent; and how do they reinforce and undermine other sources of difference?

Models of Residential Areas

Sjoberg (1960) developed a model of the pre-industrial city in which the city centre is the hub of government and religious activity, and this is where the elite live; a lower class of merchants and artisans are grouped around the elite; and on the extremities of the city are outcast groups of slaves, and minority ethnic and religious groups. The city is very cellular, with little separation between home and work place and a close juxta-position of different land uses. Residences are often both living areas and sites of work and small-scale production. The residential areas are divided into quarters based on regional, religious or ethnic origins. In Islamic cities, for example, there were Jewish and Christian districts, while in Christian cities Jews were restricted to a ghetto. Dwellings were often built with windows facing away from the street into an inner courtyard that ensured the privacy of family life; houses in family compounds were inhabited by extended kinship groups. Social status declines as one moves further away from the central city. The patterns may be complicated by the existence of domestic servants in the elite area and the existence of distinct ethnic and occupational districts, but the general model holds of a rigid class structure and racial ethnic differences mapped directly on to urban space. This model has been tested in variety of circumstances (Langton, 1975; Radford, 1979).

While Sjoberg's work was concerned with cities of the ancient world, his model still has some relevance today as elements of the preindustrial city can still be found, particularly in cities that did not experience such profound industrialization as the cities of Europe and North America. A whole variety of models of Third World cities, for example, include important pre-industrial elements. Models of African cities contain 'stranger' communities, models of south Asian cities include the wealthy elite sections, and models of southeast Asian cities have an 'alien' commercial zone (McGee, 1967; Brunn, Williams and Ziegler, 2003; Dutt and Pomeroy, 2003).

Consider just one element, elite residences. They play a significant part in Latin American cities that lack a mass middle class. The Griffin–Ford model suggests that the typical Latin American city can be divided into five major zones: a central business district, an elite residential zone and three concentric zones of housing in which residential quality declines with distance (Griffin and Ford, 1980; Ford, 1996). Crowley (1998) suggests a more complex model in which commercial and industrial land uses overlap residential zones. A key element in most models of Latin American cities is the importance of the elite residential areas. In highly polarized societies with a relatively small middle class, the elite residential areas are a very important element in the urban environment that signifies wealth and privilege. They are not insignificant parts of the urban scene and the urban imagination. One dominant model suggests that the elite residential areas are continually on the move as the rich seek the latest in housing form with the housing stock filtering down the socioeconomic scale.

In cities with a small middle class and limited public housing provision, the filtering of housing is an important element in the housing market. Ryder (2004) tests this assumption in Quito. The elite area of Mariscal Sucre was first developed in the 1920 with extravagant homes. Until 1975 it retained its exclusivity and residential status. In the mid-1970s the fashionable residential areas experienced the influx of up-market businesses meeting the commercial needs of local residents. By the 1980s there was sustained commercialization of area so that by 1993 it was a fully-fledged business area. In the mid- to late 1990s the areas experienced another change, as it became a destination for low budget tourists, a place of language schools and a red-light district. Ryder's study shows the diversification of land use in elite residential areas and its changing character as up-market business are replaced by less salubrious commercial uses.

Two major changes caused a substantial rupture in the residential patterning of urban space. The first was the imprint of colonialism on cities around the world. With primary reference to the British in Egypt, although capable of wider usage, Timothy Mitchell (1988) identifies three broad strategies for the framing of colonial states: producing a plan of urban segmentation that includes racial segregation; creating a fixed distinction between inside and outside; and constructing central spaces of observation to keep an eye on things and to show the presence of colonial power. Colonization involved a rewriting of urban space to show who was in control and who was controlled. Take the case of Tunis and Hanoi. Tunis came under French rule in 1881. A new town was laid out on a grid-iron plan right beside the old Islamic city. The garden suburbs of the French colonizers provided a rich contrast to the spontaneous settlement at the edge of the city that housed the huge influx of migrants from the countryside. The planned differences in the colonial city between public and private and between home and work stood in stark contrast to the cellular structure of the old Islamic city. When the French established Hanoi as the capital of French Indochina in 1887, they created a city in their own image. Long wide boulevards, reminiscent of Haussmann's Paris, were cut through the city, public parks were laid out and new buildings were constructed that would not look out of place in Paris or Bordeaux. After 1954 street names were changed from French to Vietnamese as part of the postcolonial re-appropriation of the city.

The major impact of colonization on the urban residential space was the containment of the natives in easily policed areas and the housing of the colonists in urban forms derived from the metropolitan centre. Cities were rewritten to be easily read and understood. Postcoloniality is in part an attempt to rewrite the city. As we have seen with reference to Calcutta, the neighbourhoods of the colonial elites became the preferred location for the new elites of postindependent nations. There were simple takeovers of urban space as well as reconstructions, erasures and re-inscriptions. Myers (2003) follows the story of urban development in Africa from colonial to postcolonial, tracing the experience of urban planning amongst three groups: the colonial power, the colonized middle and the urban majority.

The second major source of rupture to the rational pattern of urban residential space was industrialization. Large-scale industrial production largely replaced domestic production and laid the basis for the erosion of a cellular city of mixed land uses. As influential residents complained of the noise and pollution, land-use controls were developed that separated out commercial and residential uses. There was a growing separation between work and home and also major changes in the very understanding of home and work: the home was visualized as place of non-work and relaxation, although it still had to be serviced by domestic labour. Industrialization in the capitalist mode of production also created new classes. The most significant element of change was the emergence of a working class that, when well organized, became a significant element in political discourse. As primitive accumulation was superseded by high mass consumption, a mass middle class was created and the distinction between very poor and very wealthy was replaced with more complex patterns of socio-economic differentiation.

A number of models were developed to explain these new patterns. The Chicago School produced a very influential model of the city in the early phases of industrialization. Burgess (1925) developed a zonal model of urban growth shaped by large-scale immigration. As new waves of immigrants moved into the cheap renting areas of the central city, there was a steady push outwards. In the Burgess model the zone of transition (zone II) encircled the central business district (zone I). The manufacturing and commercial land uses of zone I kept invading the deteriorating residential areas of zone II. In zone III were the workers who had escaped from the deteriorating conditions of the zone II, but who needed to keep close to their work in the central city. Zone IV consisted of high-class apartment buildings and the exclusive areas of single-family dwellings. Zone V, the commuter zone, was the suburban area of single-family dwellings.

The Burgess model, developed in Chicago in the 1920s, has a number of assumptions, including a mono-nucleated city and the constant out-movement of population. The Burgess model rests very firmly on the experience of Chicago when the vast majority of immigrants were poor and only able to afford the cheap inner-city accommodation. A test of the model by Schnore (1965) found the Chicago model was only one of three possible types. While the Chicago model assumed low income groups in the centre and high income groups in the suburbs, two other patterns were possible: high and low income groups in the centre and the middle income groups in the suburbs, such as in New Orleans; and a Fort Smith type where the rich were in the centre and the poor in the suburbs. Schnore went on to propose an evolutionary model of residential structure. In the pre-industrial city high status groups lived close to the city centre; with the onset of modernization the central city became the location of both high and low income groups; and in the mature modern city the higher income groups moved out to the more distant suburbs.

The Burgess model reflects a private housing market where effective housing demand is dominated by the private market. Prior to 1945 in the US the poor had limited purchasing power and the middle class had restricted access to credit that would have enabled owner occupation. The new housing market was dominated by the affluent. In this context Homer Hoyt (1939) developed a sector model in which the high status residential sectors form zones which radiate out from the CBD along transport routes towards the homes of community leaders. The rich keep moving out to new housing and their abandoned housing filters down the income scale. Remember that Hoyt was writing when socialism seemed to hold out a promise for better management of a system that seemed stuck in depression. The model's process of filtering chimes in with arguments that the private market does work to provide housing. Leave the rich to their wealth and the housing market to private forces and housing will be provided, if the primate market works. We may agree or disagree with Hoyt about the efficacy of the process but most would agree that high status areas to tend to have a sectoral pattern. And here the point needs to be made that while similar patterns of urban residential structure can be found in different cities, the underlying processes may sharply differ.

The Burgess and Hoyt models have had a huge impact in urban studies throughout the late twentieth century. Burgess's zones were tested across many different societies. Hoyt's sector model, and especially his identification of filtering, were also evaluated in many cities. As classic works they have stimulated research and provided points of origin as well as points of departure.

The data analysis employed by the early model builders was crude. A new level of sophistication was added by Shevky and Williams (1949). To identify different residential areas in Los Angeles they used indices of social rank, urbanization and segregation derived from many different variables. The three indices were used to construct an eighteen-cell classification of census tracts with similar values. They called their cells *social areas*, and the method became widely known as social area analysis. The early reviews of their work criticized the lack of theoretical justification of

th
so(
is t
soc
Nev
forc
ethn
ent p;

M(
of the
have a
capital
occupa
(and as
househo
around t
racial gro
dimensio
trial restru
of social s
important
World capi

located where they are. It is strong on pattern but we
structuring of urban residential space is largely
traditional social areas analysis. In the 1970s
on pattern analysis there was the developm
sought to understand the behavioural de
patterning of urban space. L.A. Bro
a model of residential relocation
urban migration. There wa
approach that concentra
choices, and the const
school of thought
study of urban
ment and i
Ray Pa
Wh

... cities of First

Social ar _ analysis is now more of an inductive investigative tool. Fine-grained residential areas are now easily found through the use of statistical techniques of factor analysis and principal components analysis. Social areas analysis is an extremely popular technique for market research. To take just one example, Weiss (2000) uses the technique to identify clusters of social groupings and associated demographic snapshots that are the basis for target marketing in the US. Amongst the more than 15 social groupings (with examples of selected snapshots) he identifies are elite suburbs (for example, blue blood estates, winner's circle); the influential (young suburban town-house couples, young white-collar suburban families); urban cores (ethnically mixed urban singles and inner-city solo parent families); and working towns (retirement town seniors and low-income blue collar families). The classification of residential neighbourhoods is now an established marketing tool, with consumer behaviour discriminated spatially for targeted advertisements and product development.

Social area analysis has proved less effective in theoretical development because it is limited to identifying patterns. It explains where certain groups are, but it cannot explain how and why certain groups are

ak on process. The
gnored or assumed in
n reaction to the reliance
nt of behavioural models that
cision-making that lay behind the
n and E.G. Moore (1970) developed
that theorizes the reasons behind intra-
also the development of an institutional
d on housing constraints as much as housing
uction of the decision-making environments. This
looked at issues of power and conflict as well at the
managers and institutions who shaped the urban environ-
stitutions such as public agencies and private corporations.
(1975) summarizes the approach in the title of his 1975 book,
e City? Urban managerialism and the institutional approach was
so an important strand in the political economy approach that looked at
the role of the wider social and economic context in shaping urban residential patterns (Bassett and Short, 1980).

The Dynamics of the Housing Market

Residential areas of the city are shaped by a complex set of forces. The
dynamics of the housing market are particularly important.
Understanding the housing market allows a deeper examination of the
process whereby certain groups are allocated to different parts of the city.

Cardoso and Short (1983) make an important distinction between
different modes of housing production. *Self-produced housing*, as the
name suggests, involves people building their own dwellings. This was
common in the past and today is still found in much less developed countries. In the housing markets of many Third World cities the self-build
sector is strong and a large body of literature has developed. Janet Abu-
Lughod (2004), for example, details the informal settlements around
Cairo, including the area of Manshiet Nasser that houses around 500,000
people. Although this began as a way of coping with the lack of affordable and available housing, informal settlements are often aided by
government intervention such as the provision of basic services of water
and sewerage.

In the *individual contract mode of housing production* buyers hire
builders to construct accommodation. It is restricted to the wealthy who
can afford the extensive costs. While of numerical insignificance, such

housing often has huge architectural significance. Frank Lloyd Wright, for example, designed and built houses for the wealthy. Houses such as Falling Water in Pennsylvania are architectural statements as well as accommodation.

The *large-scale contract mode of production* involves builders constructing large numbers of houses for public or private customers. The contract mode in the private sector emerges in a private market system in which housing is fully commodified. The contract mode also occurs in the public sector in the construction of public sector housing.

Speculative production has emerged as the single most important mode of production in the advanced capitalist countries. It involves the construction of dwellings by builders for a general demand rather than an individual customer. It is associated with owner occupation. It is dependent on a system of fiscal arrangements that allows builders to extend credit lines and enables buyers to purchase housing on credit. Housing is expensive, and immediate house purchase is beyond the reach of many households. A mass market of owner occupation can only be created by complex fiscal arrangements and a sophisticated credit system. A mass of owner occupiers is only possible with government intervention that enables financial institutions to lend large amounts of money to individuals over long periods of time: the typical mortgage ranges from 25 to 30 years. Speculative housing is now an important part of the national economy; it is an index of general economic health as well as being a sector which is stimulated and deflated by government changes in interest rates.

These different modes of production are not mutually exclusive; the precise mix will vary across the world by city. In less developed countries self-produced housing is likely to be a substantial element, while in cities in advanced capitalist countries speculative housing will dominate. The mix of modes will vary over time as increasing economic development and the increasing commoditization of economic transaction are reflected in changes in housing production.

Housing is very expensive. It signifies the single biggest cost to most households. Immediate house purchase is not possible except for a few wealthier households. We can theorize the three main tenure categories – private renting, public housing and owner-occupation – as different mechanisms to overcome the high cost of housing. In the case of private renting landlords own property that they let out to tenants. There is often conflict between landlords and tenants. Landlords would like to maximize rents and tenants would prefer to minimize rent payments. The history of urban social movements is studded with rent struggles. In many countries legislative frameworks that lay out the rights and obligations (and sometimes even set maximum rent levels) guide landlord–tenant relations. Private renting is common in very big cities with an older housing stock.

In the case of public housing the landlord is the government or a government-chartered public entity. The rise of public housing is a function of the power of the social welfare movement and the organized working class, and a reflection of the government's commitment to extensive social welfare. Public housing is most established in societies with powerful labour organizations and strong traditions of social welfare. The rise and fall of public housing is an indicator of the rise and fall of social welfare. In UK, for example, public housing constituted almost 34 per cent of the total housing stock by the early 1970s before beginning a steady decline as public housing was sold off and little new public housing was constructed.

Owner occupation has emerged as the dominant tenure form in many cities in the advanced capitalist world. In the first half of the twentieth century, owner occupation was a minority tenure limited to the wealthy. Most people lived in private renting. The high cost of housing meant that most people could only become owner occupiers with cheap credit that enabled them to take out a large loan to purchase the dwelling and then pay the debt off over a large number of years. Financial institutions had to be encouraged to make large loans over extended time periods. Owner occupation was an important tenure category in Australian cities in the early twentieth century, but in North America and western Europe owner occupation was first encouraged in the 1930s as a way to stimulate the building industry during the Depression. Since 1950 it has become an important policy of governments to encourage owner occupation.

One argument is that the encouragement of owner occupation is an ideological attempt to create nation of small property owners whose values chime with the property basis of capitalist societies. The encouragement of owner occupation produces a nation of property owners with a stake in society. Another argument points to the economic rationale for encouraging owner occupation: it is an important stimulant of effective demand in the economy. Once established as a major tenure type, owner occupation becomes an important element in political decision-making. At the national level, owner occupiers are immediately affected by interest rate increases since their mortgages are so dependent on credit conditions. At the local level, owner occupiers play an important role in shaping land-use decisions. For owner occupiers, the value of their dwelling is often their biggest single asset. Negative externalities can bring down the value while positive externalities can raise the value.

Owner occupiers form pressure groups to deflect negative and attract positive externalities; the NIMBY (Not In My Back Yard) phenomenon is only properly understood as a hard material interest.

The built environment can be theorized as a physical space that represents the conflict and compromises between capital circulation, capitalist reproduction and the struggles of social groups with a stake in the built environment. Mass owner occupation is a very good example of this nexus of interests. Encouraged by governments eager to reproduce capitalist social relations, and produced by capitalist firms, it also involves a social group which is particularly sensitive to changes in the built environment. Whether protesting about a highway or an airport extension, owner occupiers as a mobilized group can influence the production and management of the built environment.

The demand for housing varies across the population. The three principal sources of variation are income, stage in the life cycle and race/ethnicity. In the private housing market the best housing in the desirable locations goes to those who can pay the most. The housing market is like a space packing problem, with the wealthier taking up the best spaces and subsequent lower income levels taking up less attractive or desired locations. At the bottom of the income scale the poorest experience the least choice. The income to housing quality relationship is mediated in markets where social housing or public housing can provide good housing for more modest income groups.

Households go through different stages in their life cycle with changing space requirements. Single-person households often merge into two-person households and then households with children, increasing the space requirements. When children grow up and leave, space requirements shrink. Short (1978) models the different housing needs associated with different stages in the life cycle. The model applies primarily to western cities. In many developing countries extended family ties are stronger and the separation of households may be less pronounced. In China, for example, it is more common for the eldest son to bring his wife to live with his parents, and sometimes several brothers may set up a joint household that includes their wives, children and parents. As housing markets commodify and cities are modernized, there is a tendency for the nuclear family to dominate the housing market.

Ethnic states and/or racial identity can affect households' housing choices. Both choice and constraints are important. People may prefer to live with people like themselves. Ethnic clustering occurs in cities around the world. Ethnic neighbourhoods provide a support system and a platform to the new society. The degree of clustering is a function of the degree of difference between the group and the dominant population. Ethnic clustering may also result from discrimination, as households are forced explicitly or implicitly to live in certain areas, through coercion or through social sanctions. We can consider two cases of ethnic/racial clustering.

The policy of spatial demarcation by race was an integral part of the apartheid system in white supremacist South Africa. When the policies of apartheid were overturned there was a deracialization of space but segregation continued. There was marked income polarization and a hyper-segregation of poor blacks. The Crankshaw and Parnell (2004) study of Johannesburg found that while interracial inequality decreased, intra-racial inequality increased dramatically. The authors point to the growing division between urbanized Africans and more recent rural migrants. Income inequality, shaped by globalization and deindustrialization, has replaced apartheid policy as the main determinant of spatial segregation. In her detailed study of Chinatown in Vancouver, Kay Anderson (1991) showed that the area was a product of the top-down use of civic power rather than a bottom-up expression of racial identity. Chinatown was a racial and spatial category created by institutional power. Anderson also examines, in a similar vein, the social construction of the 'Aboriginal' Redfern area of Sydney in Australia (Anderson, 1993).

The operating of the housing market in its meshing of supply and demand acts as a sieve to shake households out into distinct residential areas of the city. The larger the city and the more heterogeneous the urban population, the more complex the residential mosaic, as income, stage in the life cycle and race/ethnicity are expressed and embodied in distinct residential areas.

Residential areas are rarely stable. We can theorize the movement of residential areas up and down the income scale, gentrification and filtering respectively, and from expansion through new building to contraction with demolition and/or abandonment. The residential areas of the contemporary city are particularly volatile because of changes in socio-spatial reorganization. Short (1989b), for example, examines Docklands in London as an example of how major changes of deindustrialization, growth of producer services, the rise of the new middle class and the decline of an old working class all work out in a particular urban place. Economic restructuring and new class formations are recorded in the instability and reorganization of urban residential space.

Residential areas have important effects. For the longer-term residents the neighbourhood can be the main locale for social behaviour. Adolescent gangs, for example, are very territorial, and like their turf marked out with gang signs. The neighbourhood effect is a well-documented phenomenon. In his classic study of Sunderland in the UK, Robson (1969) shows that people of similar status but living in different areas had different attitudes to educational attainment, and people with differing status but living in the same area held similar attitudes. Urban social areas seemed to have an effect on an individual's attitudes as well as voting patterns.

Home Sweet Home

Housing is not an ordinary commodity. We spend much of lives in the home, and our primary emotional and connections are shaped in the domestic arena of the home; where we live and how we live are important determinants of our social position, physical health and individual well being. Home is a central element in our socialization into the world. The home is also a place of loathing and longing. The flippant remark by George Bernard Shaw, to the effect that a hotel is a refuge from home, can be counterposed to the deep feeling expressed in the spiritual refrain that a band of angels were 'coming for to carry me home'.

A strange paradox: given its huge significance, there is comparatively little work on the meaning of the home (but see Cieraad, 1999). There is a lopsided understanding of the world; the domestic places of our lives are not given as much attention as the public spaces. We have a lot more work on the work place than the home place. This book corrects some of this imbalance and focuses attention on one of the most important places.

The home is a key site in the social organization of space. It is where space becomes place; where family relations, gender and class identities are negotiated, contested and transformed. The home is an active moment, in both time and space, in the creation of individual identity, social relations and collective meaning. The home is an important site of ideological meanings.

Home is often idealized. What isn't? But it is idealized more often than other places. It is almost as if it has become one of the places where the songs of innocence are sung. Outside the songs of experience are heard. It does not matter that home is a source of work, abuse and exploitation as well as rest, love and nourishment. In the early seventeenth century John Fletcher wrote, 'Charity and beating begins at home.' Domestic abuse and child abuse are nasty in themselves, but public outrage is often heightened by the fact that they take place in the home. It is like a murder in the cathedral; a sacred place defiled. It is no accident,

I feel, that in recent years the home has been seen as a sanctuary just at a time when domestic tensions are increasing. We are losing our sense of the fairness of the polity but hang on to the notion of a domestic harmony. The image of a serene home life haunts our collective and individual imaginations.

The home is a nodal point in a whole series of polarities: journey–arrival; rest–motion; sanctuary–outside; family–community; space–place; inside–outside; private–public; domestic–social; spare-time–work time; feminine–masculine; heart–mind; Being–Becoming. These are not stable categories; they are both solidified and undermined as they play out their meaning and practice in and through the home. The home is a place riven by ambiguities. Contrast the assertion that there is no going home to the belief of the poet Robert Frost that home was the place that, when you go there, they have to take you in. The home is a place of paradoxes.

Beyond Social Area Analysis

Traditional social area analysis identifies the home and the immediate residential area as an important context for community formation, group identity and the shaping of individual attitudes. But our residences are only part of the life we lead in the city, only one node in our socio-spatial networks, an important (although not the only) resting place in the space–time paths we weave across the city. More recent work focuses on the networked communities and the far-flung diasporic communities that transcend the immediate social area. Paul Adams (2005) makes a strong case for more radical ideas of personal borders in space and time. He echoes what Mel Webber (1964) described over 40 years earlier as the elastic mile in his discussion of the non-place urban realm. Identity is shaped by the local and the non-local. Traditional urban studies focuses on communities created in bounded places around local identities. While place and locality are still important, they are just one part in a wider network of complex community ties that can transcend the immediate locality. Space and place are being restructured and reorganized, and we need new urban theories that can make sense of this new world.

Consider the case of citizenship. There has been a renewed interest in the concept as transnational identities, diasporic communities and multicultural societies undermine the more obvious connections between place and citizenship (Kymlicka, 1995). The idea of citizenry is broadened to include issues of access to resources, belonging and the international citizenship formed by the regime of global human rights. Citizenship itself is decon-structed for its variance by gender, class, race and sexual difference. Rogers (2000) considers some of the connections between the city and citizenship: the possibility of the city becoming a site for forms of citi-zenship between the nation state and global regimes; the fact that cities with large and often heterogeneous populaces are sites of pressing ques-tions of identity and belonging; cities are centres of urban social move-ments that generate demands for new forms of citizenship; cities in effect encourage active citizenship. An active citizenship is contested in cities. Cities are the space in which citizenship is created, contested and denied. Holston (2001) looks citizenship in São Paulo, Brazil. From the 1950s to the mid-1970s, rapid urbanization resulted in the growth of squatter settlements on the periphery of the city. The illegalization of these resi-dences was a denial of citizenship. In the mid-1970s urban social move-ments organized around rights to the city and access to health services, education and childcare. The demands for human services were in part a demand for full citizenship. It was an example of the experience of the city leading to new types of citizen, with the urban poor demanding polit-ical rights based on needs rather than abstract political principles. In many globalizing city regions in the developing world the urban experi-ence is the background and platform for new formulations of citizenship. Isin (2001), for example, examines the demands of an Islamic citizenship that grew out of the experience of a globalizing Istanbul. The demand was less a fundamentalist outburst and more a call for a city of virtue.

14

The City and Disorder

According to *Webster's Dictionary*, the term 'disorder' has a number of meanings: first, lack of order, confusion. It also has more social connotations of breach of order, disorderly conduct, and a public disturbance; even a derangement of physical or mental health. In this chapter I want to pursue some of the recurring themes of the city as a site of disorder.

Mapping Disorder

The rapid growth of towns and cities in the nineteenth century was often a cause for alarm amongst many middle- and upper-class commentators. While Karl Marx saw the rapid growth of industrial cities as a source for revolutionary change and a cause for optimism, this prospect worried many others. This fear is the background to the mapping of social differences common in the nineteenth century.

The term 'moral statistics' first appeared in an essay by Andre-Michel Guerry in 1833. It was used to refer to crime, pauperism and a wide range of social phenomena. Such statistics were an important part of nineteenth-century thematic mapping. Maps of crime in France first appeared in 1829 when Balbi and Guerry used data from 1825 to 1827 to plot, for each of the *départements* in the country, the incidence of crimes against persons, crimes against property and educational instruction. Mapping in the early nineteenth century predated the development of statistical techniques. Maps and mapping were an important way to identify causal connections. The Balbi–Guerry maps were not simply mapping crime: they were analysing the covariation of criminal statistics with educational level. The Belgian statistician, Adolphe Quételet, also used maps to suggest connections. His 1831 maps of France, the Low Countries and parts of the Rhineland show statistics on crimes against the property and crimes against people as carefully gradated shading maps. Quetelet was an influential figure in Europe and his work and maps were translated into other languages. In Britain in the 1840s Joseph Fletcher published maps of England and Wales that plotted, amongst others, the number of people of independent means, poverty, levels of literacy, and different types of crime. Fletcher was also on the hunt for the cause of crime, but he disagreed with Quételet that there was no relationship between educational instruction and crime.

Guerry's early efforts developed by the mid-1860s into more sophisticated maps of specific types of crime such as murder, rape, theft by servants and suicide. He used data in both France and England and Wales. His work was eagerly appreciated in the US as well as Germany, and the mapping of crime became an accepted part of cartographic endeavours. The Chicago School mapped urban social variations as predicators of crime rates. A classic study by Shaw and McKay (1942), for example, maps the covariation of various social conditions with reported incidences of juvenile delinquency.

Today the mapping of crime is an important element in contemporary policing. Keith Harries (1999) summarizes the now vast material on the mapping of crime. Maps of crime allow a spatial visualization which is vital to patrol officers, investigators, police managers, policy makers and community organizations. Improvements in GIS (geographic information systems) now allow data to be mapped, presented and correlated. Maps are used to identify areas of high crime activity (so-called hot spots), and mapping the timing and spacing of crimes allows a more efficient use of police resources. In 1994 New York City initiated Computerized Statistics (COMSTAT). Police commanders were made responsible for reducing crime in the rib districts. The accurate and timely flow of intelligence allowed more effective tactics and rapid deployment of personnel and resources. COMSTAT maps were recreated to map the density of various crimes as well potential targets areas for these crimes. A map that showed the days of highest average reported crime density varied in certain districts. Crime was more likely to be committed in some places on certain days. This information allowed police commanders to deploy patrol officers in different strengths in different places on different days. Knowing when crime was more likely to occur allowed a more efficient deployment of officers. There is now a real time response to changing patterns of crime. COMSTAT was so successful that it is widely adopted by many other city police departments. Large urban police departments around the world are at the forefront of the crime mapping.

Not only are crimes mapped, but mapping is also used to help solve crimes. Geographic profiling, like psychological profiling, has become an important part of law enforcement. Geographic profiling assumes that criminal activity is place-specific and that criminals like to use known areas that are not too close to their home location. Criminals do not travel too far from their anchor points to commit crime. Plotting a series of crimes geographically can thus be used to create a probability surface of the location of criminals. Dates and places of crime are mapped in order to provide clues to the location of the criminal.

The mapping of crime is now an important element in the management of urban crime. Keith Harries' book was published by the US Department of Justice, which maintains a website explicitly devoted to crime mapping (see http://www.ojp.usdoj.gov/cmrc). There is now a variety of software for crime mapping and geographic profiling.

The concern with social unrest, the availability of statistics and the work of pioneers all provide the context for numerous mappings of moral statistics. Moral statistics also include the mapping of vice. In 1833 Guerry mapped the numbers of illegitimate children in France. While there have been different definitions of what constitutes vice, as well as virtue, the mapping of such characteristics has been an important part of urban mapping. Mapping vice in cities has been a favourite topic of city maps from the time that the first brothels were marked on maps for the benefit of visitors to the city. Such maps have also been used by the authorities to clamp down on vice.

The background to the mapping of moral statistics is the concern to know where social deviance occurs, but also to look for the covariance of other factors so that the deviance can be understood, controlled and negated. The mapping of moral statistics is not innocent of wider political considerations.

Public anxiety in the early nineteenth century over the public health of industrial cities in Britain led to the creation of the Poor Law Commission which prompted the Ordnance Survey, the government mapping agency, to produce detailed maps of towns and cities. In 1840 cities with a population of over 4,000 were mapped at the detailed scale of 1:1,056. The secretary of the Poor Law Commission, Edwin Chadwick, published an analysis in 1842 that included maps of housing types and incidence of diseases in the city of Leeds, a rapidly expanding industrial city, and Bethnal Green in London, a working-class neighbourhood. The 'less clean' houses were coloured, in obvious cartographic significance, in dark brown, and the key identifies houses of the working class, houses of tradespeople and houses of the first class. Blue spots identified cholera outbreaks and red spots highlighted sites of contagious diseases. Public health was important issue in its own right as well as a reflection of social stability and an embodiment of political control. By the end of the century all cities were mapped at the even more detailed scale of 1:500. These maps provide the authorities with plans of the cities that allowed public health issues to be investigated, and also enabled the authorities to keep a cartographic surveillance on centres of social radicalism. Social control and political surveillance remain important themes in the mapping of cities.

City health authorities also used maps to identify the disorder of breakdowns in public health. Robert Perry, a doctor in Glasgow, mapped the course of an epidemic through the different areas of the city. (The maps were drawn by the inmates of the local Lunatic Asylum in order to 'exercise their facilities'.) One of the most famous medical maps was drawn by Dr John Snow, a doctor working in mid-nineteenth-century London. He was convinced that cholera was communicated by contaminated water. His 1855 work, *On the mode of communication of cholera* (2nd edition), contained two maps. The first showed the areas of London served by two different water companies. These companies used different sources for their water supply to the city. While the area served by one company had death rates of only 5 per 1,000, the other had rates of 71 per 1,000. Snow went further and plotted the distribution of cholera cases and showed that they clustered around particular pumps; people using the water pump in Broad Street were more likely to go down with cholera. Snow with his maps provided a convincing argument that the water pump was transmitting cholera.

Snow's maps are rightly famous. They proved a case and solved a problem. The mapping of disease was not just a passive activity; it could be actively employed to identify causes and find solutions. Today there is constant surveillance of public health indicators as the fear of contagion, the sense that disease can spread and multiply, continues to exercise the cartographic imagination of government agencies.

As cities increase in size and the rich and poor are separated out into different neighbourhoods, this urban segregation becomes a source of cartographic interest. The 1841 census of Ireland provided the basis for a whole series of maps of social characteristics. In a special report on Dublin, a map was produced that colour-coded streets from 1st Class (high-class residences), through varying degrees of 2nd and 3rd Class that were inhabited by 'artizans, huxters, low population'; a similar type of classification was adopted by Charles Booth in his study of London. His *Life and Labour of the People in London* contains a number of maps that depict a social classification. The worst areas are inhabited by the 'very poor', whom Booth further characterized as 'lowest class' and 'vicious, semi-criminal'. The maps are revealing in two main ways. First, they provide us with an interesting snapshot of urban life in the nine-teenth century. Second, the classifications used and the underlying ideol-ogy tell us much about the world-view of middle- and upper-class commentators. For many of them the cities were a volcano that could erupt at any time. The urban mapping exercises were ways to understand where the source of social seismic activity was strongest and the social threats the most extreme.

The mapping of social differences not only represents reality, but can affect urban reality. In order to lift itself out of the Great Depression, the US government in the 1930s decided to underwrite mortgages for house purchase. A national inventory was undertaken to establish the credit-worthiness of different neighbourhoods. Local real estate professionals were involved in the survey which began in 1936. Neighbourhoods were rated A–D (with corresponding colours) on a map of green, blue, yellow and red. Grade A neighbourhoods were considered up and coming, in demand; grade B was good; grade C was full of older buildings and infil-trated by 'lower grade populations' (a code for blacks, Jews and foreign immigrants); while grade D was evaluated as poor quality housing with an 'undesirable population'. The maps and accompanying texts were sent to banks and mortgage lenders. Loans were not forthcoming for people seeking housing in areas graded D and rarely in C. The red areas were starved of federally protected mortgage funds. This mapping exercise was a federal codification of the biases and prejudices of the overwhelm-ingly white, Anglo, middle-class, real estate industry. This bias was repli-cated in postwar mortgage lending until redlining, the explicit policy of denying mortgage funds to certain neighbourhoods, was officially ended by the Department of Housing and Development in 1965. Denied the lifeblood of mortgage finance, many inner-city neighbourhoods experi-enced a downward spiral. The areas in cities that were coloured red invariably experienced population loss, physical deterioration and neigh-bourhood decline.

The mapping of pathologies emerges as an important topic in the nine-teenth century. Rapid industrialization, an increase in levels of urbaniza-tion and the emergence of new social classes all created a ferment of social change and political concern. The authorities had started to gener-ate, collect and centralize data so that social phenomenon could be quan-tified and analysed. Maps were used as a way to plot and understand some of the changes and their consequences. The mapping impulse continues. Rapid improvements in GIS technology, data gathering and storage have allowed the mapping of moral statistics in the city to grow in size and sophistication.

Identifying Disorder

Disorder is a socially defined condition. It is defined by those at the centre and is imposed on those on the periphery. Underlying the distinction between order and disorder are brute facts of political power. Let us look at one example.

On 19 May 2005, Robert Mugabe's government in Zimbabwe launched a new urban policy. It was called Operation Murambatsvina, literally translated as 'Drive Out the Rubbish'. As part of a nationwide campaign to beautify the cities, destroy the black market, reduce crime and undermine the support base of their political opponents, the government authorized the bulldozing of squatter settlements that fringed the larger cities. The campaign destroyed the homes of 700,000 people and wiped out the informal economy that provided a living for 40 per cent of the population. Almost 2.4 million poor people were faced with increased economic hardship. A new urban policy was imposed by the power of the state.

The disorder that Mugabe saw was in part a threat to his continued political power. The squatter settlements had long been the main source of opposition to his rule, so the new urban policy eradicated the physical basis of his political difficulties.

Operation Murambatsvina is an extreme case. But if we look at even the most recent urban past then elements of this story can be found across different cities. Disorder is identified primarily as a threat to the existing order and it is repressed. This disorder is defined in different ways but tends to circulate around the discourses of crime, disease, social difference and perceived social opposition.

Crime is a principal source of disorder. As I have shown, much of the nineteenth-century development of urban mapping and urban social investigation was concerned with identifying the sources and haunts of criminality. This has persisted down through the years although more recently the differences have become subtle. It is not only that centralized power defines a problem; the general population can become part of the process. Stanley Cohen (1972) defines moral panics as mass movements that see individuals or groups as deviants and threats (potential and actual) to society. The folk devil is front of stage in the moral panic, the source of threat and disorder. The particular nature of the folk devil of the moral panic changes but always seems to be there; sometimes in the shadows of the collective imagination, other times in the full glare of public discourse. Cohen's work looks at the rise of moral panics in the post-Second World War UK. Similarly, Stuart Hall *et al.* (1978) argue that in the 1950s the postwar construction of consensus based on social welfare provision and rising real incomes was built on an unstable moral basis. The lumpen bourgeoisie most keenly felt the rising social unease at the pace and scale of change; they were disturbed by the increase in working-class living standards, the new-found confidence of the lower orders and the loss of deference in society. Their unease fastened on to the problems of youth and the Teddy Boy cult. The 1950s witnessed a series of moral panics centring on the decline of the family and the growth of hooliganism. A law and order discourse was inaugurated that was not just a response to increased crime but a refractor for wider social tensions and deeper class conflict.

Moral panics are not confined to the UK. Law and order emerges throughout much of the world in the 1960s and persists to this day as an important discourse; in part a response to rising crime levels, but also a response to changing social configurations and new social tensions. In a very careful study, David Wilson (2005) explores the social construction of a 'black-on-black violence' discourse that emerges in the US in the 1980s.

The creation of moral panics, the construction of folk devils and the stigmatization of the periphery by the centre are at the heart of the identification of urban disorder. The devils may change their features but they remain, and panics may disappear only to sweep down through the years. The dangerous 'other' may change in particularity – homosexuals, paedophiles, communists, blacks, welfare recipients – but they remain a general category, a continual source of disorder to be identified and disciplined.

Moral panics ebb and flow. At times of relative calm, they ebb away into the shadows; at times of rapid social change, they reemerge, stronger and more virulent, with new dangerous others to replace the old folk devils. The last 50 years has seen wrenching social changes. Wide-ranging forces of deindustrialization, industrialization, immigration, globalization and technological innovation have undercut traditional social values and established cultural norms. The last half-century has also seen a series of moral panics in cities and nations as different groups have been designated the folk devil. Rapid change has prompted a rise of fundamentalism that seeks solace in unchanging verities, unambiguous texts and unchallenged obedience to authority. 'Things fall apart', the poet W.B. Yeats wrote in 1921, ' the centre cannot hold;/Mere anarchy is loosed upon the world'. For many there is not only a need to return to the purity of the traditional but also to identify the defiled and unclean who cause this anarchy.

Operation Murambatsvina stands as a stark and brutal example of the operation of state power. The state in its various forms and levels can act as a repressive force. The state also sets the stage by crafting legislation and by policing the city. At the heart of the public life of a city is the regulation and control of urban public space. Don Mitchell (2003) addresses this concern and makes the point that public space is always an achievement against steep odds. He links struggles over public space with movements for social justice. Political dissent is regulated by the freedoms afforded to public space. Kathryn Mitchell (2000) argues that public space needs to be regulated. What is at issue is who is doing the regulation, the level of regulation and the real political space that public space affords for political dissent and social difference.

Ogborn (1993) reminds us that the issue of the policing of urban space is not recent: it emerged with full force in the nineteenth century. However, this is a particularly telling moment in the history of public space as a new round of terrorism provokes substantial changes in surveillance, fortress architecture, bunker mentality and spatial policing. The rise of security policing, new forms of surveillance and control of urban spaces is a subject scholars have explored for some time (Fyfe and Bannister, 1998; Gold and Revill, 2000). Davis (1990) diagnoses what he calls 'fortress cities' as a response to perceived urban disorder and decay, primarily from domestic sources. Since the car bomb and the suicide bomber are now very real threats, many urban authorities have created fortress-style rings of steel as a counterresponse. Pawley (1998) wonders if the 'architecture of terror' will replace the signature building in the future; others have prophesied the demise of the skyscraper.

The fortress metaphor describes a landscape that is demarcated by physical borders (such as gates and walls) as well as by often invisible surveillance devices (such as closed-circuit television) that watch city streets, parks and gated communities. This is a vision of a city that can be controlled. Much of the work examining the fortress city has focused on semi-public space (such as shopping malls or urban gardens) or private space (gated communities or privately owned businesses). Much less attention has focused on the fortification of genuine public space, and few have looked at such open public space as national parks or historic sites. Benton-Short (in press) provides a detailed case study of the National Mall in Washington, DC, a public open space, a place of national memory and international signification.

Restrictions on public space are worrisome to those who have analysed the historically important role of public space as a site for the formation of citizenship, and as a conduit for discussions on civil society

(Habermas, 1989). Other scholars have described the decline of urban public space at the expense of the rise of more privatized spaces that don the carnival mask or provide a theme park environment (Sorkin, 1992). The large body of literature examining public space has made important contributions to seeing urban public spaces as sites of important discourse and change, and as significant places for the practice of democracy and the exercise of active citizenship (see Sennett, 1970).

The events of 11 September 2001 and the subsequent global war on terrorism have altered the articulation of security and fortifications of both private and public space in cities around the US and also in many other countries. Urban scholars have examined the threat of terrorism on cities such as London (Coaffee, 2004) or Belfast (Brown, 1985; Jarman, 1993). Many accounts present bleak portrayals of future urbanism and design as the invocation of 'national security' may trump issues of public access and public space (Coaffee, 2003). The stakes have changed, but it is unclear how the need to improve security translates into acceptable levels of fortification and loss of public access to public space.

Commentators have discussed the costs and benefits of adopting counterterrorism measures in the face of real or perceived terrorist threats (Graham, 2002). Until the early 1990s, many cities had no comprehensive security and defensive strategy; attempts to design out terrorism occurred specific target by specific target, and often after an event raised the issue or vulnerability, or a direct threat was made. Reconceptualized ideas about terrorism have led to new and dramatic urban counter-responses. Terrorists now target global cities to attract global media publicity. Since the 1990s terrorists have focused on economic infrastructure and financial zones, and as a result so did many counterterrorism measures. Since 11 September 2001, however, it is clear that symbolic targets – such as monuments, memorials, landmark buildings and other important public spaces – are increasingly at risk. The responses have been highly intense and visible counterterrorist measures.

The everyday policing of the city is the most obvious control of disorder. Steve Herbert's (1997) *Policing Space* concentrates on the formal working of police departments, drawing particular attention to the role of territoriality in the everyday actions of police as they control space and exercise power. Urban police departments are ultimately the formal managers of urban spaces. Their practices vary over time and across space, and so a historical geography of urban policing would tell us that story of police strategies, social difference and patterns of discipline and punishment.

The recent history of the New York Police Department (NYPD), for example, encapsulates the changed priorities of the policing of urban apace. In the 1990s the emphasis was on reducing crime. Statistical analysis, crime mapping, rapid response and the broken window hypothesis were guiding principles in reducing crime levels. After the attacks on the Twin Towers, the emphasis changed to securing the city from terrorist attacks. Before 9/11 only a few officers were assigned to counterterrorism; by 2005 there were over a thousand. NYPD officers were stationed in Singapore, Britain, Canada, France and Israel to learn from the experience of other countries; a new intelligence-gathering system was introduced to track suspicious business activities (such as the purchase of bomb-making equipment); and the department has a special counterterrorism bureau that collects and sifts through information from overseas as well as in the city. The NYPD has a more sophisticated information-gathering network than the FBI and, drawing upon the large and diverse immigrant population in the city, employs more foreign speakers than the federal agency. Tanker spills, for example, which used to be treated as a traffic accident are now, because of their potential threat, considered a crime unless proved otherwise. In some ways the NYPD needs to better than the FBI because the Federal Government has proved so inept, because the FBI has wider responsibilities rather than the narrow focus on one city, and because the politics of federal spending meant homeland security funds were disbursed in the fiscal year 2004 in a bizarre pattern that led to Wyoming receiving $37.74 per capita, North Dakota $30.82 and New York only $5.41. The estimated annual costs of security measures in New York City are now close to $200 million per year.

NYPD now has a special unit, the Hercules team, that consists of a rapid response unit of heavily armed officers. In a standard operation armoured trucks roll up, and out come officers in full riot gear, M-4 assault weapons with motorcycle patrols, and dogs. The deployments are unpredictable, with no obvious source of threat visible; they are random displays of force meant to intimidate and create a hostile environment for terrorists planning an attack. They are meant to repel the bad guys, but they can create a sense of discomfort for ordinary citizens. William Finnegan (2005) describes one deployment when an officer was asked by a woman why they were on the street. 'There used to be two buildings right over there', the officer said pointing to the site of the Twin Towers. 'That was just one event', the woman responded. 'It's being used to justify all kinds of horrible things.'

The Contested City: Creating New Urban Orders

Disorder and order are not separate categories: they are parts of a symbiotic process as successful resistances to old orders provide the basis for new orders. The city is a contested site. From individual acts of resistance and rebellion against the prevailing social and moral orders to collective protests, the city is a place of informal tactics and agency as well as official strategies and structure. The city is also the stage where the centre is challenged by those on the rim of social, sexual, ethnic, racial and economic power, and where order is transgressed and contested as well as imposed and policed.

We can distinguish between urban protests and urban social movements. Urban protests tend to be spontaneous eruptions of disorder. On 26 June 2005, Lui Liang, a student, was cycling in the Chinese city of Chizhou. According to reports, he was hit by a Toyota sedan driven by a wealthy investor and well-connected administrator. In the ensuing dispute the investor's two bodyguards, who were riding in the car, beat the young student. This minor incident sparked a large-scale urban protest. The investor and his bodyguards were taken to the police station. A large crowd formed outside the station, eager to see the rich outsiders punished. Almost 10,000 people milled around the station and riot police were called. Thinking that the bodyguards were being treated too leniently, the crowd threw rocks and bottles at the police. The crowd, now emboldened, overturned the investor's car as well as two police cars, set them alight and ransacked a supermarket. The rioting continued until the evening. At 11 p.m. 700 riot police arrived and the looting ended.

The roots of the riot lay in the sense of grievance against a system that enriched well-connected officials. The rioters felt that the system worked against them and for the rich elite. As one man said, 'When the anger boils up in your heart so long, it has to burst' (Cody, 2005).

The history and contemporary geography of cities is full of instances of such urban protest. The urban crowd can protest over specific incidents but their grievances are generally more long standing and refer to a sense of injustice, a denial of rights, relative immiseration or a sense of betrayal. A riot is at bottom, Martin Luther King Jr once remarked, the language of the unheard.

The streets can and do become a place where social grievances are given shape and form and substance. Taking to the streets is an integral part of the urban story. The fear of the crowd has influenced architecture, town planning and urban morphology down through the centuries, and the city tends to be the eye of the revolutionary storm. Protest activity is concentrated in the big towns and cities, especially those with a culture of resistance that can be more easily mobilized into popular protest than the rural areas. In this regard, Marx was right when he wrote that cities had a more revolutionary edge. Even the expression, *taking to the streets*, captures the urban bias of social protest. In late eighteenth-century France, revolutionary events took their most dramatic effects in Paris. The Russian Revolution was concentrated in the big cities. Similarly, in Eastern Europe in the late 1980s; it was the cities (especially the capital cities) where protests against communist governments were strongest, most dramatic and most successful. The taking of the Bastille, the storming of the Winter Palace, and the toppling of the Berlin Wall are all examples of symbolic events in cities that both signified and codified revolutionary change.

Urban protest can be fleeting, like the riot in Chizhou, an eruption of social discontent, perhaps a harbinger of things to come and a echo from deep-seated feelings of alienation, but not necessarily a source of immediate change from the authorities. There may be changes in policing and surveillance, but not necessarily a redress of grievances. Larger-scale and more long-lasting social improvements tend to arise from sustained collective actions. Wilkinson (1971) defines a social movement as a deliberate collective endeavour to promote change, with a minimum degree of organization and a commitment to change based on the active participation of members. A variety of social movements can be identified expressing religious sentiment, simple discontent, nationalism, race and ethnic identity, age and gender movements, and movements for civil rights. The most important questions about social movements revolve around *context* (how, why, when and where do movements occur), *organization, mobilization* (how does it exercise power and what are the range of collective actions), *opportunity* and *consequences*.

Consider the case of the Civil Rights Movement in the US. Throughout the first half of the twentieth century racial segregation was a common practice in the South, where a form of apartheid in principle and practice shaped the lives of people. It was reinforced by violence. Lynchings were common and in August 1955 a young boy, Emmet Till, was killed by two white men for talking 'fresh ' to a white woman. An all-white jury took only one hour to find the two men held responsible 'not guilty'. In December of that same year, Mrs Rosa Parks boarded a bus in Montgomery, Alabama. The driver told her and three other black people to move to the back of the bus, the designated place for blacks when whites entered the vehicle. Mrs Parks refused and was arrested. The black community declared a boycott of the buses in the city. People walked and car-pooled and forced the bus company to stop its racist practice. A Supreme Court ruling prohibited segregation on all public buses. The Montgomery bus boycott had a number of characteristics that were repeated throughout the South in the late 1950s and 1960s. Acts of civil disobedience were undertaken by many ordinary people as protests, boycotts, sit-ins and marches kept the issue alive. The movement had some successes at the federal level. The Supreme Court had ruled against school segregation in a 1954 ruling, and eventually in 1964 a Civil Rights Act prohibited racial discrimination. Civil rights were won through protest and action.

Urban social movements, a common term for collective actions that occur in the city and about the city, can arise over conflicts over the use, meaning and management of cities (see Castells, 1983). Arnstein (1971) identifies a ladder of citizen participation, from non-participation at the bottom where residents are simply manipulated or their problems and issues are simply ignored. The rioters in the Chinese city that erupted were clearly at the bottom of the ladder. The ladder moves through varieties of tokenism to full public control. In many cities most people are at the bottom of the ladder, and those at the top tend to come from the wealthy and connected.

Between the precondition for urban social movements and their creation lies the mobilization of opinion. Groups are formed either through promotion by outside agencies and/or the perception of potential members that issues can be solved or affected by collective action. In most groups a small active core provides the vast majority of the energy and commitment. Most urban social movements adopt two broad types of strategy. *Service strategies* arise over the provision of public services. These strategies involve the mobilization of the community's own resources through *complementary strategies* that augment existing service erosion, *alternative strategies* that demonstrate new ways of meeting a need and providing an alternative, and *substitute strategies* that replace existing forms of service provision. *Influence strategies* connect with the formal levels of power and include *collaborative strategies* (when there is a shared assumption between authorities and the group), *campaign strategies* (where the community groups seek to demonstrate the need for additional resources) and *coercive strategies* (where the group confronts the authorities).

To focus on urban social movements is to focus on the more visible signs of community concerns and political action. Non-action and failure are as much a feature of the city as action and success. Political exclusion is the fate of many groups as their grievances may not be formulated, and even when needs are articulated they can be ignored or deemed illegitimate. Let us consider three examples where struggles managed to change things.

In 1970 a plan to build 57 houses in the Sydney suburb of Hunter's Hill met with local resistance (see Short, 1988). A group of local women resisted the development on public open space and wrote to the state and local governments. They had little success so they approached the Builders Labourers Federation (BLF). This union had grown in strength and radicalism in the late 1960s as a building boom in the city raised the demand for building labour and thus increased the power of the union, which was led by men committed to improving members' working conditions but also with a commitment to broader social reforms. The BLF supported the residents of Hunters Hill and placed a ban on the development. The BLF used their union muscle to place permanent 'green' bans around the city, including plans for an Olympic Stadium in Centennial Park, an underground car park across from the Opera House and the demolition of the Theatre Royal; temporary bans were also placed on building work at Macquarie University because a homosexual student had been expelled, and at Sydney University because two women were not allowed to give a course on women's studies.

The BLF was successful because the building boom had increased their organizational strength and bargaining power. The union forged successful alliances with residents' groups and urban social movements. By the mid-1970s the building boom was over and the radical union leadership out of power. However, the social struggles left an enduring legacy in the city. Fig trees still grow opposite the Opera House, Centennial Park is still a green space and much public space remains open. Subsequent heritage and planning legislation crafted to create a more liveable city carries on the spirit of the green bans.

Around 3 a.m. on 27 June 1969, police raided a gay bar, the Stonewall Inn, in New York's Greenwich Village. This was a habitual occurrence, part of what D'Emilio (1983) reports as the renewed repression against gays after the ending of the Second World War. The postwar world in the US enforced conformity. Police raids against the urban places of emerging gay communities were common. A raid with subsequent arrests in an uncontested police action was the usual story. This time, however, events did not follow the usual script. As police took people into the paddy wagons, customers pelted them with stones and coins. The currency was both a weapon and metaphor for the payoff system in which police shook down homosexuals for payment. News of the event soon spread through the community and soon hundreds of people were milling around the bar with the police now trapped inside. Riot police were called in. The crowd increased to around 2,000, and some of the protesters chanted 'Gay Power'. That first night, 13 people were arrested and many were injured. Crowds came back the next night and five days later more than 1,000 people turned up at the bar to protest against police harassment against gays.

The Stonewall riots were a rallying point for the gay movement. A month after the protests, the Gay Liberation Front was formed in New York City and soon similar organizations had been formed in cities around the world. In 1970, in commemoration of the event, between 5,000 and 10,000 people marched from the village to Central Park. Gay Pride Marches are now held in many cities on the last Sunday of June in commemoration of the protests. It was not an easy journey from the Stonewall riots to acceptance of gay rights. The *New York Times*, for example, on 29 June 1969 described how 'hundreds of young men went on a rampage'; the 'liberal' newspaper placed the blame squarely on young men rather seeing it as an act of resistance against police harassment. Gays still do face harassment and discrimination, but what Stonewall showed was that a sustained resistance could effectively resist the arbitrary and repressive use of police power, change political consciousness and provide a rallying point for the open articulation of gay identity and the promotion of gay rights.

In 1965 Ferdinand Marcos became president of the Philippines. A fervent anti-communist, he was an important ally of the US. President Johnson described him as 'our strong right arm man in Asia'. He ran a kleptocracy. Between 1972 and 1986 he siphoned off $20 billion, almost a half of the country's entire gross national product. His wife, Imelda, was reported to have 3,000 pairs of shoes, each pair costing as much as the average Filipino's annual income. Popular resistance against his rule grew over the years. Marcos responded by declaring martial law and suspending even the most basic democratic rights. In 1983 the popular politician, Benino Aquino, was assassinated at the airport as he returned from exile in the US. He was in opposition to Marcos and his death was widely seen as a desperate attempt by Marcos to eradicate resistance to his rule. Marcos lost popular support as well as the backing of the US, who now felt that he was more of a liability than a help in the fight against communism. The US forced him to hold an election in 1986. Aquino's widow, Cory Aquino, ran against him. Tampering, intimidation and outright fraud marred the election held in February. When Marcos was declared the winner, resistance to his rule stiffened. Some military leaders withdrew their support and the Church condemned the election result.

On the 23 February 1986, hundreds of thousands of people filled the main highway, EDSA (Epifanio de los Santos Avenue), in a festive atmosphere as whole families, nuns and priests, performers and children prayed sang and chanted (Mercado and Tatad, 1986). They risked their lives as government troops could have opened fire on them. The vast crowd in the centre of the capital city became a huge political fact that further delegitimized Marcos's rule. On the 25 February Cory Aquino was inaugurated as the new President. The US provided a plane to fly Marcos and his family to Hawaii. With them reportedly went assets of over $10 million, including 48 feet of pearls.

The events of February 1986 in Manila were soon referred to as People Power; they showed that a mass movement, in collaboration with military support, could topple dictatorships. The widely publicized images of People Power were transmitted around the world and may have provided a role model for the popular resistance to communist rule in Eastern European in the late 1980s. A shrine was erected on the EDSA in commemoration. The shrine became a setting for subsequent mass movements. In January 2001 almost a million people converged on the EDSA shrine to protest against the corruption of President Joseph Estrada. Later, hundreds of thousands of supporters gathered at the same place in his support. A debate ensued about whether People Power had become mob rule (Spaeth, 2001).

These three examples are important in a general sense because they show that urban protest and urban social movements can successfully challenge the existing order. Change and development comes from the bottom as well as the top, and urban studies needs to tell the story of change from below as well as the operation of power from above.

I began Chapter 2 with a discussion of two cinema classics, *Metropolis* and *Berlin: Symphony of a City*. It is fitting, then, that I end this section of the book with another cinema classic, the *Battle of Algiers* (1965). The movie was commissioned by the Algerian government and directed by an Italian, Gillo Pontecorvo, who used non-professional actors, many of whom played a part in the actual events. The black-and-white movie has a documentary feel; there is a grainy realism that allows an easy suspension of disbelief. The setting of the movie is the city of Algiers during an insurgency against French colonial rule. One of the principal characters is Ali La Pointe, who organizes terrorist/resistance cells in the city for the Algerian resistance movement. Bombs are set off in public places – two cafés and an air terminal – and innocent bystanders are killed. French paratroopers under Colonel Mathieu are called in and undertake a massive police operation, involving cordoning off the 'native city' and the heavy policing of all the Arabs. The action soon involves outright violence and torture.

The movie could have been a hack propaganda piece. Commissioned by the Algerian government and directed by an Italian communist, it could have been a justification for the liberation movement or an easy condemnation of the French. Instead, the movie is an excellent piece of film making, a taut political thriller that embraces moral ambiguity. The victims of the bombs, for example, are depicted innocently at play before they are killed. They are shown as real people rather than political ciphers. The movie shows the context, strategies and tactics of an urban social movement in a dramatic depiction of actual events. The creation of an urban network and the policing of urban space are central elements of the story.

The movie has contemporary resonance. It was re-released in 2004, and a special showing at the Pentagon was not accidental. The strategy and tactics of a 'police' action in a hostile country was particularly appropriate for an American military engaged in Iraq. The movie ends with the French success, but it was a hollow victory. The country achieved independence from France in 1962. There are obvious parallels between the battle for Algiers and the battle in Baghdad.

15

The Future City: Rethinking Urban Theory

We live in exciting times. Cities are on the edge of the cusp of social and economic transformation. Deindustrialization and the global shift in manufacturing, the growth of global cities, increasing polarization, new technologies, a new urban geopolitics of war and terror, and a whole host of social and economic processes are reshaping urban hierarchies, rewriting urban structure and renewing urban identities. We are in the middle of an urban revolution.

These dramatic changes are forcing us to rewrite urban theory. The theories of the modern city, and now even the postmodern city, no longer provide such a comforting embrace. Let me outline some of the constituent elements of a new urban theory for a new urban condition.

The Question of Scale

Over the course of the last 600 years we have moved from an ability to conceive of cities as semi-autonomous economic units, the era of the city-states, to seeing cities as part of the nation state where the city was just one element in a predominantly national organization of political space. This was the city as a function of the national. Now we need to conceptualize the city at the multiple and interacting scales of global, national and local.

The nation state is not disappearing. In some cases, there is a renewed relationship between nation states and selected cities. In countries such as Britain and France, the respective capital cities receive massive amounts of public investment as the preferred platform for global connectivity. London and Paris benefit enormously from state investment by central governments eager to keep and enhance global connectivity. The urban primacy in many countries means an intimate connection between the nation states and the major city. It is at the level of smaller, less primate cities that an uncoupling of nation and urban is most apparent. A neo- liberal agenda and resultant privatization situates more cities on a surface of pure market competition which is less softened by public sector interventions.

We should be careful to recognize the continuing importance of the nation state in the affairs of the city. Since the early nineteenth century, there has been a string of steady assertions of the nation state over the city. Angus Cameron (in press) writes that 'despite the promises of globalization, urbanization and network space, we are still living in an era of what might be called state-cities that remain relatively powerless with respect to the states they inhabit'. Accumulated state power still hangs heavy over even the largest cities. The current fascination with the death of the nation states ignores the embedding of cities in national systems of economic regulation and identity. We are not in an era of the death of the state but of a subtle reworking of state–city relationships.

It would also be wrong to see global forces simply overwhelming local urban economies. Global forces have their limits. In cities where the bulk of employment is in the public sector, the global pull of cheap labour is less meaningful. In many other sectors, economic globalization is the unfettering of the mobility of capital, with consequent differential effects on the people living and working in, and the fixed capital concretized in, existing cities.

There is a dramatic rescaling as global forces and national systems of reregulation impact cities. Some rapidly globalizing cities are successfully breaking away from the national economic landscape into more semi-autonomous city-states. In others, combinations of economic globalization and reduced public sector interventions are creating problems of economic viability. In yet others, on the other side of the global shift in manufacturing employment, economic globalization and changes in national policy are creating rapid growth, rapid marketization of labour and land markets and increasing inequality. Global, national and urban processes are affecting individual cities around the world, while globalizing cities are the site and platform for shifts in national and global articulations. A new urban theory will be sensitive to cities as sites of intersecting scalar processes. As a (probably unworkable) reminder, we should henceforth place the term 'city' in the middle of *global–city–national*.

From City to Globalizing City Regions

Perhaps it is time to dispense with the term 'city'. It conjures up notions of continuity between small bounded urban places and contemporary cities. But contemporary cities are now only one point in wider urban regions: they are urban force fields that stretch into suburban and peri-urban sprawls. The 'city' is simply one more element in regional economic agglomerations, just one point in complex, dense, overlapping circulation patterns and social network flows. We have moved from the city to the urban region. The continuing centrality of the city in this urban force field varies enormously; places such as New York City, for example, are still sites of concentrated economic activity and residential occupation. There are still sectors and cities that retain their centrality. Advanced producer services in global cities, for example, retain their central city locations. In other cities and other economic sectors, dispersal, deconcentration, and polycentrality are now the hallmarks of the new urban fields. We can see cities as emerging from the changing balance of forces between the competing forces of concentration and dispersal: concentration for spectacles, conviviality, and the outcome of individual human actions as well as the massing effects of large investments such as metro stations, ballparks, stadiums and events, and entertainment zones; dispersal to cheaper sites, new sites, the snowball effects of people moving, and then jobs and services moving to be close to the suburbanites and so on until the one urban centre is a dim memory in a far-off place. New urban regions are emerging from these competing centrifugal and centripetal processes.

The urban regional field is uneven. There are pockets of concentration across a dispersing urban field which is creating problems of linkages and flows. The old monocentric pattern was in part a function of the traditional transport technologies. The motor car, now a ubiquitous presence in most cities, allows a wider, more even, spread and yet it can also cause strangulation of flow, negative environmental impacts and the wear and emotional tear on commuters in gridlock.

The large urban regions unified on maps and statistics are on a finer grained, detailed scale, composed of multiple and often only occasionally intersecting paths traced by different people as they make space–time paths through the region. Networks of flows into housing submarkets and job niches are creating new forms of segregation as people from certain housing markets put their children into certain schools, occupy certain sectors of the job market, and have very different urban life experiences. The flows of the urban region are sometimes mutually exclusive, as in the residential segregation of the rich and poor, and at other times interconnecting, as when a rich executive employs a poor immigrant to landscape the garden.

These large city regions are the prime hubs of economic globalization. These new globalizing city regions are the site of multinational corporations investments and new techniques of manufacturing, and also centres of service industries. Three GCRs have been identified in Asia Pacific: Bangkok (11 million people), Seoul (20 million people) and Jakarta (20 million people) which have between 35 and 25 per cent of all foreign direct investment into their respective countries and constitute between 20 per cent and 40 per cent of their respective national gross domestic product. GCRs possess a number of distinctive features: the core has specialized producer services such as banking, accountancy, legal and advertising services; in effect, they are centres of economic transactions and surveillance and hubs in the global network of flows in producer services. Also in the core are the hotels, communications and transport centres that link the country to the rest of the world. In the periphery are the more intensive land uses, such as manufacturing and mass housing. In rapidly expanding GCRs an outer ring of recently urbanized countryside can also be identified as the metropolis extends its influence across the landscape.

Unfettered capitalism rewards winners and punishes losers. Globalization exacerbates this trend, which is even more reinforced in the GCRs with the shift from closed to more open economies. The form of the opening varies from planned economies (in the case of China) and former centrally-planned economies in former communist-controlled areas, and from import-substitution economic strategies (in the case of Mexico and many other developing countries) towards a more direct integration into the global economy. The restructuring involves a social reorganization of the national space economy and growing inequalities between globally successful and less successful sectors and workers. Those in the upper echelons of advanced producer services, such as investment banking, now operate on a more global metric of remuneration, while those in traditional sectors see the disappearance of their safety net and a decline in their job security. In the short term there is a growing tension between those profiting from globalization and those being punished by globalization. Some economic theorists would argue that while this may be true in the short to medium term, in the long term globalization would promote greater economic efficiency and ultimately greater income growth for everyone. However, we tend to live our lives in the short to medium term. In the long term, as Keynes reminded us, the one true certainty is that we are all dead.

The Entrepreneurial City

The tensions in global and globalizing cities are reinforced by the decline of the Keynesian city in the West, the globalization of the planned economies in the East and the reduction of even limited social welfares in the South. It is not economic globalization per se that is causing the social tensions within cities: it is the governmental responses to economic globalization. Studies that measure social polarization and income distribution in different cities reveal that the range varies according to how the national society responds to market inequalities (Fainstein, 2001). Some societies defuse economic inequalities while an increasing number are reinforcing them. The city is the arena in which this tension is being played out in the starkest of forms.

Cities are being restructured as political terrains. Commitments to generous welfare arrangements are being undermined in the richer countries, and the whole notion of cities as places of collective living is being challenged by a sense of cities as simply sites of economic transactions. The shift from the Keynesian city to the entrepreneurial city involves a transformation of urban governance, involving a reorientation of policy objectives and practices from welfare to economic competitiveness, and a broader shift in political sensibilities from the cities as places of collective living to cities as sites of competitive economic advantage. The reimagining of cities involves a rewriting of the urban experience and an enthronement of a competitive capitalism in the polis.

The Cosmopolitan City

Cosmopolitanism is the hallmark of truly global cities. Martha Nussbaum (1994) triggered a substantial discussion when she noted that one important strand of contemporary identity is the notion of global citizenship, involving more universal concerns and aspirations. The debate has twisted and turned, but the sense that cosmopolitanism (often in opposition to, yet sometimes in conjunction with, patriotism and other pulls on identity) is an important element in personal identity and group solidarity remains. Much of this debate, which I will term the political philosophy of cosmopolitanism, has been rooted in a placeless realm with only perhaps a passing nod to the city. It has been characterized by a lack of spatial imagination. It is only with the more recent debates (that have extended a formal recognition of cultural issues) that there has been a sharper identification of the connections between the city and cultural globalization. The cosmopolitan city is both a cause and an embodiment of cultural globalization. What we also need is an ambitious theory of the cosmopolitan city that connects global, national and urban identities as well as developing notions of what citizenship means in this complex pull of identities and allegiances.

Nomadic Geographies

It may seem perverse in a discussion of such fixed places as cities to raise the issue of nomadic geographies. However, it is important to examine the emotional consequences from living in a space of flows and a world of movement.

The airport lounge is an excellent example of the connections between movement and anxiety, a space where we make connections, a chamber for the space–time compression of modern jet travel; it is also place of serial monotony where a sense of displacement (coupled with movement) fills the air. The airport lounge experience is the opposite of the sense of embeddedness that is both a prison for, and an asylum from, modern life. We are travelling when we are in the lounge, but we are stuck in a strange place.

Movement was always associated with freedom, the ability to escape. Now it has a sense of dislocation, or placelessness. The geographical cure is also the spatial curse as a sense of fluidity erodes our sense of permanence and order.

Martin Heidegger's notion of 'throwness' describes the disorientating feeling of being 'thrown' into existence without any warning, preparation or chance on our part to choose to be thrown or not. Today this existential condition magnifies into a sense of being shot out of a cannon. The searching for a soft landing lies behind the rise of fundamentalism found in the major denominations, including Christianity, Islam and Judaism. Even the Mormons have witnessed a fundamental revival as polygamists seek to recreate the original promise of Joseph Smith.

An anxiety, a sense of permanent displacement and a feeling of reluctance about participation mark life in the contemporary city. The rate of technological change has left most of us with feelings of incompetence, uncertainty and a need to trust the technology yet with a distrust of technological. A *New Yorker* cartoon has a mother cooing softly to her young daughter, 'It's all right, sweetie', she says, 'In the information age, everybody feels stupid.' Anxiety arises not so much from the traditional existential crisis of lack of meaning as from the postmodern sense of too much meaning.

The sense of infinite freedom that a fully capitalist economy promises creates a space between the people we are and the people we want to be. Even traditional morality no longer holds the power to constrict. A mature capitalism has cast off its remaining bourgeois shackles to become the full market economy of its original promise. Capitalism of the late eighteenth, nineteenth and most of the twentieth century had to work its way slowly through accumulated centuries of traditional bourgeois respectability and age-old moral concerns. Now the sex, desire and longing that remained so hidden, and so private, is now just one more commodity in the seemingly endless ability of the market economy to commodify even the deepest recesses of our imagination. The fantasy city of fully formed market capitalism is a place of pleasure and profit (Hannigan, 1998). A commodified pleasure principle replaces the urban romanticism that flourished when moral constraints were in place. And as we become fully-fledged consumers, other sides of our character, rather like rarely-used muscles, begin to atrophy and die. Another *New Yorker* cartoon depicts a man obviously recovering from a panic attack who says to his friend, 'Really, I'm fine. It was just a fleeting sense of purpose – I'm sure it will pass.'

The City of Light and Dark

De Certeau begins one of his essays by dedicating it to 'the ordinary man, the common hero'. This emancipatory impulse has been a strong feature of urban theorizing. Henri Lefebvre (2003), for example, writes of the right to the city and outlines a better city marked by self-determination, creativity and authenticity.

I have also posed the question of how we should create cities in which ordinary people can lead dignified and creative lives (Short, 1989a). This was set in a more general context of identifying those forces that created cities as if only capital matters and as if only some people matter. We still need ideas for cities as if people matter. The emancipatory impulse remains because the need for it persists. Cities continue to be sites of oppression, containment and exclusion. To make cities places of freedom, liberation and inclusion we need both a theory and practice of progressive urban politics.

Technology has long promised a better world and a rosier future, but the computer revolution has created the digital divide as much as the bounty of the World Wide Web. Technology on its own does not create a better world. The technological fix is important but partial. Graham and Marvin (2001) write tellingly of the splintering urbanism of the new technologies.

We are at a pivotal point in recent history. It did not take long for the peace dividend of the immediate post-Cold War world to quickly evaporate. Now, in the world of post-9/11, cities are again being explicitly recognized as targets of terror and warfare. Indeed, Graham (2004, 168) notes, 'contemporary warfare and terror now largely boil down to contests over the spaces, meanings, support systems and power structures of cities and urban regions'. The nexus of cities, war and terror is back on the academic agenda as well as in the evolution of a new urban geopolitics. The securitization of urban public spaces, the renewed vigour in surveillance, the targeting of cities and the attacking of cities is now a reality that we must all acknowledge. There is an urbanization of modern conflict. The city is once again at the centre of the practice of terrorism and the technology of destruction.

An urban Thanatos competes with the construction of bright city on a hill. The forces of light and dark are drawing battle lines in the city.

A Question of Method

No single method or approach is able to capture the complexity of the new urban forms. Complex phenomena require the use of varied and different approaches. While it is impossible to envision a serious study of urban development that does not utilize a historic–geographic materialism, or a study of urban economies that does not utilize a political economy, it also difficult to see how these approaches will give us all the answers. Quantitative and qualitative methods, data analysis and participant observation, and the employment of multiple techniques in a variety of perspectives seem the only way to capture the flux and flow of the new cities. The urban condition needs to be seen from the social science equivalent of the telescope and the microscope.

The rise of the modern city is intimately connected to the development of film and cinematic culture (Brooker, 2002). It is fitting, then, that the variety of filmic techniques can be used to tell urban stories: the long positioning shot that sets the scene, the wide angle that contextualizes, the close-up, the dissolved time sequences, the judicious cross-editing that connects people and places separated by time and space. Utilizing the social science equivalent of the film genres of action, documentary, comedy, fantasy, film noir, magical realism and science fiction (and others) are just some of the different ways that we can understand the city and tell its multiple truths.

References

Abu-Lughod, J. L. (2004) 'Cairo: too many people, not enough land, too few resources', in J. Gugler (ed.), *World Cities beyond the West*. Cambridge: Cambridge University Press.

Adams, P. (2005) *The Boundless Self: Communication in Physical and Virtual Spaces*. Syracuse: Syracuse University Press.

Aglietta, M. (1987) *A Theory of Capitalist Regulation: The US Experience* (originally published in French, 1974). London: Verso.

Alves, M. H. M. (2004) 'São Paulo: the political and socioeconomic transformations wrought by the New Labor Movement in the city and beyond', in J. Gugler (ed.), *World Cities beyond the West*. Cambridge: Cambridge University Press.

Amin, A. (ed.) (1994) *Post-Fordism: A Reader*. Oxford: Basil Blackwell.

Amin, A. (2000) 'The economic base of contemporary cities', in G. Bridge and S. Watson (eds), *A Companion to the City*. Oxford and Malden: Basil Blackwell.

Anderson, E. (1990) *Streetwise: Race, Class and Change in an Urban Community*. Chicago: University of Chicago Press.

Anderson, K. (1991) *Vancouver's Chinatown: Racial Discourse in Canada, 1875–1980*. Montreal: McGill University Press.

Anderson, K. (1993) 'Constructing geographies: "race", place and the making of Sydney's Aboriginal Redfern', in P. Jackson and J. Penrose (eds), *Constructions of Race, Place and Nation*. Minneapolis: University of Minnesota Press.

Anzaldua, G. (1987) *Borderlands/La Frontera*. San Francisco: Aunt Lute Press.

Arnstein, S.R. (1971) 'A ladder of citizen participation in the USA', *Journal of Town Planning Institute*, 57: 176–82.

Ashworth, G. and Voogd, H. (1990) *Selling the City: Marketing Approaches in Public Sector Urban Planning*. London: Belhaven Press.

Bailey, J. (1989) *Marketing the Cities in the 1980s and Beyond*. Cleveland American Economic Development Council and Cleveland State University Press.

Baran, P. and Sweezy, P. (1966) *Monopoly Capital*. New York: Monthly Review Press.

Barke, M. and Harrop, K. (1994) 'Selling the industrial town: identity, image and illusion', in J. R. Gold and S. V. Ward (eds), *Place Promotion: The Use of Publicity and Marketing to Sell Towns and Regions*. Chichester: John Wiley.

Bassett, K. (1993) 'Urban cultural strategies and urban regeneration', *Environment and Planning A*, 25: 1,773–88.

Bassett, K. A. and Short, J. R. (1980) *Housing and Residential Structure: Alternative Approaches*. London: Routledge.

Beaverstock, J. V. (2002) 'Transnational elites in global cities: British expatriates in Singapore's financial district', *Geoforum*, 33: 525–38.

Beaverstock, J. V. (2004) 'Managing across borders: Transnational knowledge management and expatriation in legal firms', *Journal of Economic Geography*, 4: 157–79.

Beaverstock, J. V. (2005) 'Transnational managerial elites in the city: British highly-skilled inter-company transferees in New York City's financial district', *Journal of Ethnic and Migration Studies*, 31: 245–68.

Beaverstock, J. V., Hubbard, P. and Short, J. R. (2004) 'Getting away with it? Exposing the geographies of the super-rich', *Geoforum*, 35: 401–7.

Beaverstock, J. V., Smith, R. G. and Taylor, P. J. (1999) 'The long arm of the law: London's law firms in a globalizing world economy', *Environment and Planning A*, 31: 1857–76.

Beaverstock, J. V., Smith, R. G. and Taylor, P. J. (2000) 'World city network: a new metageography', *Annals of Association of American Geographers*, 90: 123–35.

Bell, D. (2001) 'Fragments for a Queer City', in D. Bell, J. Binnie, R. Holliday, R. Longhurst and R. Peace, *Pleasure Zones*, Syracuse: Syracuse University Press.

Bell, D., Binnie, J., Holliday, R., Longhurst, R. and Peace, R. (2001) *Pleasure Zones*. Syracuse: Syracuse University Press.

Benjamin, W. (1999) *The Arcades Project*. Translated by H. Eiland and K. McLaughlin. Cambridge, MA and London: Belknap Press of Harvard University Press.

Benton-Short, L. (in press) 'Bunkers and barriers: securing the National Mall in Washington, DC', *Society and Space*.

Benton-Short, L. and Price, M. (2006a) 'Globalization from below: the ranking of global immigrant cities', *International Journal of Urban and Regional Research* (in press).

Benton-Short, L. and Price, M. (2006b) 'A typology of global immigrant destinations', *Population, Space and Place* (in press).

Berger, R. (2004) *Immigrant Women Tell their Stories*. New York: Haworth Press.

Berman, M. (1982) *All That is Solid Melts into Air; The Experience of Modernity*. New York: Simon & Schuster.

Bevan, R. (2005) *The Destruction of Memory: Architecture and Cultural Warfare*. London: Reaktion.

Bhabha, H. (1994) *The Location of Culture*. London: Routledge.

Binnie, J. (2004) *The Globalization of Sexuality*. London: Routledge.

Bondi, L. (1992) 'Gender symbols and urban landscapes', *Progress in Human Geography*, 16: 157–70.

Bondi, L. and Rose, D. (2003) 'Constructing gender, constructing the urban', *Gender, Place and Culture*, 10: 229–45.

Booth, C. (1892–1903) *Life and Labour of the People in London*. London: Macmillan.

Boyer, R. (1990) *The Regulation School: A Critical Introduction*. Translated by C. Charney. New York: Columbia University Press.

Bromley, R. (1988) 'Working in the streets: survival strategy, necessity or unavoidable evil', in J. Gugler (ed.), *The Urbanization of the Third World*. New York: Oxford University Press.

Brooker, P. (2002) *Modernity and Metropolis: Writing, Film and Urban Formations*. New York: Palgrave.

Brown L. A. and Moore, E. G. (1970) 'The intra-urban migration process: a perspective', *Geografiska Annaler*, 52B: 1–13.

Brown, S. (1985) 'Central Belfast's security segment – an urban phenomenon', *Area*, 17: 1–8.

Brunn, S., Williams, J.F. and Ziegler, D. J. (eds) (2003) *Cities of the World: Regional Urban Development*. Lanham, MD: Rowman & Littlefield.

Burgess, E. W. (1925) 'The growth of the city', in R. E. Park, E. W. Burgess and R. D. McKenzie (eds), *The City*. Chicago: University of Chicago Press.

Califia, P. (1994) *Public Sex: The Culture of Radical Sex*. Pittsburgh: Cleis.

Callaway, H. (1981) 'Spatial domination and women's mobility in Yorubaland, Nigeria', in A. Ardener (ed.), *Women and Space*. London: Croom Helm.

Cameron, A. (in press) 'State-cities', in T. Hall, P. Hubbard and J. R. Short (eds), *The Compendium of Urban Studies*. London:Sage.

Cannadine, D. (2001) *Ornamentalism: How the British Saw their Empire*. Oxford: Oxford University Press.

Cardoso, A. and Short, J. R. (1983) 'Forms of housing production', *Environment and Planning A*, 15: 917–28.

Caro, R. A. (1974) *The Power Broker: Robert Moses and the Fall of New York*. New York: Knopf.

Castells, M. (1983) *The City and the Grassroots*. London: Edward Arnold.

Castells, M. (2000) *The Rise of the Network Society*. Oxford: Basil Blackwell.

Castree, N., Coe, N.M., Ward, K. and Samers, M. (2004) *Spaces of Work: Global Capitalism and Geographies of Labour*. London: Sage.

Certeau, M. de (1984) *The Practice of Everyday Life*. Berkeley and Los Angeles: University of California Press.

Cesaire, A. (2000) *Discourse on Colonialism*. New York: New York University Press.

Chakravorty, S. (2000) 'From colonial city to globalizing city: the far from complete spatial transformation of Calcutta', In P. Marcuse and R. Kempen (eds), *Globalizing Cities: A New Spatial Order*. Oxford: Basil Blackwell.

Chang, T. C., Huang, S. and Savage, V. R. (2004) 'On the waterfront: globalization and urbanization in Singapore', *Urban Geography*, 25: 413–36.

Chauncey, G. (1994) *Gay New York*. New York: HarperCollins.

Cheng, L. and Gereffi, G. (1994) 'The informal economy in East Asian development', *International Journal of Urban and Regional Research*, 18: 194–219.

Chow, R. (1991) *Women and Chinese Modernity: The Politics of Reading between the West and East*. Minneapolis: University of Minnesota Press.

Cieraad, I. (ed.) (1999) *At Home: An Anthropology of Domestic Space*. Syracuse: Syracuse University Press.

Clark, G. L. (1981) 'The employment relation and the spatial division of labor', *Annals of Association of American Geographers*, 71: 412–24.

Coaffee, J. (2003) *Terrorism, Risk and the City*. Aldershot: Ashgate.

Coaffee, J. (2004) 'Rings of steel, rings of concrete and rings of confidence: designing out terrorism in central London pre and post September 11', *International Journal of Urban and Regional Research*, 28: 201–11.

Cody, E. (2005) 'A Chinese city's rage at the rich and powerful', *The Washington Post*, 1 August: A1 and A14.

Cohen, D. Spear, S., Scribner, R., Kissinger, P., Mason, K. and Walden, J. (2000) 'Broken windows and the risk of gonorrhea', *American Journal of Public Health*, 90: 230–6.

Cohen, L. (2003) *Consumers' Republic: The Politics of Mass Consumption in Postwar America*. New York: Knopf.

Cohen, S. (1972) *Folk Devils and Moral Panics*. London: MacGibbon & Kee.

Crankshaw, O. and Parnell, S. (2004) 'Johannesburg: race, inequality and urbanization', in J. Gugler (ed.), *World Cities beyond the West*. Cambridge: Cambridge University Press.

Crenson, M. (1971) *The Un-Politics of Air Pollution: A Study of Non-Decisionmaking in Cities*. Baltimore: Johns Hopkins University Press.

Cross, J. (1998) *Informal Politics: Street Vendors and the State in Mexico City*. Stanford: Stanford University Press.

Cronon, W. (1991) *Nature's Metropolis: Chicago and the Great West*. New York: Norton.

Crowley, W. K. (1998) 'Modeling the Latin American city', *The Geographical Review*, 88: 127–30.

Dahl, R. (1961) *Who Governs?* New Haven: Yale University Press.

Davie, M. (1983) 'The great flat roof disaster', *The Sunday Observer*, 11 September: 40.

Davis, M. (1990) *City of Quartz*. London: Verso.

Davis, M. (1998) *Ecology of Fear*. New York: Holt.

Dear, M. (2000) *The Postmodern Urban Condition*. Oxford: Basil Blackwell.

D'Emilio, J. (1983) *Sexual Politics, Sexual Communities*. Chicago: University of Chicago Press.

Derudder, B. and Witlox, F. (2005) 'On the use of inadequate airline data in mappings of a global urban system', *Journal of Air Transport Management*, 11: 231–7.

Doel, M. and Hubbard, P. (2002) 'Taking world cities literally', *City*, 6: 351–68.

Douglas, I. (1981) 'The city as an ecosystem', *Progress in Physical Geography*, 5: 315–67.

Douglas, M. and Friedmann, J. (1998) *Cities for Citizens*. Chichester: John Wiley.

Duncan, N. (1996) 'Renegotiating gender and sexuality in public and private spaces', in N. Duncan (ed.), *BodySpace: Destabilizing Geographies of Gender and Sexuality*. London and New York: Routledge.

Dutt, A. K. and Pomeroy, G. M. (2003) 'Cities of South Asia', In S. Brunn, J. F. Williams and D. J. Ziegler (eds), *Cities of the World: Regional Urban Development*. Lanham, MD: Rowman & Littlefield.

Ehrenreich, B. (2001) *Nickel and Dimed*. New York: Henry Holt.

Engels, F. (1973) *The Condition of the Working Class in England in 1844*. Moscow: Progress.

Etzel, R. A. (2003) 'How environmental exposures influence the development and exacerbation of asthma', *Pediatrics*, 112: 233–9.

Evans, P. (ed.) (2002) *Livable Cities: Urban Struggles for Livelihood and Sustainability*. Berkeley and Los Angeles: University of California Press.

Fainstein, S. (2001) 'Inequality in global-city regions', in A. J. Scott (ed.), *Global City-Regions*. Oxford: Oxford University Press.

Finnegan, W. (2005) 'The terrorism beat', *The New Yorker*, 25 July: 58–71.

Forbes, D. (2004) 'Jakarta: globalization, economic crisis and social change', in J. Gugler (ed.), *World Cities beyond the West*. Cambridge: Cambridge University Press.

Ford, L. R. (1996) 'A new and improved model of Latin American city structure', *Geographical Review*, 86: 437–40.

Freestone, R. and Gibson, C. (2004) 'City planning and the cultural economy', Paper presented at *City Futures* Conference, Chicago, 8–10 July.

Friedmann, J. (1986) 'The world city hypothesis', *Development and Change*, 17: 69–83.

Friedmann, J. (1998) 'The new political economy of planning: the rise of civil society', in M. Douglas and J. Friedmann (eds), *Cities for Citizens*, Chichester: John Wiley.

Friedmann, J. (2005) *China's Urban Transition*. Minneapolis: University of Minnesota Press.

Friedmann, J. and Wolff, G. (1982) 'World city formation: an agenda for research and action', *International Journal of Urban and Regional Research*, 3: 309–44.

Fyfe, N. R. (ed.) (1998) *Images of the Street*. London and New York: Routledge.

Fyfe, N. R. and Bannister, J. (1998) 'The eyes upon the street: closed-circuit television surveillance and the city', in Nicholas R. Fyfe (ed.), *Images of the Street: Planning, Identity and Control in Public Space*.

Gaffikin, F. and Warf, B. (1993) 'Urban policy and the post-Keynsian state in the UK and US', *International Journal of Urban and Regional Research*, 17: 67–84.

Galbraith, J. K. (1958) *The Affluent Society*. London: Hamish Hamilton.

Gandy, M. (2002) *Concrete and Clay: Reworking Nature in New York City*. Cambridge: MIT Press.

Garff, J. (2005) *Søren Kierkegaard: A Biography*. Translated by B. Kirmmse. Princeton, NJ: Princeton University Press.

GAWC (Globalization and World Cities) (2005) http://www.lboro.ac.uk/gawc/publicat.html.

Gilfoyle, T. (1992) *City of Eros: New York City, Prostitution and the Commercialization of Sex, 1790–1920*. New York: Norton.

Gilroy, P. (1993) *The Black Atlantic*. Cambridge, MA: Harvard University Press.

Gladwell, M. (1996) 'The science of shopping', *The New Yorker*, November: 66–75.

Glass, T. A. and Balfour, J. L. (2003) 'Neighborhoods, Aging, and Functional Limitations', in Ichiro Kawachi and L. F. Berkman (eds), *Neighborhoods and Health*, New York: Oxford University Press.

Glazer, N. and Moynihan, D. (1963) *Beyond the Melting Pot*. Boston: MIT Press.

Gleber, A. (1999) *The Art of Taking a Walk: Flanerie, Literature, and Film in Weimar Culture*. Princeton, NJ: Princeton University Press.

Goffman, E. (1959) *The Presentation of Self in Everyday Life*. New York: Anchor.

Gold, J. R. and G. Revill (eds) (2000) *Landscapes of Defence*. London: Prentice Hall.

Gold, J. R. and Ward, S.V. (eds) (1994) *Place Promotion: The Use of Publicity and Marketing to Sell Towns and Regions*. Chichester: John Wiley.

Gordon, D. (1984) 'Capitalist Development and the History of American Cities', in W. Tabb and L. Sawyers (eds), *Marxism and The Metropolis*. Oxford: Oxford University Press.

Goss, J. (1993) 'The magic of the mall', *Annals of Association of American Geographers*, 83: 18–47.

Gottdiener, M. (1987) *The Decline of Urban Politics*. Newbury Park, CA: Sage.

Gottmann, J. (1961) *Megalopolis*. New York: Twentieth Century Fund.

Graham. S. (2002) 'Reflections on cities, September 11th and the "war on terrorism" – one year on', *International Journal of Urban and Regional Research*, 26: 589–90.

Graham, S. (2004) 'Postmortem city; towards an urban geopolitics', *City*, 8: 165–96.

Graham, S. and Marvin, S. (2001) *Splintering Urbanism*. London: Routledge.

Grant, R. (in press) *Transnational Spaces: Urban Transformation in Greater Accra, Ghana*. Syracuse: Syracuse University Press.

Grant, R. and Nijman, J. (2002) 'Globalization and the corporate geography of cities in the less developed world', *Annals of Association of American Geographers*, 92: 320–40.

Grant, R. and Short, J. R. (eds) (2002) *Globalization and the Margins*. Basingstoke and New York: Palgrave Macmillan.

Griffin, E. and Ford, L. (1980) 'A model of Latin American city structure', *Geographical Review*, 70: 397–422.

Griffiths, R. (1993) 'The politics of cultural policy in urban regeneration strategies', *Policy and Politics*, 21: 39–46.

Grosz, E. (1992) 'Bodies-Cities', in Colomina, B. (ed.), *Sexuality and Space*, New York: Princeton Architectural Press.

Guano, E. (2002) 'Spectacles of modernity; transnational imagination and liberal hegemonies in neoliberal Buenos Aires', *Cultural Anthropology*, 17: 181–209.

Gugler, J. (ed.) (1988) *The Urbanization of the Third World*. Oxford: Oxford University Press.

Gugler, J. (ed.) (2004) *World Cities beyond the West*. Cambridge: Cambridge University Press.

Gumprecht, B. (1999) *The Los Angeles River: The Life, Death and Possible Rebirth*. Baltimore and London: Johns Hopkins University Press.

Habermas, J. (1989) *The Structural Transformation of the Public Sphere*. Trans. by T. Burger and F. Lawrence. Cambridge, MA: MIT Press.

Haider, D. (1992) 'Place wars: new realities of the 1990s', *Economic Development Quarterly*, 6: 127–34.

Hake, S. (1994) 'Urban Spectacle in Walter Ruttmann's *Berlin, Symphony of a City*', in T.W. Kniesche and S. Brockmann (eds), *Dancing on the Volcano: Essays on the Culture of the Weimar Republic*, Columbia, SC: Camden House.

Hall, P. (1966, reprinted 1984) *The World Cities*. London: Weidenfeld & Nicolson.

Hall, P. (1988) *Cities of Tomorrow*. Oxford: Basil Blackwell.

Hall, P. (1998) *Cities in Civilization*. London: Weidenfeld & Nicolson.

Hall, S., Critcher, C., Jeffreson, T., Clarke, J. and Roberts, B. (1978) *Policing the Crisis: Mugging, the State and Law and Order*. London: Macmillan.

Hall, T. and Hubbard, P. (eds) (1998) *The Entrepreneurial City: Geographies of Politics, Regime and Representation*. Chichester: John Wiley.
Hamnett, C. and Shoval, N. (2003)' Museums as flagships of urban development', in L. M. Hoffman, S. S. Fainstein and D. R. Judd (eds), *Cities and Visitors*. Oxford: Basil Blackwell.
Hannigan, J. (1998) *Fantasy City: Pleasure and Profit in the Postmodern Metropolis*. London: Routledge.
Hanser, A. (2005) 'The gendered rice bowl: the sexual politics of service work in urban China', *Gender and Society*, 19: 581–600.
Hanson, S. and Pratt, G. (1995) *Gender, Work and Space*. London: Routledge.
Harries, K. (1999) *Mapping Crime: Principle and Practice*. Washington, DC: US Department of Justice .
Harvey, D. (1969) *Explanation in Geography*. Oxford: Basil Blackwell.
Harvey, D. (1973) *Social Justice and the City*. Oxford: Basil Blackwell.
Harvey, D. (1982) *The Limits to Capital*. Oxford: Basil Blackwell.
Harvey, D. (1989a) *The Condition of Postmodernity*. Oxford: Basil Blackwell.
Harvey, D. (1989b) 'From managerialism to entrepreneurialism: the transformation in urban governance in late capitalism', *Geografiska Annaler*, 71B: 3–18.
Harvey, D. (1996a) *Justice, Nature and the Geography of Difference*. Oxford: Basil Blackwell.
Harvey, D. (1996b) *The Limits to Capital*. Oxford: Basil Blackwell.
Harvey, D. (2000) *Spaces of Hope*. Edinburgh: Edinburgh University Press.
Harvey, D. (2003) *Paris: Capital of Modernity*. New York: Routledge.
Haughton, M. (1999) 'Environmental justice and the sustainable city', in D. Satterthwaite (ed.) *Sustainable Cities*. London: Earthscan.
Hayden, D. (1980) 'What would a non-sexist city be like', *Signs*, 5: 170–87.
Hayes, E. (1972) *Power Structure and Urban Policy: Who Rules in Oakland*. New York: McGraw-Hill.
Hays-Mitchell, M. (2002) 'Globalization and women: gender and resistance in the informal sector of Peru', in R. Grant and J. R. Short (eds), *Globalization and the Margins*. Basingstoke: Palgrave Macmillan.
Herbert, S. (1997) *Policing Space: Territoriality and the Los Angeles Police Department*. Minneapolis: University of Minnesota Press.
Herod, A. (ed.) (1998) *Organizing the Landscape: Geographical Perspectives on Labor Unionism*. Minneapolis and London: University of Minnesota Press.
Herod, A. (2001) *Labor Geographies: Workers and the Landscapes of Capitalism*. New York: Guilford Press.
Hewison, R. (1987) *The Heritage Industry*. London: Methuen.
Higonnet, P. (2002) *Paris: Capital of the World*. Translated by Arthur Goldhammer. Cambridge, MA: Harvard University Press.
Holcomb. B. (1994) 'City make-overs: marketing the post-industrial city', in J. R. Gold and S. V. Ward (eds), *Place Promotion: The Use of Publicity and Marketing to Sell Towns and Regions*. Chichester: John Wiley.
Holston, J. (2001) 'Urban citizenship and globalization', in A. J. Scott (ed.), *Global City-Regions*. Oxford: Oxford University Press.
Hough, M. (2004) *Cities and Natural Process; A Basis for Sustainability*, 2nd edn. London: Routledge.
Howard, E. (1898) *To-morrow: A Peaceful Path to Real Reform*. London: Swann Sonnenschein.

Howard, E. (1902) *Garden Cities of Tomorrow*. London: Swan Sonnenschein.

Hoyt, H. (1939) *The Structure and Growth of Residential Neighborhoods in American Cities*. Washington, DC: Federal Housing Administration.

Hubbard, P. (1996) 'Urban design and city regeneration: social representations of entrepreneurial landscapes', *Urban Studies*, 33: 1,441–61.

Hubbard, P. (1999) *Sex and the City: Geographies of Prostitution in the Urban West*. Chichester: Ashgate.

Hubbard, P. (2000) 'Desire/disgust: mapping the moral contours of heterosexuality', *Progress in Human Geography*, 24: 191–217.

Hubbard, P. (2003) 'Making space for sex work: female street prostitution and the production of urban space', *International Journal of Urban and Regional Research*, 27: 75–89.

Hudson, R. (2001) *Producing Places*. New York: Guildford.

Hudson, R. (2005) *Economic Geographies*. Thousand Oaks, CA: Sage.

Hunter, F. (1953) *Community Power Structure: A Study of Decision Makers*. Chapel Hill: University of North Carolina Press.

Ingram, G. B., Bouthillette, A.-M. and Retter, Y. (1997) *Queers in Space*. Bay Press: Seattle.

Isin, E. F. (2001) 'Istanbuls' conflicting paths to citizenship: Islamization and globalization', in A. J. Scott (ed.), *Global City-Regions*. Oxford: Oxford University Press.

Jacobs, J, (1961) *The Death and Life of Great American Cities*. New York: Random House.

Jacobs, J. (1969) *The Economy of Cities*. New York: Random House.

Jarman, N. (1993) 'Intersecting Belfast', in B. Bender (ed.), *Landscape – Politics and Perspectives*. Oxford: Pergamon Press.

Jayne, M. (2005) *The City and Consumption*. London: Routledge.

Jonas, A. and Wilson, D. (eds) (1999) *The Urban Growth Machine: Critical Perspectives Two Decades Later*. Albany: State University of New York Press.

Jordan, D. P. (1995) *Transforming Paris: The Life and Labors of Baron Haussmann*. New York: Free Press.

Judd, D. and Kantor, P. (eds) (1992) *Enduring Tensions in Urban Politics*. New York: Macmillan.

Kaika, M. (2005) *City of Flows: Modernity, Nature and the City*. London: Routledge.

Katz, C. and Monk, J. (eds) (1993) *Full Circles: Geographies of Women over the Life Course*. London: Routledge.

Katznelson. I. (1979) *City Trenches: Urban Politics and the Patterning of Class in the United States*. New York: Pantheon.

Kawachi, I. and Berkman, L. F. (eds) (2003) *Neighborhoods and Health*. New York: Oxford University Press.

Kearns, G. and C. Philo (eds) (1993) *Selling Places: The City as Cultural Capital, Past and Present*. Oxford: Pergamon Press.

Keil, R. (1998) *Los Angeles: Globalization, Urbanization and Social Struggles*. New York: John Wiley.

Kelman, J. (1994) *How Late It Was, How Late*. London: Secker & Warburg.

Kennedy, B. P., Kawachi, I., Lochner, K. and Jones. C. P. (1999) '(Dis)respect and black mortality', in Ichiro Kawachi, B. P. Kennedy and R. G. Wilkinson (eds), *The Society and Health Reader: Income Inequality and Health*. New York: The New Press.

Kim, Y.-H. (2002) 'Globalization and financial crises in Seoul, South Korea', in R. Grant and J. R. Short (eds), *Globalization and the Margins*. Basingstoke and New York: Palgrave Macmillan.

Kim, Y.-H. (2004) 'Seoul: complementing economic success with Games', in J. Gugler (ed.), *World Cities beyond the West*. Cambridge: Cambridge University Press.

King, A. (2003) 'Speaking from the margins: "postmodernism", transnationalism, and the imagining of contemporary Indian urbanity', in R. Grant and J. R. Short (eds), *Globalization and the Margins*. Basingstoke and New York: Palgrave Macmillan.

Klinenberg, E. (2002) *Heat Wave: A Social Autopsy of Disaster in Chicago*. Chicago and London: University of Chicago Press.

Knopp, L. (2001) 'A Queer Journey to Queer Geography', in P. Moss (ed.), *Placing Autobiography in Geography*, Syracuse: Syracuse University Press.

Kong, L. and Yeoh, B. S. A. (2003) *The Politics of Landscape in Singapore*. Syracuse: Syracuse University Press.

Kotler, P., Haider, D. H. and Rein, I. (1993) *Marketing Places: Attracting Investment to Cities, States and Nations*. New York: Free Press.

Kymlicka, W. (1995) *Multicultural Citizenship*. Oxford: Oxford University Press.

Langton, J. (1975) 'Residential patterns in pre-industrial cities', *Transactions of Institute of British Geographers*, 65: 1–27.

Le Corbusier (1923) *Vers une architecture*. Paris: Crès.

Le Corbusier (1923) *La ville radieuse*. Paris: Crès.

Lefebvre, H. (1968) *Le doit a la ville*. Paris: Anthropos.

Lefebvre, H. (1991) *The Production of Space*. Oxford: Basil Blackwell.

Lefebvre, H. (2003) *The Urban Revolution*. Translated by Robert Bononno. Minneapolis: University of Minnesota Press.

Lieberson, S. (1980) *A Piece of the Pie*. Berkeley: University of California Press.

Lipietz, A. (1987) *Mirages and Miracles: The Crises of Global Fordism*. Translated by David Macey. London: Verso.

Lloyd, D. (1993) *Anomalous States: Irish Writing and the Post-Colonial Moment*. Durham, NC: Duke University Press.

Lloyd, R. (2005) *Neo-Bohemia: Art and Commerce in the Postindustrial City*. London: Routledge.

Logan, J. (ed.) (2002) *The New Chinese City: Globalization and Market Reform*. Oxford: Basil Blackwell.

Logan, J. and Molotch, H. (1987) *Urban Fortunes: The Political Economy of Place*. Berkeley and Los Angeles: University of California Press.

Longhurst, R. (2001) *Bodies: Exploring Fluid Boundaries*. London and New York: Routledge.

Lowe, M. (1993) 'Local hero! An examination of the role of the regional entrepreneur in the regeneration of Britain's regions', in G. Kearns and C. Philo (eds), *Selling Places: The City as Cultural Capital, Past and Present*. Oxford: Pergamon.

Lukes, S. (1974) *Power: A Radical View*. London: Macmillan.

Lynd, R. S. and Lynd, H. M. (1929) *Middletown*. New York: Harcourt Brace.

Lyotard, J.-F. (1993) *Libidinal Economy*. Translated by I. H. Grant. London: Athlone.

Ma, L. and Wu, F. (eds) (2005) *Restructuring the Chinese City*. London: Routledge.

MacIntyre, S. and Ellaway, A. (2000) 'Ecological Approaches: Rediscovering the Role of the Physical and Social Environment', in Lisa F. Berkman and Ichiro Kawachi (eds), *Social Epidemiology*. Oxford: Oxford University Press.

Maltby, R. (1989) *Passing Parade: A History of Popular Culture in the Twentieth Century*. Oxford: Oxford University Press.

Malvery, O. C. (1906) *The Soul Market*. London: Hutchinson.

Marcuse, H. (1964) *One-Dimensional Man: Studies in the Ideology of Advanced Industrial Society*. Boston, MA: Beacon Press.

Marshall, A. (1922) *The Principles of Economics*. London: Macmillan.

Massey, D. (1984) *Spatial Divisions of Labour*. Basingstoke: Macmillan.

Massey, D. (1994) *Space, Place and Gender*. London: Polity.

Massey, D. (1995) 'Masculinity, dualisms and high technology', *Transactions of Institute of British Geographers*, 20: 487–9.

Matrix (1984) *Making Space: Women and the Man Made Environment*. London: Pluto Press.

Mazey, M. E. and Lee, D. (1983) *Her Space, Her Place; A Geography of Women*. Washington, DC: Association of American Geographers.

McClintock, A. (1992) 'The angel of progress: pitfalls of the term "postcolonialism"', *Social Text*, Spring: 31–2.

McDowell, L. (1997) *Capital Culture: Gender at Work in the City*. Oxford: Basil Blackwell.

McDowell, L. (1999) *Space, Place and Gender*. London: Polity.

McDowell, L. (2003) *Reluctant Masculinities*. Oxford: Basil Blackwell.

McDowell, L. (2005) *Working Memories*. London: UCL Press.

McGee, T. R. (1967) *The Southeast Asian City: A Social Geography of the Primate Cities of South East Asia*. New York: Praeger.

Mearns, A. (1883) *The Bitter Cry of Outcast London*. London: James Clarke.

Mercado. M. A. and Tatad, F. S. (1986) *People Power: The Philippine Revolution of 1986*. Manila: Reuter Foundation.

Merrifield, A. (2002) *Dialectical Marxism: Social Struggles in the Capitalist City*. New York: Monthly Review Press.

Mitchell, T. (1988) *Colonizing Egypt*. Cambridge: Cambridge University Press.

Mitchell, D. (2003) *The Right to the City*. New York: Guildford.

Mitchell, K. (2000) 'The culture of public space', *Urban Geography*, 21: 443–9.

Moore, T. (1997) *The Re-Enchantment of Everyday Life*. New York: HarperCollins.

Moore, T. (1998) *The Soul of Sex*. New York: HarperCollins.

Morris, B. (2004) 'What we talk about when we talk about "Walking in the City"', *Cultural Studies*, 18: 675–97.

Mudimbe. V. Y. (1988) *The Invention of Africa*. London: James Currey.

Mumford. L. (1961) *The City in History*. New York: Harcourt Brace.

Munro, M. and Madigan, R. (1999) 'Negotiating space in the family home', in I. Cieraad (ed.), *At Home: An Anthropology of Domestic Space*. Syracuse: Syracuse University Press.

Murdie, R. A. (1969) 'Factorial ecology of metropolitan Toronto, 1951–1961', *Research Paper 116*. Chicago: University of Chicago, Department of Geography.

Myers, G. A. (2003) *Verandahs of Power: Colonialism and Space in Urban Africa.* Syracuse: Syracuse University Press.

Nelson, N. (1988) 'How women and men get by: the sexual division of labour in the informal sector of a Nairobi squatter settlement', in J. Gugler (ed.), *The Urbanization of the Third World.* New York: Oxford University Press.

Neumann, D. (1994) 'The Urbanistic Vision in Fritz Lang's *Metropolis*', In T.W. Kniesche and S. Brockmann (eds), *Dancing on the Volcano: Essays on the Culture of The Weimar Republic,* Columbia, SC: Camden House.

Newman, O. (1972) *Defensible Space: Crime Prevention through Urban Design.* New York: Macmillan.

Newman, O. (1996) *Creating Defensible Space.* Washington, DC: US Department of Housing and Urban Development.

Nijman, J. (1999) 'Cultural globalization and the identity of place: the reconstruction of Amsterdam', *Cultural Geographies,* 6: 146–64.

Nijman, J. (2002) 'The effects of economic globalization: land use and land values in Mumbai, India', in R. Grant and J. R. Short (eds), *Globalization and the Margins.* Basingstoke and New York: Palgrave Macmillan.

Nussbaum, M. (1994) 'Patriotism and cosmopolitanism', *Boston Review,* October/November: 1–10.

Ogborn, M. (1993) 'Ordering the city: surveillance, public space and the reform of urban policing in England, 1835–56', *Political Geography,* 12: 505–21.

Paddison. R. (1993) 'City marketing, image reconstruction and urban regeneration', *Urban Studies,* 30: 339–50.

Pahl, R. (1975) *Whose City?*, 2nd edn. Harmondsworth: Penguin.

Panayotou, T. (2001) 'Environmental sustainability and services in developing global city-regions', in A. J. Scott (ed.), *Global City-Regions.* Oxford: Oxford University Press.

Park, R. E. (1952) *Human Communities: The City and Human Ecology.* New York: Free Press.

Park, R. E., Burgess, E. W. and McKenzie, R. D. (1925) *The City,* reprinted 1967. Chicago and London: University of Chicago Press.

Pawley, M. (1998) *Terminal Architecture.* London: Reaktion.

Peck, J. (1996) *Workplace: The Social Regulation of Labor Markets.* New York: Guildford.

Peck, J. and Tickell, A. (1995) 'Business goes local : dissecting the "business agenda" in Manchester', *International Journal of Urban and Regional Research,* 19: 55–78.

Peterson, P. E. (1980) *City Limits.* Chicago: University of Chicago Press.

Porter, M.E. (1995) 'The competitive advantage of the inner city', *Harvard Business Review,* May–June: 53–71.

Portes, A. *et al.* (1989) *The Informal Economy: Studies in Advanced and Less Developed Countries.* Baltimore: Johns Hopkins University Press.

Pratt, G. (2004) *Working Feminism.* Philadelphia: Temple University Press.

Preston, D. (1998) 'Cannibals of the canyon', *The New Yorker,* 30 November, 76–89.

Purcell, M. (2002) 'Politics in global cities: Los Angeles charter reform and the new social movement', *Environment and Planning A,* 34: 23–42.

Putnam, R. (2000) *Bowling Alone: The Collapse and Revival of American Community.* New York: Simon & Schuster.

Radford, J. P. (1979) 'Testing the model of the pre-industrial city: the case of ante-bellum Charleston, South Carolina', *Transactions of Institute of British Geographers New Series*, 4: 392–410.

Reynolds, B. and Fitzpatrick, J. (1999) 'The transversatility of Michel de Certeau', *Diacritics*, 29: 63–80.

Riesman, D. (1950) *The Lonely Crowd*. New Haven: Yale University Press.

Riis, J. A. (1890) *How the Other Half Lives: Studies among the Tenements of New York*. New York: Scribner's Sons.

Robson, B. T. (1969) *Urban Analysis*. Cambridge: Cambridge University Press.

Rogers, A. (2000) 'Citizenship, multiculturalism and the European city', in G. Bridge and S. Watson (eds), *A Companion to the City*. Oxford: Basil Blackwell.

Ross, K. (1996) 'Streetwise: the French invention of everyday life', *Parallax*, 2: 67–75.

Rutheiser, C. (2000) 'Capitalizing on Havana: the return of the repressed in a late socialist city', in G. Bridge and S. Watson (eds), *A Companion to the City*. Oxford: Blackwell.

Ryder, R. H. (2004) 'Land use diversification in the elite residential sector of Quito, Ecuador', *Professional Geographer*, 56: 488–502.

Sahlins, M. (1972) *Stone Age Economics*. Chicago: Aldine-Atherton.

Said, E. (1978) *Orientalism*. New York: Pantheon.

Said, E. (1993) *Culture and Imperialism*. London: Chatto & Windus.

Sampson, R., Raudenbush, S. and Felton, E. (1997) 'Neighborhoods and violent crime: a multilevel study of collective efficacy', *Science*, 277: 918–24.

Sandercock, L. (1998) *Towards Cosmopolis: Planning for Multicultural Cities*. Chichester: Wiley.

Sandercock, L. (2003) *Cosmopolis II: Mongrel Cities in the 21st Century*. London: Continuum.

Sassen, S. (1991; 2001 2nd edn) *The Global City: New York, London, Tokyo*. Princeton: Princeton University Press.

Sassen, S. (1994) *Cities in a World Economy*. Thousand Oaks, CA: Pine Forge.

Sassen, S. (2000) 'The global city: strategic site/new frontier', in E. Isin (ed.), *Democracy, Citizenship and the Global City*, New York: Routledge.

Sassen, S. (2002) 'Globalization and the formation of claims', in R. Grant and J. R. Short (eds), *Globalization and The Margins*. Basingstoke and New York: Palgrave Macmillan.

Schnore, L. F. (1965) *The Urban Scene*. New York: Free Press.

Scott, A. J. (1988) *Metropolis: From Division of Labor to Urban Form*. Berkeley and Los Angeles: University of California Press.

Scott, A. J. (2000) *The Cultural Economy of Cities*. London: Sage.

Scott, A. J. (ed.) (2001) *Global City-Regions*. Oxford: Oxford University Press.

Scott, A. J. and Soja, E. (eds) (1996) *The City: Los Angeles and Urban Theory at the End of the Twentieth Century*. Berkeley and Los Angeles: University of California Press.

Sedgwick, E. K. (1990) *Epistemology of the Closet*. New York: Harvester Wheatsheaf.

Sennett, R. (1970) *The Uses of Disorder: Personal Identity and City Life*. New York: Knopf.

Sennett, R. (1994) *Flesh and Stone: The Body and the City in Western Civilization*. New York: Norton.

Shaw, C.R. and McKay, H. D. (1942) *Juvenile Delinquency and Urban Areas*, reprinted 1969. Chicago: University of Chicago Press.

Shevky, E. and Bell, W. (1955) *Social Area Analysis*. Stanford, CA: Stanford University Press.

Shevky, E. and Williams, M. (1949) *The Social Areas of Los Angeles*. Los Angeles: University of California Press.

Short, J. R. (1978) 'Residential mobility', *Progress in Human Geography*, 2: 419–27.

Short, J. R. (1984) *The Urban Arena: Capital, State and Community in Contemporary Britain*. London: Macmillan.

Short, J. R. (1988) 'Construction workers and the city', *Environment and Planning A*, 20: 719–40.

Short, J. R. (1989a) *The Humane City: Cities as if People Really Mattered*. Oxford: Basil Blackwell.

Short J. R. (1989b) 'Yuppies, yuffies and the new urban order', *Transactions of Institute of British Geographers*, 26: 173–88.

Short, J. R. (1993) *An Introduction to Political Geography*. London: Routledge.

Short, J. R. (1999) 'Urban imaginers; boosterism and the representation of cities', in A. Jonas and D. Wilson (eds), *The Urban Growth Machine: Critical Perspectives Two Decades Later*. Albany: State University of New York Press.

Short, J. R. (2004a) *Global Metropolitan*. London: Routledge.

Short, J. R. (2004b) *Making Space*. Syracuse: Syracuse University Press.

Short, J. R. (2006) *Alabaster Cities*. Syracuse: Syracuse University Press.

Short, J. R. and Kim, Y.-H. (1998) 'Urban crises/urban representations: selling the city in difficult times', in T. Hall and P. Hubbard (eds), *The Entrepreneurial City*. Chichester: Wiley.

Short, J.R. and Kim, Y.-H. (1999) *Globalization and the City*. Harlow: Longman.

Short, J. R., Benton, L., Luce, B. and Walton, J. (1993) 'The reconstruction of the image of a postindustrial city', *Annals of Association of American Geographers*, 83 (2): 207–24.

Short, J. R., Boniche, A. Kim, Y. and Li, P. (2001) 'Cultural globalization, global English and Geography journals', *Professional Geographer*, 53: 1–11.

Short, J. R. Kim, Y.-H., Kuus, M. and Wells, H. (1996) 'The dirty little secret of world cities research', *International Journal of Urban and Regional Research*, 20, 697–715.

Simmel, G. (1950) 'The Metropolis and Mental Life', in K. Wolff (ed.), *The Sociology of Georg Simmel*. Glencoe: Free Press, 409–26.

Sjoberg, G. (1960) *The Preindustrial City*. New York: Free Press.

Smith, N. (1996) *The New Urban Frontier*. London: Routledge.

Snow, J. (1855) *On the Mode of Communication of Cholera*. London: Churchill.

Soja, E. (1989) *Postmodern Geographies: The Reassertion of Space in Critical Society Theory*. London: Verso.

Soja, E. (1996) *Thirdspace: Journey to Los Angeles and Other Real-and-Imagined Places*. Oxford; Basil Blackwell.

Soja, E. (2000) *Postmetropolis*. Oxford: Basil Blackwell.

Sorkin, M. (ed.) (1992) *Variations on a Theme Park: The New American City and the End of Public Space*. New York: Hill & Wang.

Spaeth, A. (2001) 'Oops, we did it again', *Time*, 157: 4–6.

Spain, D. (1992) *Gendered Spaces*. Chapel Hill: University of North Carolina Press.

Spivak, G. (1987) *In Other Worlds*. New York: Methuen.

Spurling, A. (1992) 'Men and women: the use and abuse of mutual space', in D. Porter (ed.), *Between Men and Feminism*. London: Routledge.

Stansell, C. (1986) *City of Women: Sex and Class in New York, 1789–1860*. New York: Knopf.

Stevens, Q. and Dovey, K. (2004) 'Appropriating the spectacle: play and politics in a leisure landscape', *Journal of Urban Design*, 9: 351–64.

Stoker, G. and Mossberger, K. (1994) 'Urban regime theory in comparative perspective', *Environment and Planning C: Government and Policy*, 12: 195–212.

Stone, C. (1989) *Regime Politics: Governing Atlanta 1946–1988*. Lawrence: University Press of Kansas.

Storper, M. (1997) *The Regional World*. New York: Guildford.

Storper, M. and Venables, A. J. (2004) 'Buzz: face to face contact and the urban economy', *Journal of Economic Geography*, 4: 351–70.

Strom, E. (2002) 'Converting pork into porcelain: cultural institutions and downtown development', *Urban Affairs Review*, 38: 3–21.

Strong, J. (1885) *Our Country; Its Possible Future and Present Origins*. New York: Baker & Taylor.

Suleri, S. (1992) *Rhetoric of English India*. Chicago; University of Chicago Press.

Swyngedouw, E. (2004) *Social Power and the Urbanization of Water*. Oxford: Oxford University Press.

Taylor, P. (2004) *World City Networks*. London: Routledge.

Terhorst, P. and van de Ven, J. (2003) 'The economic restructuring of the historic city center', in S. Musterd and W. Salet (eds), *Amsterdam Human Capital*. Amsterdam: Amsterdam University Press.

Thompson, E. P. (1963) *The Making of the English Working Class*. Harmondsworth: Penguin.

Thompson, E. P. (1971) \The moral economy of the English crowd in the eighteenth century', *Past & Present*, 50: 76–136.

Thrift, N. (2005) *Knowing Capitalism*. Thousand Oaks: Sage.

Torres, R. M. and Momsen, J. D. (2005) 'Gringolandia: the construction of a new tourist space in Mexico', *Annals of Association of American Geographers*, 95: 315–35.

Townsend, A. (2001) 'Networked cities and the global structure of the Internet', *American Behavioral Scientist*, 44: 1,698–717.

Valance, G. (2000) *Haussmann le grand*. Paris: Flammarion.

Valentine, G. (1989) 'The geography of women's fear', *Area*, 21: 385–90.

Valentine, G. (1996) '(Re)negotiating the "heterosexual" street', in N. Duncan, (ed.), *BodySpace: Destabilizing Geographies of Gender and Sexuality*. London and New York: Routledge.

Vandegrift, D. and T. Yoked (2004) 'Obesity rates, income, and suburban sprawl: an analysis of U.S. States', *Health and Place*, 10: 221–9.

Waldinger, R. (2001) 'The immigrant niche in global city-regions: concept, patterns, controversy', in A. J. Scot (ed.), *Global City-Regions*. Oxford: Oxford University Press.

Walker, R. A. (1981) 'The theory of suburbanization: capitalism and the construction of urban space in the United States', in M. Dear and A. J. Scott (eds), *Urbanization and Urban Planning in Capitalist Society*. London: Methuen.

Ward, S. V. (1994) 'Time and place: key themes in place promotion in the USA, Canada and Britain since 1870', in J. R. Gold and S. V. Ward (eds), *Place Promotion: The Use of Publicity and Marketing to Sell Towns and Regions*. Chichester: John Wiley.

Ward, S. V. (1998) *Selling Places: The Marketing and Promotion of Towns and Cities, 1850–2000*. London: Span.

Watson, S. (1991) 'Gilding the smokestacks: the new symbolic representations of deindustrialized regions', *Environment and Planning D, Society and Space*, 9: 59–70.

Webber, M. M. (1964) 'The urban place and the nonplace urban realm', in M. M. Webber (ed.), *Explorations in Urban Structure*. Philadelphia: University of Pennsylvania Press.

Weber, M. (1922) *Wirtschaft und Gesellschaft*. Tübingen: J. C. B. Mohr.

Weikart, L. (2003) 'Follow the money: mayoral choice and expenditure policy', *American Review of Public Administration*, 35: 209–32.

Weiss, M. J. (2000) *The Clustered World: How We Live, What We Buy, and What it all means about Who We Are*. Boston, MA: Little, Brown.

Whelan, Y. (2002) 'The construction and destruction of a colonial landscape: monuments to British monarchs in Dublin before and after independence', *Journal of Historical Geography*, 24: 508–33.

Whyte, W. H. (1980) *The Social Life of Small Urban Spaces*. Washington, DC: Conservation Foundation.

Wilkinson, P. (1971) *Social Movements*. London: Macmillan.

Willis, P. (1978) *Learning to Labour*. London: Gower.

Wilson, D. (1996) 'Metaphors, growth coalition discourses and black poverty neighborhoods', *Antipode*, 28: 72–96.

Wilson, D. (2005) *Inventing Black-on-Black Violence*. Syracuse: Syracuse University Press.

Wilson, E. (1991) *The Sphinx in the City*. London: Virago.

Wilson, E. (2001) *The Contradictions of Culture: Cities, Culture, Women*. London: Sage.

Wilson, K. and Portes, A. (1980) 'Immigrant enclaves: an analysis of the labor market experiences of Cubans in Miami', *American Journal of Sociology*, 88: 295–319.

Women and Geography Study Group (1984) *Geography and Gender: An Introduction to Feminist Geography*. London: Hutchison.

Woolf, V. (1929) *A Room of One's Own*. London: Hogarth Press.

Wrigley, N. and Lowe, M. (eds) (1996) *Retailing, Consumption and Capital*. Harlow: Addison-Wesley-Longman.

Wrigley, N. and Lowe, M. (2002) *Reading Retail*. London: Arnold.

Wrong, M. (2001) *In the Footsteps of Mr. Kurtz: Living on the Brink of Disaster in Mobutu's Congo*. New York: HarperCollins.

Wu, F. (2000) 'Place promotion in Shanghai, PRC', *Cities*, 17: 349–61.

Wu, F. (2005) *Globalization and the Chinese City*. London: Routledge.

Wu, W. and Yusuf, S. (2004) 'Shanghai; remaking China's future global city', in J. Gugler (ed.), *World Cities beyond the West*. Cambridge: Cambridge University Press.

Yeoh, B. S. A. (2001) 'Postcolonial cities', *Progress in Human Geography*, 25: 456–68.

Zukin, S. (1995) *The Cultures of Cities*. Oxford: Basil Blackwell.

Zukin, S. (2001) 'How to create a culture capital: reflections on urban markets and places', in I. Blazwick (ed.), *Century City: Art and Culture in the Modern Metropolis*. London: Tate Gallery.

Index